This book is a study of ancient Greek theories of learning and discovery. It begins by examining Plato's theory of recollection, arguably the first theory of innate knowledge, and then traces the way in which Aristotle, Epicurus and the Stoics developed their own explanations of learning. The first section of the book presents an entirely new interpretation of the theory of recollection. The central chapters explore how this changes the way in which the subsequent development of ancient philosophy should be understood. Among the issues raised are the ancients' attitudes to the formation of ordinary concepts, and to their role in inquiry, especially moral inquiry. The final section uses the revised account of the ancient period to draw a comparison with the seventeenth century debate about innate ideas, and finds that the relation between the two periods is far more interesting and complex than is usually supposed.

*Recollection and Experience* will be of interest to scholars and students of ancient philosophy, as well as philosophers interested in the more recent debate about innate ideas.

# RECOLLECTION AND EXPERIENCE

# RECOLLECTION AND EXPERIENCE

## Plato's theory of learning and its successors

DOMINIC SCOTT

*Lecturer in Philosophy in the University of Cambridge, and Fellow of Clare College*

CAMBRIDGE
UNIVERSITY PRESS

Published by the Press Syndicate of the University of Cambridge
The Pitt Building, Trumpington Street, Cambridge CB2 IRP
40 West 20th Street, New York, NY 10011-4211, USA
10 Stamford Road, Oakleigh, Melbourne 3166, Australia

First published 1995

Printed in Great Britain at the University Press, Cambridge

*A catalogue record for this book is available from the British Library*

*Library of Congress cataloguing in publication data*

Scott, Dominic.
Recollection and experience: Plato's theory of learning and its
successors / Dominic Scott.
p.   cm.
Includes bibliographical references and indexes.
1. Plato–views of learning.   2. Learning.   3. Innate ideas (Philosophy).
4. Plato–Influence.   5. Philosophy, Ancient.   6. Philosophy, Modern–17th
century.   I. Title.
B398.L3S36   1995
121'.3–dc20   94–32443   CIP

ISBN 0 521 47455 8 hardback

EBF

# Contents

## Contents

# Acknowledgements

In the course of writing this book I have incurred numerous intellectual debts. I have received invaluable help from Margaret Atkins, Monique Canto-Sperber, Gail Fine, Geoffrey Lloyd, Terry Moore, Malcolm Schofield and Robert Wardy. I would particularly like to thank Tony Hubbard, who first got me interested in philosophy and in Plato's theory of recollection, M. M. McCabe, who nurtured my interest into an obsession, David Sedley, who has helped on innumerable occasions with his acuity and judgement and above all Myles Burnyeat, for his insight and inspiration over the last few years.

I have benefited enormously from the support of Clare College, Cambridge and, more recently, of the Philosophy Faculty of Cambridge University. The project was also helped by a change of atmosphere made possible by a visit to the Philosophy Department of Princeton University in 1992–3. I would like to thank all my students at Cambridge and Princeton who have, perhaps unwittingly, exerted an influence on the writing of this book.

I would also like to thank Nicole Monnier for reading the manuscript in the final stages and David Coleman for a number of extremely helpful suggestions.

Earlier versions of parts of this book have already appeared in print as follows:

Chapter 2: Scott (1987)
Chapter 7 [1]: Scott (1989)
Chapter 8 [3]: Scott (1988)

I would like to thank the editors of the *Classical Quarterly* and of the *Proceedings of the Cambridge Philological Society* for permission to reprint this material.

# Abbreviations

| | |
|---|---|
| *An.* | Aristotle, *De Anima (On the Soul)* |
| *An. Po.* | Aristotle, *Posterior Analytics* |
| D. L. | Diogenes Laërtius |
| *EE* | Aristotle, *Eudemian Ethics* |
| *M* | Sextus Empiricus, *Adversus Mathematicos (Against the Professors)* |
| *Met.* | Aristotle, *Metaphysics* |
| *ND* | Cicero, *De Natura Deorum (On the Nature of the Gods)* |
| *NE* | Aristotle, *Nicomachean Ethics* |
| *Phys.* | Aristotle, *Physics* |
| *SVF* | *Stoicorum Veterum Fragmenta*, see von Arnim (1903–24) |

*General Introduction*

Socrates thought that an awareness of our own ignorance should create a desire for the knowledge that eludes us. Plato agreed with him, but went on to ask how such knowledge, which had managed to elude even Socrates, could ever be acquired. He found his answer in the theory of recollection, one of his most notorious philosophical legacies. What we now call learning, he claimed in the *Meno*, is in fact the recollection of knowledge had in a prenatal existence. None of his successors, Aristotle, Epicurus or the Stoics, found this suggestion convincing, but all of them were sufficiently impressed by the importance of the questions that he was trying to answer to go to considerable lengths to present their own alternatives, their rivals to recollection. Aristotle, in obvious reaction to Plato, placed great emphasis upon perception and experience both in scientific and ethical learning. Epicurus and the Stoics also developed sophisticated accounts of the role of experience in learning and, in addition, showed an increasing interest in distinguishing between those elements of our thinking that arise naturally and those that derive from cultural influences. Seen in this light, Plato's theory of recollection acted as the catalyst for what was to be a long-running philosophical debate about the origins of knowledge.

Precisely because Plato's successors acknowledged the importance of his questions but replaced his answers with their own, we have the opportunity to compare these different theories diachronically, to see how a certain theme develops over the course of ancient philosophy. Such a project, if it were to do justice to all the issues involved over so large a span of time, would result in the compilation of a modest encyclopaedia. This book has no such ambitions; its focus will be more selective, concentrating on three issues to do with learning and discovery.

3

The first concerns the well known distinction between innatist and empiricist theories of learning. To give a preliminary characterisation, this is a distinction between theories that appeal to the mind's internal resources to explain many of its cognitive achievements and those that explain them from the external input of sense perception. The debate between these positions has been prominent in post-Renaissance philosophy, especially in the seventeenth century when it involved Descartes, Locke and Leibniz, among many others. It has also reappeared on the agenda very recently, helped in large part by Chomsky's espousal of innateness in a linguistic context.

A version of this debate took place in antiquity and one concern of this study will be to determine what positions the major figures of this period took on the issue. In Plato's case we shall be able to answer the question without much difficulty, but with the other philosophers the task becomes more problematic. The difficulties here do not simply arise from the state of the texts themselves, but also from the fact that the terms innatism and empiricism are not transparently clear and hence should only be applied to the ancient philosophers with caution. In particular, exactly what do we mean by saying something is innate to the mind? No one is trying to claim that, from the very moment of birth, babies are in conscious possession of certain beliefs or concepts. Do we mean then that such beliefs or concepts are merely latent in the mind from birth? Or do we mean instead that the person has an inborn predisposition to form certain beliefs, in the same way that someone might have a congenital tendency towards catching a particular disease? But how exactly is this different from the claim that we have the capacity to form beliefs and concepts, which is presumably what empiricism amounts to? The issue here is complex, and when trying to determine which of the many available positions were adopted in the ancient period it is in some cases not enough simply to scrutinise the texts; we also need to clarify the different meanings of the terms 'innate' and 'empirical' and the various distinctions implied by them.

That we should be discussing the innateness question needs little explanation. Determining where the ancient philosophers stood on this issue is essential for any work that purports to talk about their theories of learning. But there are two further issues which will give this book its special focus. Throughout the course of the innateness debate, the learning of all manner of different things has been discussed: mathematical theorems, the existence of God, the relation of cause and effect, principles of morality, rules of grammar, logical laws and so on. But in addition to differences of subject matter there is another way of distinguishing theories of learning from one another. This concerns the level of learning to be explained and it provides the second focus for this book. All the ancient philosophers included in this study made some distinction between different levels of thinking: the philosophical or technical and the mundane or pre-philosophical. In his earlier dialogues, Plato portrays Socrates as being prepared to talk to anyone, whether young or old, citizen or foreigner (*Apology* 30a2–3). But in the course of such encounters, a gulf typically emerges between the interlocutors' somewhat unreflective responses and the level of philosophical rigour that Socrates demands of them. In the *Republic* this distinction is hardened into a political divide between the philosopher-rulers and the other classes in the state. Aristotle not only accepted a distinction between two levels of cognitive achievement, he invented terminology for it as well: 'the more familiar to us' and 'the more familiar in nature'. Often, he used these terms to contrast the perspective that we have of the world prior to scientific or philosophical investigation with the way the world is understood as a result of that investigation, the way the world is in itself, as seen from a God's-eye view. When applied to ethics, the distinction was one between the pre-philosophical intuitions of ordinary people and a sophisticated theory. Similarly, the Hellenistic philosophers sharply distinguished the more technical achievements of philosophy or science from the concepts and beliefs that constitute the very faculty of human reason itself.

Corresponding to these two different levels of cognitive achievement will be two quite distinct explanations one can expect from a theory of learning. One is concerned with the process by which we reach the more familiar to us and so attempt to explain concept formation and the acquisition of language. I shall refer to this, for want of a better expression, as 'ordinary learning'. The other attempts to explain the movement from the more familiar to us to the more familiar in nature, the discovery of scientific, moral and, more generally, philosophical knowledge. There was undoubtedly a strong interest on the part of all the ancient philosophers in these later phases of learning. Plato's theory of recollection was clearly intended to explain how we can attain philosophical understanding, and when his successors attempted to formulate their rivals to recollection, they were concerned with the same problem. But it is less clear whether they were also interested in explaining the earlier stages of learning. Determining the extent to which the ancient philosophers were interested in ordinary learning as well as more advanced forms of discovery will be the second concern of this book.

The third arises from the distinction between these two cognitive levels. Whatever we decide to think about their interest in ordinary learning, the ancient philosophers were certainly concerned with the question of higher learning or, to use Aristotle's terminology once again, the movement from the more familiar to us to the more familiar in nature. But how did they conceive of the relationship or, better, the distance, between these two perspectives? When someone makes a scientific discovery, do they find their previous perspective utterly transformed, or is the new scientific perspective recognisably similar to their earlier perceptual perspective, only more clearly understood? In the case of ethical discovery there is an analogous question. Is the philosophical journey from received opinion and pre-reflective intuition a transformation to a perspective that may seem perhaps shockingly different as one first approaches it, or is it more akin to the refinement and distillation of one's earlier intuitions?

A philosopher who thinks that there is a considerable gap between the two perspectives is likely to take a pessimistic attitude towards the cognitive achievements of ordinary people, the amount of work that lies ahead of them and their chances of achieving any success. The nature of discovery, if it does take place, will be seen as revisionary and disorientating. There is a discontinuity between perception or common sense on the one hand and science or philosophy on the other. Very importantly, this affects the way one sees the role of philosophy itself. It begins to be seen as having an essentially critical function.

At the other extreme, a philosopher who thinks that the gap between the two perspectives is much narrower will show greater optimism about the more familiar to us, in particular about its ability to prompt us to ask the right questions and guide us in the right direction. The path between the two perspectives will be a continuous one, a gradual articulation of our starting-points; the end result will be recognisably similar to our initial expectations or presuppositions. Refinement replaces rejection as the dominant attitude towards appearance and intuition, so that, again, the way one sees the nature of philosophy is affected. It now plays out the role of developing the widely held beliefs of the time.

This shows how, in both science and ethics, we can mark out two extreme positions about the relationship between the perspectives. And now, in between these two positions, pessimistic and optimistic, we can then see the potential for a whole variety of other positions to appear. To locate where the ancient philosophers stood on this continuum will be the third concern of this book. This task is made difficult because in some cases, a philosopher may profess to be taking one attitude – that of the friend and ally of common sense, for instance – but when it comes to working out a philosophical theory, may trample the intuitions freely under foot.

These, then, are the three issues that will concern us in this study: the opposition between innatism and empiricism, the distinction between ordinary and philosophical levels of learning and the relation that holds between them. As we have seen, it should be no surprise that we are discussing the first issue, but what makes the second and third ones salient? The answer arises from the fact that, at present, there is a controversy about Plato's theory of recollection in which these two issues are central. From the current state of the literature, it seems that most votes at the moment would go to one side in this controversy. As a result, not only has the theory itself been misunderstood but the whole way in which we look at the later development of the learning debate has been distorted.

Everyone would agree that the theory of recollection is intended to explain how philosophical and mathematical discoveries are made. But in most people's view, this is not all it does. For them, Plato is attempting to explain not only higher learning but ordinary learning as well. Recollection explains how we all form the concepts of ordinary thought, concepts of equality and beauty, for instance. The theory also helps account for our linguistic capacities. It then goes beyond this by explaining how we can develop these innate concepts into fully fledged definitions, but this is a continuation of the process of recollection.

This, as I shall argue in section I, is wrong. Instead we should come to understand Plato's theory in an entirely different way. Plato proposes recollection only to explain the later stages of learning. Ordinary learning, in which he is little interested, is accounted for externally; we acquire our concepts of equality or beauty from sense perception, and moral notions from hearsay or tradition. Recollection only enters the story when we have already reached the level of ordinary conceptual thought and start to become puzzled and dissatisfied with the perspective thus gained of the world. Those who do not become puzzled in this way do not even begin to recollect, and the extraordinary resources latent within them remain completely unused.

It should be clear that this controversy involves the second of our three issues, the question of what level of learning is being explained. But, as I shall argue, it also involves the polarity between pessimism and optimism, because in the first interpretation philosophy is not seen as marking a radical transition from ordinary thought, but as the continued recollection of concepts that have, to some extent, already come to light in our pre-philosophical thinking. The second interpretation, on the other hand, involves a strict discontinuity between the two perspectives and presents Plato as the severe critic of common sense. The few who do start to recollect find that their perspective of the world, both metaphysical and moral, becomes utterly transformed. That Plato adopted this kind of approach to philosophy elsewhere, for instance in the central books of the *Republic*, is very often conceded. What is not appreciated is that he also took this line when he proposed the theory of recollection itself, especially in the *Phaedo*.

The first section of this book, then, is designed to dislodge a widespread reading of Platonic recollection. But the point of the book as a whole is that this misunderstanding blights not only our appreciation of Plato but also of the rest of the learning debate in antiquity and even, as we shall see, beyond. If we misread Plato's own theory, we shall find affinities between him and his successors where no such affinities exist. Equally, we may find differences where there are none.

After our discussion of Platonic recollection in section I, we shall go on to examine its rivals, specifically from the point of view of the three issues just laid out. The first of these rivals, Aristotle's theory of learning, represents a somewhat rude rebuff to Plato's theory. In a famous chapter about the discovery of first principles, Aristotle appears to write off recollection as 'absurd'. His exact reasons for saying this, which have not often been discussed, will be examined in chapter 3. We then turn to two issues of special importance that will arise from our reassessment of Platonic recollection. There can be no doubt that just after Aristotle, among the Hellenistic philosophers, there was a very strong interest in how our most mundane concepts are formed. If this interest was not something brought into philosophy by Plato, was it a Hellenistic innovation or had Aristotle already filled the gap?

Aristotle, as we shall see in chapter 4, shows almost as little interest in the earlier phases of cognitive learning as Plato. Instead he focuses all his attention on the progress from the more familiar to us to the more familiar in nature. But the theory that he gives, as it is usually conceived, appears to be very different from Plato's theory of recollection as we have characterised it in section I. There, Plato emerges as the stern critic of perception and common sense; Aristotle, on the other hand, is often held up as their champion. But how sharp is this contrast? There are many places in which Aristotle seems to profess an intention to conform to perception and common sense. But in his ethics, for instance, there are passages that suggest he is deviating from them in a spirit of almost Platonic revisionism. How, for instance, can the status he accords to intellectual contemplation in his account of human happiness be said to conform to the opinions held by the majority of people? In chapters 5–6 we shall be looking more closely at his views on scientific and ethical discovery to see how clear the contrast with Plato really is.

One thing we can be sure about in the next phase of the debate, the Hellenistic era, is that there was considerable interest in ordinary learning. In the light of our conclusions in sections I–II, this immediately raises the question of why such an interest arose in this period and not before. But the chief focus of attention in this section of the book will be the emergence in this period of a new version of the innateness theory. This was a theory infused with the Hellenistic interest in explaining the origin of our ordinary concepts. In other words, we have something that is precisely what Platonic recollection is not; the Hellenistic theory of innateness claims that certain concepts and beliefs that are acknowledged by everyone have been sown into us at birth by Nature or God. (It also differs from Plato's theory in being free of any associations

with reincarnation and recollection.) Furthermore, not only is it
concerned to explain the formation of ordinary moral concepts,
but it has exactly the kind of optimism we found lacking in Plato.
The innate beliefs in question are operative in everyone's thought,
as a result of which they are said to command universal consent. To
put it the other way round, beliefs that are common to everyone
are held up as the handiwork of Nature herself.

There can be no doubt that this theory was around in the first
century BC. Many scholars have thought that it was invented only
in that century. But among our sources, some texts point much
earlier – some to Epicurus, others to the early Stoa. To settle this
question we shall have to establish first of all whether either of
these took a favourable attitude to common sense and second, of
course, whether they espoused any form of innateness.

The chapters on Hellenistic philosophy will build on the way we
reinterpreted Platonic recollection in section I. They provide a
good example of how interpreting recollection as a theory about
ordinary concept formation can mislead us into finding an affinity
between Platonic and Hellenistic theories of learning. Once we
restore Plato's theory to its true colours, on the other hand, we
can appreciate the real discontinuity that the Hellenistic theory
of innateness represents. As a result, that theory will emerge not
as the product of a Platonic revival but as a significant innovation
in its own right.

The full importance of this comes out when we realise the
influence that this theory was to have later on in the history
of philosophy, in particular during the most famous episode in
the debate about innatism, in the seventeenth-century. In talking
about that period, philosophers very often now refer to 'the theory
of innate ideas'. What is so significant for us is that such a theory
attempts to explain, among other things, the formation of concepts
involved in ordinary thought. Leibniz, for instance, referred to the
innate ideas as the 'inner core and mortar of our thoughts'. Now,
if the conclusions of sections I and III are accepted it becomes clear
that the theory of innate ideas was a Hellenistic invention, and has
far less to do with Platonic innatism than is usually supposed. In
section IV I shall substantiate these claims, in particular bringing
out the affinities between the Hellenistic and seventeenth-century
theories. Many philosophers of the later period tended to equate
innate ideas with common conceptions and innate principles with

beliefs that commanded widespread assent. They often betrayed their Hellenistic influence by using the terminology of that period or even by quoting from the relevant sources.

By the end of chapter 9 it should be clear how inappropriate the word 'Platonism' is to describe the thought of this period. What is even more remarkable, though, is the way in which one empiricist philosopher, the most famous opponent of innatism in the seventeenth century, subjected these theories to attack. In the first book of his *Essay Concerning Human Understanding*, John Locke lambasts his opponents by latching onto their distinctively Hellenistic feature of linking innatism to a respect for common notions. Empiricist though he was, he attacks these theories by using arguments that show an extraordinary similarity to Plato's revisionist epistemology in such dialogues as the *Meno*. Such a strange convergence is only intelligible when one accepts the great discontinuity between Plato and the 'Platonist' advocates of innate ideas in the seventeenth century.

This should give an idea of the way in which I shall be using the diachronic approach in this study. The first three sections will attempt to cast light on the ancient debate about learning by throwing the different theories into relief against each other. The fourth section then uses the conclusions of its predecessors to trace the true lineage of the seventeenth-century debate. The study as a whole is intended to be of interest to philosophers as well as historians of philosophy, both ancient and modern. In recent years there has been a renaissance of the innatist–empiricist debate instigated by Chomsky's rationalist linguistics and fuelled by the opposition of the likes of Goodman, Putnam and Quine. In company with other writers, Chomsky has brought out the importance of reading the seventeenth- and eighteenth-century participants in this debate. One of the aims of this book is that the voices of the ancients are also heard above all the commotion.

I have tried to ensure that this book can be read on different levels. On many of the issues there is already a large scholarly literature, but I have used the footnotes to indicate my debts and disagreements, and in the main text have tried not to lose sight of the points of broader philosophical interest. A certain familiarity with the relevant texts is presupposed. For readers who are more familiar with some of these than with others, here is a guide to which are particularly important to the different sections of the book:

Section I – Plato, *Meno*; *Phaedo* 57a–84b; *Phaedrus* 246a–257b.

Section II – Aristotle, *Posterior Analytics* I 1–3, II 8–10, 19; *Physics* I 1; *Metaphysics* I 1; *Nicomachean Ethics* I 1–8, VI, X 7–9. These texts can all be found in Ackrill (1987).

Section III – There is now an invaluable collection of Epicurean and Stoic texts in Long and Sedley (1987). For Epicurus, see sections 17–19, 23, 25, and for the Stoics, sections 39–40, 54.

Section IV – On the seventeenth-century debate over innate ideas see:

John Locke, *An Essay Concerning Human Understanding* I ii (1–5) and iii; G. W. Leibniz, *New Essays on Human Understanding* I.

SECTION ONE

*Platonic Recollection*

# Introduction

Although Plato's theory of recollection is one of his most well-known doctrines, there are only three works in which it appears – the *Meno*, the *Phaedo* and the *Phaedrus*.[1] The earliest of the trio, the *Meno*, starts like one of the early Socratic dialogues. Socrates claims not to know what virtue is and asks his interlocutor Meno to give him a definition of it. After three separate attempts, Meno's confidence falters and, when asked for a fourth time to define virtue, objects. If neither of them has any idea of what virtue is, how can they make any progress towards a discovery? Socrates introduces recollection to meet this objection. The soul pre-exists the body, and was consciously in possession of knowledge in its earlier state. Upon entering the body the soul forgets its knowledge, but retains it latently in the form of a memory. What makes discovery possible, therefore, is our ability to recollect and revive these memories within us. Socrates then attempts to find some support for his theory in the famous examination of the slave boy.

At the end of the examination he professes himself to be none too certain about the theory, or at least its details, so it is not surprising to find him making another attempt to establish it in the *Phaedo* (72eff.). Socrates is trying to prove the immortality of the soul, and, as part of an intricate argument for this, wishes to show that the soul must have existed before the body. Socrates assumes the existence of a class of entities, or 'forms', such as those of beauty, goodness, justice and equality, which are not accessible to sense perception, and distinguishes them from their sensible instances, claiming that the instances 'fall short of' the form itself.

---

[1] For the purposes of quotation, I shall be using the following translations (with occasional modifications): for the *Meno* Guthrie (1956), for the *Phaedo* Gallop (1975) and for the *Phaedrus* Hackforth (1952).

He goes on to claim that we must have had knowledge of the form before we made the judgement that a particular falls short of it, and then, in a crucial but difficult stretch of argument, attempts to convince his interlocutor that we must have had this knowledge before we began to use our senses, i.e. before we were born. He concludes that we had the knowledge in a previous state, forgot it at birth and, in time, can regain it by a process of recollection.

The only other place in which recollection figures is in the *Phaedrus*, in the course of the famous allegory describing the fall of the human soul and its incarnation into bodily form. The allegory makes free use of the notion of reincarnation and the way in which a fallen soul may find itself not just in a human body but in almost any kind of animal body. As in the *Phaedo*, the claim is that at the moment of incarnation the soul forgets the knowledge that it once had, but at least when in human form it has the ability to recollect its knowledge of the forms.

It is usually claimed, and rightly so, that the theory of recollection is a theory of innateness. Plato believed that there are certain items in the mind present from birth which explain acts of learning later on in our lives. This is alluded to in the *Phaedo*[2] but is also a feature of the *Meno*, where, towards the end of the slave boy demonstration, Socrates says that in recollecting the slave boy will be recovering knowledge that is within him.[3] This implies that all along there is some knowledge already in the boy. Similarly, in his next question Socrates refers to 'the knowledge which the boy *now has*' (85d9). Thus, although the knowledge is forgotten at birth, it remains latent and is not erased from the soul altogether.[4] This means that Plato's theory has a substantial amount in common with other theories of innateness. Where he differs from other innatists, of course, is in his claim that not only are we in possession of such knowledge at birth, but we have been in possession of this

---

[2] *Phaedo* 73a9 talks of 'knowledge present within us' (ἐπιστήμη ἐνοῦσα). Note that this is a back-reference to the *Meno*.

[3] 85d6–7: τὸ δὲ ἀναλαμβάνειν αὐτὸν ἐν αὑτῷ ἐπιστήμην οὐκ ἀναμιμνήσκεσθαί ἐστιν; See also *Meno* 86b1–2, where Socrates talks of the truth of everything being forever in the soul.

[4] Fine (1992) 213 with n. 41 and (1993) 138 has denied that there is knowledge within the boy. Despite my agreement with almost everything else she has to say about recollection, I would take issue with her on this point. Her view is undermined by the reference in 85d9 to 'the knowledge that the boy now has'. She claims that this reference is forward-looking, but I find this implausible given that Plato not only uses the present tense but adds in the word 'now' as well.

knowledge before birth as well. This is a genuine difference, and we should not try to purge the theory of any commitment to pre-existence and literal recollection by claiming that Plato was only speaking metaphorically. This fails to do justice to the fact that in the *Phaedo* Plato sets out to prove the pre-existence of the soul, for which he needs to claim quite literally that the soul was once in possession of its innate knowledge. Even in the *Meno*, where the emphasis is more epistemological, there is still a short argument for the claim that the soul has been in existence from eternity (85d9–86b4).

Despite his commitment to pre-existence, however, Plato's theory should still be considered a variety of innateness. Later on in this study, when we have had the opportunity to consider other kinds of innateness, we shall ask why Plato should have decided to adopt this one in particular.[5] This chapter, however, will start by addressing a different question, namely, what level of learning the theory is supposed to explain. In the General Introduction I set out two interpretations that give very different answers to this question; they now need to be described in more detail.

According to one interpretation, Plato starts by drawing attention to the way we classify particulars under certain concepts in everyday thought. For example, we might think that a particular object is beautiful or that two objects are equal to each other. From where do we acquire these concepts of beauty and equality? Plato, it is thought, considered such concepts to be too complex for sense perception to provide on its own; so they have instead to come from the soul's internal resources. It is by recollection that we can apply such concepts to the world of our experience. Plato therefore breaks our mundane thoughts down into two components: those that derive from perception and those that derive from the memories of the soul.

Human understanding now comes out as the product of an interaction between the information that our senses give us about particular physical objects and the concepts, for instance, of equality or beauty, under which we classify those particulars. This makes Platonic recollection rather Kantian in tone, for just as Kant made intuitions and concepts the two essential sources of our empirical knowledge, Plato – according to this interpretation – uses

---

[5] See pp. 213–16 below.

perceptions and our innate knowledge of the forms. Of course, the recollection that we all engage in must be extended into knowledge by the philosopher, but that is the next stage on, and does not upset the 'Kantian' nature of the first one.[6] In other words, everyone has achieved a dim recollection of the forms even though they may not have brought their knowledge out into the full light of day.

So much for the first interpretation which I shall call 'K' (for Kant). To illustrate the second, I shall follow the lead of one ancient interpreter[7] and use an analogy adapted from a story in Herodotus. In the midst of the Persian wars against Greece and with a Persian invasion of Greece imminent, the Greeks had a stroke of luck. One of their number, a Spartan named Demaratus, who lived in Persia and had hitherto been no friend of the Greeks, nevertheless decided to commit an act of spite against the Persians. He turned spy for the Greeks and warned them of the invasion. He did this by sending them a letter, a wooden tablet with wax melted on top. What he did, however, was to inscribe the message about the invasion onto the wood and then conceal it beneath the layer of wax. In Herodotus' story, Demaratus leaves the wax surface blank and the tablet is allowed to pass back to Greece where eventually the trick is discovered; the wax is scraped away and the message underneath revealed (VII 239). For my purposes, however, I shall change the story slightly. Imagine that Demaratus had not left the surface wax blank but had inscribed upon it something innocent for Persian consumption. We would now have two messages, one obvious but unreliable, the other true but completely hidden away from view.

Certain details of this analogy force us to look at Plato's theory

---

[6] It is fascinating to note, however, that one person who disassociates himself from this 'Kantian' view of recollection is Kant himself. In the *Critique of Pure Reason* he talks of the laborious process of recollection and identifies it with philosophy: see A 313/B 370 = Kemp Smith (1933) 310. Elsewhere, he makes recollection a very recondite affair and says that we recollect the ideas *only* with difficulty (Kant (1928) 434–5). What lies behind this interpretation is his view that the ideas are not categories or concepts of pure reason, which combine with sensible intuitions to make experience possible, but intellectual intuitions of things as they are in themselves, which is a very different matter.

[7] Plutarch. His interpretation of the theory of recollection is preserved in this fragment: 'there are items of knowledge inside us, but they are concealed beneath the other things which come in from outside, like the case of the tablet sent by Demaratus' (ἔνεισιν μὲν αἱ ἐπιστῆμαι, κρύπτονται δ' ὑπὸ τῶν ἄλλων ἐπεισοδίων ὁμοίως τῇ ὑπὸ Δημαράτου πεμφθείσῃ δέλτῳ). For the origin of this fragment, see Sandbach (1969) 388–9 and Westerink (1976–7) II 166.

of recollection from an unusual perspective. The first important detail is that a message was inscribed on the wax which made complete sense to its Persian readers; the second that these same readers had no inkling at all that there was a message underneath; and the third that they were deceived by the message written on the wax. What happens if we apply all these features to Platonic recollection?

In one sense we are, on this interpretation, blank tablets at birth. We rely upon external sources, perception or hearsay, to form all sorts of notions and opinions about the world around us and about morality. Furthermore – and this is crucial – we can form all these opinions without any help from our innate knowledge whatsoever. Just as the Persians could understand the surface message without being aware of the message inscribed underneath, we can make sense of externally formed views without ever drawing upon our innate resources, without even beginning to recollect. Deep in our souls, however, is knowledge of entities that exist in separation from the particulars, entities of which most people have no consciousness at all; most people would deny that there exist those entities that Plato talks of as forms. But just as the Persians were misled about Demaratus' intentions, so most people are deceived by the surface message into thinking that the world of particulars is all there is. Only the philosopher, who has become puzzled by the confusions and contradictions inherent in our external sources, takes so different a view of reality.

This reading of recollection – call it 'D' for Demaratus – differs sharply from K on the question of what exactly is innate and what is supplied from external sources. D in fact makes Plato more generous about what the senses, for instance, are capable of giving us. They can inform us that a particular object is beautiful or that two particulars are equal without any help from our innate knowledge of the forms. He uses innateness only to explain a philosopher's knowledge of the transcendent entities, the forms, with which particulars are to be unfavourably compared as being deficient.

As a result, recollection ceases to be an account of ordinary thought. Whereas K uses a co-operation between the innate and the empirical to explain ordinary thought, D allows us to make 'Kantian' sense of our experience without invoking any innate knowledge of forms at all. In other words, recollection is used to cover different stretches of intellectual development according to which interpretation one follows. K takes the broader stretch. It attempts to explain our intellectual activity from infancy through to maturity in terms of a continuous path of recollection. One theory is made to embrace the earliest glimmers of intelligence and the vertiginous heights of philosophical achievement at once. On D, Plato only uses recollection to cover the period of later or higher learning, the movement from the mundane perspective to the philosophical. The earlier stages are taken care of externally.

There is also a difference in the number of people who actually recollect. Although both theories agree that everyone has the knowledge inside them, K again takes a broader approach to the issue of who actually recollects. If recollection is necessary for conceptual thought, and if everyone engages in conceptual thought, then everyone recollects to some degree, even if few complete the process through to the end. On D, the fact that everyone engages in conceptual thought does not show that everyone recollects. Recollection only starts with the process of philosophising, and thus only a rather limited number of people recollect. Associated with this is a further point. On D recollection is right from the start a difficult process, on K its first stages are automatic and easy.

This brings us to yet another important difference between the two interpretations. K allows Plato far more optimism in his approach to learning and discovery than D. Perhaps the most important aspect of Herodotus' story was that Demaratus fooled the Persians. In the D interpretation of recollection the counterpart for this feature of the story is that the opinions we derive from external sources, whether from perception or hearsay, in some way mislead us about how things really are. The Demaratus theory thus attributes to Plato a sense of gloom about the cognitive achievements of ordinary people and about the difficulty of philosophical discovery. It also entails that if the inquiry is successful we shall come to revise our earlier beliefs in quite a drastic way. The discovery will be a shock to us just as the Persians would have been disconcerted to learn what lay beneath the message they had believed.

Notice that what gives D this pessimistic character is not merely the way it limits the achievement of recollection to so few. Its message is still more depressing than this because it says something not only about the fortunate few who recollect but about the many who do not. They are not merely missing out on something, but are in some way actually deceived. There are then two senses in which D is pessimistic.

Now in one of these senses K is obviously more optimistic than D. All human beings go through the process of concept formation and, according to K, all human beings – tyrants and sophists included – thereby recollect. But this, it might be argued, still allows for a heavy dose of pessimism in the other sense, for one could say that although ordinary thought involves recollection, it involves only a very partial recollection, only the first glimmers of truth. In completing the process of recollection the philosopher must refine and revise their earlier opinions, and the refinements that philosophy will have to make may be enormous; thus a revisionary approach to philosophy is still compatible with K. Nevertheless, there remains a substantive contrast between D and K. Consider the status of the opinions that arise with perception. In K these represent the results of partial recollection and the movement from them to the final goal is in some sense continuous. They are starting points to be built upon, parts of an overall picture that has to be filled in. On D, however, things are very different. In the image of Demaratus' tablet they are messages to deceive us and are to be scraped away. We discard them, not build on them. There is a radical discontinuity as we become aware of the deception. This makes for an important difference between the two interpretations.

Now that we have the two interpretations of Platonic recollection before us, it is time to turn to the texts. As we have seen, there are only three dialogues in which the theory appears, the *Meno*, the *Phaedo* and the *Phaedrus*. A first perusal of each of these passages may well incline one towards K. The *Meno* does, after all, say that learning and research are *wholly* recollection (81d4–5). Does this not suggest that recollection must cover the wider learning span that K advocates? On D, only *some* learning is recollection. As far as the *Phaedo* is concerned, there is quite a wide consensus that Plato is, among other things, drawing attention to the way in which we all recognise universals in particular sense perceptions by virtue of our pre-existent knowledge of the forms. Furthermore, by imposing a severe limit on the number of people who actually recollect, D is inviting the following problem: if Plato is not talking about something everyone does, how can he prove that everyone's soul is immortal?

Perhaps the strongest evidence for K, though, is to be found in the *Phaedrus*. At one point, Socrates talks of the choice that the fallen souls must make every thousand years as to what type of creature they wish to become. Some, having once been humans, may choose to turn into animals; others may turn back into human form after a spell as an animal. But a soul which has never seen the truth can never take on human form, since human beings are required 'to understand the language of forms, passing from a plurality of perceptions to a unity gathered together by reason', and this is nothing other than the recollection of the vision which we had before incarnation (249b). The K interpretation very plausibly asserts that the argument of this passage requires recollection to explain the cognitive activity of all humans. It is the hallmark of human intelligence to classify the data of sense perception under universals, and Plato's claim is that this would not be possible if we had not already had knowledge of general concepts. D must have a very different interpretation of this argument to offer, but it is not immediately clear what it will be.

Before we begin on the business of looking at the texts in more detail we should take note of some problems concerning two of them. Recollection in the *Meno* is a tentative doctrine, and one should be wary of expecting too determinate an interpretation of it. Once the theory of forms has been introduced in the *Phaedo* the theory of recollection is clearer, at least in relation to the role of sense perception, and it is possible to argue for more determinate interpretations. So it is with the *Phaedo* rather than the *Meno* that both sides in the dispute are making their strongest claims. For much of my discussion I shall be limiting myself to the negative claim that the *Meno* provides no evidence for K.

But if one has to be cautious about the *Meno* one also has to be cautious about the *Phaedrus*, though for slightly different reasons. The whole passage is presented as a myth, not a proof, and so it may be objected that the text requires different treatment and cannot be used straightforwardly as evidence for a particular interpretation of recollection. So here I shall adopt a conditional strategy and argue that if one does use the myth as evidence in this way, then it is D, not K, that emerges as the most convincing interpretation of recollection. With these qualifications in mind we are ready to begin, starting with the *Meno* in chapter 1 and then going on to the *Phaedo* and the *Phaedrus* in chapter 2.

# CHAPTER I

# *The* Meno

The first two parts of this chapter will focus specifically on the question of whether Plato shows any interest in ordinary learning in the *Meno*. In [1] I shall tackle this question by examining Meno's paradox (80d5–e5), the problem that provokes Socrates into proposing recollection in the first place. Is this a problem about ordinary learning, higher learning or both? In [2] I shall look at the initial statement of the theory and at the examination of the slave boy (81c5–85d1) to see if recollection is actually used to explain ordinary concept formation. In both [1] and [2] I shall argue that there is no evidence that the theory was meant to explain such learning. Finally, in [3], I shall look at the second half of the dialogue and argue that, although it would be unwise to press for a fully determinate version of the Demaratus interpretation in these pages, we can find it in an embryonic form. Recollection is used to account for philosophical discovery that results in knowledge; but Plato also draws our attention to the existence of a certain class of true beliefs which are not formed by recollection, even partial recollection, but derive from a kind of surrogate for perception – hearsay or tradition.

## [1] MENO'S PARADOX

The dialogue opens with Meno asking Socrates whether virtue is acquired by teaching, practice or nature. In reply, Socrates professes himself to be unable to answer the question. So far from knowing what virtue is like, he does not even know what it is (71a5–7). Meno appears surprised by this but is happy to remedy Socrates' ignorance, and so the cross-examination begins. Meno's first way of answering the question 'what is virtue?' is to give a list of different virtues without saying what it is they all have in common. When he tries again with a definition of virtue as the power to rule men, Socrates points out that there must be other virtues and so we are no nearer a unitary definition than before. At this point Socrates decides to give some examples to Meno to show what giving a definition involves. The inquiry into virtue is then resumed with a new definition – virtue is the desire for noble things and the ability to procure them. Socrates persuades Meno that the first half of the definition applies to everyone, whether virtuous or not, so that it is only the ability to acquire noble things that counts as a definition. Furthermore, virtue is not a matter of acquiring them in any old way, but doing so with justice and piety. But justice is agreed to be a part of virtue, so it turns out that Meno has defined virtue by citing a part of virtue. Socrates then points out that we cannot know what a part of virtue is when we do not know what the whole is.

At 79e5 Socrates appears to expect the inquiry to go on as before with Meno submitting another definition for examination. But it is not to be; Meno revolts. Despite his surprise at the opening of the dialogue when he heard that Socrates was ignorant about virtue, he now admits to having been warned about Socrates' reputation for reducing people to perplexity. He goes on to compare Socrates to the sting-ray, a fish that numbs anything with which it comes into contact. Meno used to give several speeches on the subject of virtue, but now, like the victim of the sting-ray, feels quite numb (80a8–b4). In his next speech, Socrates takes up this simile and says that he is only like the sting-ray if it, like its victim, is numb. Like Meno he has no idea what virtue is, though he concludes, 'nevertheless I am ready to carry out, together with you, a joint investigation and inquiry into what it is'.

But Meno is not so pliable. Instead he objects (80d5–8):

But how will you look for something when you don't in the least know what it is? How on earth are you going to set up something you don't know as the object of your search? To put it another way, even if you come right up against it, how will you know that what you have found is the thing you didn't know?

To this Socrates replies (80e1–5):

I know what you mean. Do you realise that what you are bringing up is the trick argument that a person cannot inquire either into what he knows or into what he does not know? He would not seek what he knows, for since he knows it there is no need of the inquiry, nor what he does not know, for in that case he does not even know what he is to look for.

It is in response to this problem that Socrates introduces the theory of recollection. It seems plausible to conclude from this that recollection is meant to solve this paradox. If so, our task of determining the nature of Socrates' theory from its context will involve asking just what that problem is. In particular, is it a problem about all learning, or only about the acquisition of philosophical knowledge?

Unfortunately, it has proved difficult for scholars to agree on the exact diagnosis of Meno's paradox. I shall give my own, but we should take stock of one crucial point. Establishing the details of Meno's paradox may be very difficult, but that the overall problem to which Plato is responding concerns higher learning is easier to see. There is no doubt that Meno raises his objection in his frustration at being encouraged to continue an inquiry in which he feels unable to have any success. The general issue must therefore concern a discovery yet to be made by someone who has nevertheless attained the normal stage of human understanding. Moreover, this discovery is not only one that has yet to be made by Meno, it has yet to be made by anyone, as far as Socrates is aware.[1] The point at issue therefore concerns a discovery that has so far proved formidably difficult to make, and so the theory brought in to address this issue is not going to be *centrally* concerned with mundane concept formation. Thus, to the extent that D focuses its interest on the higher learning, it is in tune with the context of the *Meno*. If recollection in this dialogue did in any way concern the acquisition of ordinary concepts it would only do so tangentially.

Having established this, we should attempt to give an analysis of Meno's paradox. The difficulty for any interpreter is that Plato does not develop the problem in any great detail. Meno raises three questions in quick succession and Socrates briefly reformulates the problem in a dilemma before moving on to an exposition of the theory of recollection.[2] But if Plato provides little exegesis of

---

[1] At least by any Athenian: Athens is said to be stricken by a drought of wisdom at 70c3–71a1.

[2] At first sight, there appear to be discrepancies between the two formulations of the paradox. I have argued in Scott (1991) 628–9 that the differences between the

Meno's problem itself after 81a1, the best clues to understanding it are to be found in the first ten pages of the dialogue, because the problem at issue is one that arises out of the previous part of the discussion.

Meno's problem has two elements. The first concerns what has become known as the priority of definition. At the beginning of the dialogue Socrates says that we cannot know what something is like without knowing what it is. Asking what virtue is like before knowing what it is would be as bad as asking what Meno is like before knowing who he is (71b4–8). This analogy is not to be interpreted as saying that Socrates is in a state of blank ignorance about virtue in the sense that he has no conception about it at all; on the contrary, the first ten pages of the dialogue show him equipped with a number of beliefs on the subject.[3] Rather, the analogy is being used to stress the priority of definitional knowledge. We may, of course, have ideas or beliefs – even true ones – about what virtue is like but these can never count as knowledge until we know the definition itself.

Socrates insists that we must know what virtue is before we can discover what it is like. This seems clear enough as far as the *Meno* is concerned.[4] What is more controversial, however, is the question of whether this should be extended into the claim that we cannot know anything at all about virtue until we know the definition. In particular, is Socrates here claiming that, without knowledge of the definition, we cannot know whether something is an example

two versions should not be exaggerated. But, be that as it may, our purpose is to learn what we can about recollection by studying the problem that provokes Socrates into proposing it; thus, what matters is *Socrates'* conception and presentation of the paradox.

[3] The belief that virtue is unitary is one example (72a6ff.). Another substantive claim is that justice is essential to virtue (73a7–c1, 73d6–8 and 78d3–79a1). For this point see Canto-Sperber (1991) 72 with n. 120.

[4] This assumption has, however, been disputed by Nehamas (1987) 290–1. He thinks that Socrates is only committed to a very limited version of the principle: 'it seems to apply only to specific issues, and not to all features of virtue ... Socrates seems to believe that we need to know the definition of a virtue in order to decide whether certain disputable features ... are true or are not true of it.' In my view there is insufficient textual support for limiting the principle in this way. On the other hand I think that there is much better evidence for restricting the principle in another way. Nehamas rightly holds that the priority of definition is not a principle to be applied to all terms, tables and chairs included. See also Burnyeat (1977) 393. The only unequivocal statements of the assumption in the dialogues concern moral or aesthetic terms.

There is an enormous literature on the question of whether Socrates or Plato was committed to the priority of definition. For a useful list of recent contributions see Benson (1990) 19–20, n. 2.

of virtue? Apart from affirming at the beginning (71b3–4) and in two other places (86d3–6 and 100b4–6) that we cannot know what virtue is like without knowing what it is, the only other stricture that Socrates explicitly makes is that we cannot define the parts of virtue without having defined the whole (79c8–9). The status of examples is not explicitly mentioned. Nevertheless, it seems plausible to suppose that he would expect the priority of definition to apply to knowledge of examples. It would be curiously asymmetrical to allow us knowledge of examples of virtue without the definition, but not of its qualities.

All this tells us something about the necessary conditions for making certain discoveries – for instance, what virtue is like and whether something counts as an instance of virtue – but nothing so far about discoveries of the definition of virtue itself. At 74b3ff., however, Socrates directs his attention to this latter question and it is here that the second element of Meno's problem comes to light. To explain some of his requirements for a proper definition he gives Meno some model definitions, defining shape at 75b9–11 as what always accompanies colour. Meno, however, dismisses this definition as 'simple-minded' on the grounds that it would be of no use to someone who did not understand what colour was (75c2–7). This leads Socrates to make an important distinction between giving a definition to someone who is arguing competitively, in which case all that matters is that the definition is true (however baffled one may leave one's interlocutor), and a more friendly or 'dialectical' approach, where the definition must not only be true, but also explanatory, i.e. given in terms that the interlocutor professes to understand. Without this our dialectical definition would never get off the ground. Now the situation envisaged is one in which the person giving the definition presumably knows, whilst the other does not but learns. But all this can equally well apply to two people neither of whom know – two people, that is, who have embarked on a joint inquiry after what they do not know. Here, too, they must start from what they know, and move on to what they do not know, and so it is no surprise to find that the conditions which were laid down for dialectical definition at 75d5–7, where Socrates had teaching and learning in mind, are applied to the joint inquiry into virtue at 79d1–4, just after Meno has given a part of virtue in his definition. Any inquiry must proceed in terms that are agreed and not themselves under investigation.

We can see how a problem about discovery arises as soon as we put the stipulation about the priority of definition together with the conditions for a dialectical definition. Once the priority of definition is assumed, it follows that discoveries about non-definitional features of virtue can only be made on the basis of knowledge of the definition. The second principle states a condition for discovering the definition itself; such discoveries must start out from knowledge.[5] But if we are asking what virtue is, so that *ex hypothesi* we do not know what it is, and if we cannot know anything else about the object without knowledge of the definition, we cannot meet the conditions for giving a definition dialectically. We have no relevant knowledge from which to start. Thus our conundrum is that we want to discover something, but in order to make that discovery need the very knowledge we are seeking.

What lies beneath the problem is that assumptions made at the outset will play a crucial part in guiding the progress of the inquiry and that mere beliefs at the outset are not enough. Anything short of knowledge introduces the risk of muddle, distortion and, of course, error, all of which could have a catastrophic effect on the outcome of the inquiry. Thus, in the absence of reliable starting-points, we have no hope of ever transcending our opinions and achieving knowledge.

Such, then, is the gist of Meno's paradox. Before we return to our overall question about the scope of recollection we need to take note of a difficulty in interpreting the paradox in this way. As I have set it out, the paradox is an attack on the possibility of discovery. The problem points to the way in which we hold all sorts of beliefs without adequate foundation, or undertake all sorts of inquiries in the false expectation that they will be successful. From this one could infer that inquiry is pointless. What one could not do, however, is to infer that inquiry is *impossible*. We have a sufficient grasp of something to ask questions and undertake investigations, but not sufficient for us to bring them to successful completion.

This is just what has been the case in the *Meno* up to 80d5. But now look more closely at the wording of the paradox at 80e1–5:

---

[5] Knowledge here should be taken in a strong sense as opposed to, for instance, mere true belief. I take this to be an implication of 79d1–4.

a person *cannot inquire* either into what he knows or into what he does not know. He would not seek what he knows, for since he knows it there is no need of the inquiry, nor what he does not know, for in that case he does not even know what he is to look for.

Because Socrates uses the word for 'inquire' rather than 'discover' he is, strictly speaking, setting out a problem not about discovery as such but about inquiry *per se*, whether that inquiry is successful or not. It is not possible even to inquire, i.e. to *attempt* to discover; there is a problem about even *asking* a question, let alone answering it. In denying that we can get even an unsuccessful inquiry going it is rather like a Zenonian argument against motion; we simply cannot move at all. With the problem of discovery, on the other hand, we merely find it impossible to reach a particular destination.[6]

Of course, if the paradox of inquiry rules out all inquiry, *a fortiori* it rules out inquiry that results in discovery, but this should not lead us to deny that the two problems are different. One way of bringing out the difference is to see that the paradox about inquiry is a trivial problem and easy to solve, whereas the paradox about discovery is more difficult. The paradox about inquiry is grounded upon a claim about knowledge that is simply false, namely, that knowledge is an all-or-nothing affair. Inquiry would indeed be impossible if knowing an object meant knowing all about it (so that no further knowledge about it is possible) and if not knowing it meant being in a state of complete ignorance about it such that one cannot even think or formulate a question. If knowledge is seen in this way as an all-or-nothing thing – either one 'hits' the object or one does not – the puzzle will work. The way to solve the problem is to point out that one can grasp something partially, without knowing it in the full sense. This will allow one to formulate a problem without simultaneously solving it. The paradox about inquiry could also be solved by an appeal to the distinction, present in the *Meno* itself, between true belief and knowledge.[7] Having a true belief about something will enable us to identify it as an object of inquiry without knowing about it.

But while the problem about inquiry collapses in the face of such distinctions, the problem of discovery, if anything, thrives upon them, because it exploits the gulf that is opened up between the

---

[6] I have discussed the difference between a problem of inquiry and a problem of discovery at greater length in Scott (1991).

[7] The distinction is first employed at 85c6–7 and then developed at 97a9ff.

two cognitive states. To undermine the problem of discovery Plato would have had to retract his espousal of the priority of definition, which would be a very different matter altogether.

The problem of discovery that I have diagnosed and the problem of inquiry are different. So the objection to my reading of the problem that provokes the theory of recollection is that it is at variance with Socrates' formulation of the problem at 80e1–5, in particular with his use of the word 'inquire' in 80e3. Should we take this discrepancy as evidence that we have the wrong diagnosis? I would suggest not. Look at this passage at the end of the slave boy demonstration which seems most likely to be a back-reference to the paradox:

one thing I am ready to fight for as long as I can, in word and act: that is, that we shall be better, braver and more active if we believe we must look for what we don't know than if we believe *there is no point inquiring because what we don't know we can never discover.* (86b7–c2)

As is clear from the lines that I have italicised, this passage refers not to a problem about inquiry *per se*, but to a problem about successful inquiry, i.e. discovery. It also refers to the suggestion that inquiry might be pointless, but not that it might be impossible. If we take these lines as a reliable account of what the original problem is, we could say that there is merely a slight inaccuracy in the formulation at 80e3 and that the word 'discover' (*heuriskein*) would have been more appropriate than 'inquire' (*zētein*).

Now that we have arrived at a diagnosis of Meno's paradox, we can give an answer to our overall question. The problem that Socrates is confronting is not one about how we first form our moral concepts; it is about how we can ever get beyond the stage of merely holding opinions to the acquisition of the kind of knowledge that could survive Socratic examination. Assuming Meno's paradox is the principal reason for recollection, then, the main focus of the theory is upon higher learning. There are, however, two qualifications we should make to this claim. First, we have not ruled out the possibility that Plato might have had other reasons for introducing recollection which are connected with ordinary learning. A second possibility is that even if the theory is primarily intended to explain higher learning, it might also explain ordinary learning incidentally or as a by-product. In other words, all we can say so far is that up to the point where Socrates begins to sketch the theory (81a10) our expectations are for a theory whose primary focus is upon higher learning. To tackle the second of these possibilities, we need to look at the presentation of the theory in the slave boy examination. This we shall do in [2] below.

As for the first, there is in fact one other reason why Socrates introduces recollection into the dialogue. But this, far from exhibiting any kind of interest in ordinary learning, merely serves to underline the point that recollection is primarily about philosophical discovery. Look at this passage where Socrates is trying to persuade Meno to accept the theory:

We ought not then to be led astray by the contentious argument you quoted. It would make us lazy and is music to the ears of weaklings. The other doctrine produces energetic seekers after knowledge; and being convinced of its truth, I am ready, with your help, to inquire into the nature of virtue. (81d5–e2)

As at 86b-c there is a strong attack on laziness and an attempt to incite Meno to do some hard work. Now previously we have been seeing recollection as the solution to a complex epistemological puzzle; here, by contrast, it is being used more straightforwardly as a way to stimulate Meno out of intellectual apathy. That Meno is inclined towards such torpor is clear from his speech at 79e7–80b7 where he complains that Socrates has made him numb. Interestingly enough, in his next speech Socrates seems to acknowledge the naturalness of this desire to give up. He admits, like Meno, to being ignorant about the nature of virtue, though he concludes, '*nevertheless* I am ready to carry out, together with you, a joint investigation and inquiry into what it is'. The use of the word 'nevertheless' betrays his admission that a perfectly natural reaction to everything he has just said would be to abandon the inquiry. Recollection thus functions as an antidote to this sort of intellectual laziness. If so, the implication is that the inquiry that Meno wanted to abandon is something of a struggle. The theory of recollection is therefore meant to incite us into a form of higher learning and to do this it needs to be primarily a thesis about higher learning.[8]

8 See Scott (1991) for a more detailed discussion of the incentive function of recollection. I also argued in that article that this is the *only* function recollection is serving in the *Meno*. My main line of reasoning was that if recollection is meant to solve any epistemological problem it would be the paradox of 80e1–5; but because of the use of the word 'inquire' (*zētein*) at 80e3, that paradox is merely a sophism about inquiry too trivial to merit either Socrates' attention or recollection as its solution; hence it

## [2] THE PRESENTATION OF THE THEORY

Socrates' reasons for introducing the theory of recollection suggest that it is a theory principally concerned with higher learning. So far we have not seen any indication that Plato is interested in using the theory to explain the formation of ordinary concepts. On my interpretation, the *Meno* continues in this vein. Recollection begins only from the moment when we encounter perplexity in the course of a Socratic examination. However, this is to say too much too soon. For all we know, it may be that Plato also used the theory to explain the formation of ordinary concepts or that it does this anyway. We need to turn to the presentation of the theory after 81c5 to see if this is in fact the case.

Socrates first describes the theory in a passage at the beginning of this section and then provides us with a demonstration of recollection in action in the interview with the slave boy. Here is the initial presentation of the theory at 81c5–d5:

Thus the soul, since it is immortal and has been born many times, and has seen all things both here and in Hades, has learned everything that is. So we need not be surprised if it can recall the knowledge of virtue or anything else which, as we shall see, it once possessed. All nature is akin, and the soul has learned everything, so that when a person has recalled a single piece of knowledge – *learned* it, in ordinary language – there is no reason why we should not find out all the rest, if he keeps a stout heart and does not grow weary of the search; for seeking and learning are in fact nothing but recollection.

At first sight this passage seems to go in favour of K. It talks of the soul knowing 'everything', and of seeking and learning being 'nothing but recollection'. These phrases appear to make the scope of recollection extremely wide. Nevertheless, we should be extremely wary of taking this passage at face value. If it is taken to imply that absolutely everything that we learn is recollected from a previous existence, it goes further than even the most devoted adherent of K would dare. Are we really to include all

is more plausible to suppose that recollection is not meant to solve the paradox but only to incite Meno into renewed inquiry. On reflection, however, I think that this argument places too much weight on the use of the word 'inquire' (*zētein*) in 80e3 at the expense of the context of the first ten pages of the dialogue and the back reference of 86b7–c1. I now think that although recollection does serve as an incentive it also functions as the solution to Meno's paradox.

learning – 'learning how' as well as 'learning that'? Does Plato
include learning how to play the lyre, for instance? And under
the label of 'learning that', do we also have to include empirical
learning and discovery of individual facts? These sorts of question
have, of course, already been raised by scholars and commentators
who have argued for various qualifications to be appended to
the sentence,[9] and they are surely right in their reluctance to
take 'all learning' absolutely literally. What we have to do is to
examine what Socrates says about recollection in the course of
the slave boy examination in order to determine the scope of
the theory. Defenders of K will gain little by insisting that the
initial statement of the theory of recollection be taken literally
because it will give them too much, and once it is conceded that
some restrictions need to be placed on the claims of 81c5–d5, K
is no longer the only interpretation available; D is back in the
running. In short, the passage is too indeterminate to decide one
way or the other.

Another point in this passage to mention is Socrates' reference to the notion that the soul 'has seen' everything in its
various incarnations (81c6). The talk of the soul 'seeing' anything suggests that the language of this passage is metaphorical. Furthermore, the implication that the soul once learnt anything is to be corrected later in the dialogue at 86a6–b4 where
Socrates argues that the soul never *learnt* anything but has been
in a state of knowing everything from eternity. In the light of
these points it is wisest to treat this passage as a provisional
sketch of the theory and not to take everything stated in it at
face value.

This is not to say, of course, that one cannot read K into these
lines taken on their own, merely that one need not, and that D,
with its more qualified interpretation, is an acceptable reading of
the lines. As to what qualifications D would make to the claim of
81d1, 'the soul has learned everything', one should look to 85e2–3

---

9 Bluck (1961) 9–10, for instance, argues against including experiences of a previous life
into the matter of recollection. Vlastos (1994) 97 construes recollection as *'any advance
in understanding which results from the perception of logical relationships'*. See also Bostock
(1988) 15 who is nevertheless one of the main proponents of K where the *Phaedo*
is concerned. For an extremely severe restriction on the meaning of the word learn
(*manthanein*) see Nehamas (1985) 21–2. On his view, the slave boy does not recollect
at all, and would only do so if he attained knowledge, not just true opinion. If this
is the case, however, it is difficult to see what the demonstration is meant to be
demonstrating if not recollection in action.

where Socrates generalises from the slave boy demonstration to say that the boy can recollect not just geometry, but also all the other technical disciplines (*mathēmata*). Plato is interested in the acquisition of knowledge about such disciplines, of which geometry is a paradigm example.

We should also note that the statement of 81d4–5, 'seeking and learning are in fact nothing but recollection', is capable of a restricted interpretation of the kind that D would favour. Why, after all, should the phrase have to mean that *all* research and *all* learning are, both of them, always cases of recollection? What about research that ends in the acquisition of false beliefs? As we shall see below, the idea that we might recollect false beliefs is deeply problematic. A more plausible reading of this sentence is to take it as a hendiadys. Learning *via* research is recollection, 'learning *via* research' referring to the deliberate efforts of the philosophically earnest. If the phrase is taken in this way, it is entirely consistent with the D interpretation.

The initial sketch of recollection should not be used on its own to decide between K and D. Let us turn to the slave boy demonstration to see if there is any evidence for finding an interest in ordinary learning. As Socrates presents it here, there are three stages of recollection:

(i) The slave boy comes to realise that what he previously believed to be right is in fact wrong. Thus, after he has elicited a false answer from the boy, Socrates says to Meno (82e12–13): 'Now watch how he recollects things in order – the proper way to recollect.' It is between this point and 84a2 that the first stage of recollection happens, and at the end of it the slave boy is in perplexity, but is at least aware that he does not know, and this awareness is the result of the first glimmers of recollection.

(ii) In the next stage of recollection (84d3–85b7) the slave boy moves from the mere awareness of his ignorance towards the acquisition of true opinions. Yet when he has these opinions, he does not yet have knowledge (85c6–10):

So someone who does not know about something, whatever it may be that he doesn't know, has in himself true opinions on a subject without having knowledge . . . and at the moment these opinions have just been stirred up in him as if he were in a dream.

(iii) It is only at the final stage of recollection that knowledge is acquired, as Socrates goes on to say in the passage immediately following the quotation. This stage is mentioned later in the dialogue, at 98a4, when Socrates describes the difference between knowledge and true opinion. When we have tied down an opinion with 'explanatory reasoning' we convert it into knowledge, and this is nothing but recollection.

The examination of the slave boy shows recollection starting only after contact with a certain type of stimulus or catalyst, in this case Socrates. There is no evidence to show that he would have started to recollect had he never met Socrates. In this passage recollection is only invoked to explain the slave boy's awareness that what he originally thought was wrong, the acquisition of certain true opinions,[10] and the movement from these opinions towards knowledge. I do not wish to try to pin down at precisely what stage in the examination the slave boy's recollection begins; the text is not sufficiently determinate. I am confining myself to the general interpretation set out above in stages (i)–(iii) and to the rejection of the idea that recollection is used in this passage to explain how the slave boy acquired the beliefs and concepts necessary to make sense of what Socrates was talking about when the examination began. This is precisely what K would have recollection do. Beginning from an analysis of propositional thought into its conceptual components, it has Plato explain the formation of concepts that make language and thought possible. On all such matters, however, the text itself remains completely silent.

One objection to my view is suggested by a sentence at 82b6–7, where Socrates, before the slave boy has even opened his mouth, says to Meno, 'see whether it seems to you that he is learning from me or simply being reminded'. Should we not infer that anything that the slave boy says after this is the result of recollection, including the mistakes and false starts that lead him into his *aporia*?

The first response to this is that even if the slave boy were recollecting from the moment he begins to speak, it would not be enough to support the K interpretation, according to which recollection is meant to explain how we come by the concepts we use in everyday thought. The slave boy has acquired these before the examination began. He speaks Greek (82b4) and seems

---

[10] Notice how in 85c9–10 Socrates talks of the arousal of opinions as something that has only just (ἄρτι) happened.

to have the conceptual apparatus sufficient to understand almost all Socrates' questions. So what happens after Socrates begins the examination is not relevant to questions about the ordinary learning in which K is interested. Indeed, this brings out why this whole passage can never provide any evidence for K. The purpose of the examination is that Meno should witness recollection actually happening. Thus there is no point Socrates saying anything about cognitive achievements that may have happened *before* the examination because Meno was not standing over the boy to check that such learning was genuine recollection. The only learning that Socrates is going to talk about is that which takes place within the demonstration for Meno to witness; mundane concept formation has taken place before the examination, and thus it cannot be what is at issue during the examination.

Even if it did help K's case to claim that recollection begins as soon as the slave boy begins to speak it would be neither necessary nor at all wise to do so. The comment of 82b6–7, 'see whether he is learning from me or simply being reminded', need not apply to the immediately following section (82b9–e3) but can be taken to apply to the demonstration as a whole in which there will indeed be some recollection. Furthermore, the consequences of making it apply to 82b9–e3, the section in which the boy gives some false answers, would be disastrous to Socrates' whole strategy in the *Meno*. This interpretation would turn recollection into something very much like the midwife story in the *Theaetetus*, where Socrates extracts from his interlocutor a number of false definitions which are 'within' him.

Now try saying that when Socrates extracts the false answer from the slave boy he is making him recollect; try saying this while at the same time remembering that Socrates is using the examination to prove to Meno that learning is recollection, as part of his programme to show that discovery is possible. Socrates' strategy in examining the slave boy is to take some subject-matter with which both he and Meno are familiar so that they can arbitrate. In the search for virtue, however, there was no one who knew, and thus no one to arbitrate. If Socrates can convince Meno that he is not teaching the boy but merely questioning him, and if Meno himself knows the answers, then he may be persuaded that when the slave boy gets it right, he is deriving knowledge from within. But if Meno sees the boy 'recollecting' false judgements,

Socrates' programme is completely ruined. If we can derive from within ourselves false as well as true judgements, we shall need to decide which are which. But how are we to make this decision? Is there to be another process of recollection to help us find out? If so, we have an infinite regress on our hands.[11] If we can spare recollection from falling into these problems, so much the better; and we can – so long as we reject any interpretation that is not content to limit Plato's interests to the problem of how the slave boy got the right answers, but how he got the wrong ones as well.

[3] RECOLLECTION AND THE CONCLUSION OF THE MENO

So far the *Meno* provides no evidence that the theory of recollection is meant to explain ordinary learning. It may seem that this is as much as we can extract from the dialogue, because, after 86, recollection is hardly mentioned explicitly again. Nevertheless, the second half of the dialogue contains some important material about the distinction between knowledge and true belief and about the means by which these are produced. All of this has a significant bearing on the theory of recollection and I wish to argue that, in these pages, we can find an embryonic version of the Demaratus theory.

The argument of the second half of the *Meno* is perplexing, marked by a series of twists and turns that show Plato at his most tentative. For the sake of clarity, let me set out the interpretation of the conclusion that I shall be defending before I start to trace a path through the maze of Plato's argument. The theme of the dialogue has been the question of whether virtue can be taught, and much of the first ten pages were concerned with trying to define virtue itself. By the end of the dialogue, Socrates concludes that there are two kinds of virtue: one is knowledge, which comes by teaching, the other is an inferior kind of virtue that is based upon mere true belief and that comes by 'divine dispensation'. On my interpretation, knowledge here is to be taken as philosophical understanding arrived at by a laborious process of recollection and prompted by questioning by a 'teacher' in the form of a Socratic questioner. The whole process essentially involves thinking for oneself. As for the true beliefs mentioned in the conclusion, the

[11] Compare this with the 'aviary' regress in *Theaetetus* 200a12ff.

only good thing about them is that they are true. Otherwise they are disparaged as the product of learning by hearsay or tradition, ironically referred to as 'divine dispensation'. True belief is marked by an absence of reflection and an unwillingness or even inability to think for oneself. Precisely because it is instilled by an external source, hearsay, its development is entirely independent of recollection. There are thus two quite independent sources, one for knowledge, the other for true opinion. This is the interpretation I shall be proposing for the conclusion of the dialogue; let us now turn to examine the text in more detail.

At 86c7, after the end of the recollection passage Meno tries to make Socrates return to the original question of how virtue is acquired. As before, Socrates insists that they must first define virtue but, in what can be seen as an apparent compromise, he proposes the method of hypothesis. They will tackle Meno's question, but not head-on. Instead of discussing the proposition that virtue is teachable they will find one equivalent to it, and discuss that instead. As an equivalent they select the proposition that virtue is knowledge on the (unargued) grounds that only knowledge is teachable. In effect this leads them back to a discussion of the nature of virtue: is it a form of knowledge?

There follows an argument in which virtue is agreed to be knowledge, and so it seems that Meno's question has now been answered. Virtue is knowledge and so it must be teachable (87c11–9c4). But then Socrates raises a doubt. They were certainly right to say that if something is knowledge it is teachable, but *is* virtue teachable? (89d3) In the next stretch of argument, much of which features the new character Anytus, it is argued that virtue is not teachable after all. If it were, why have none of the most distinguished men at Athens succeeded in teaching it to their sons? (90b7–94e2) And why is there no agreement on the question as to whether it is teachable? Why are there no generally acknowledged teachers of it? In such conditions virtue seems not to be teachable (95b1–6c10).

It now looks as if we have a straight contradiction on our hands: one argument (87–9) demonstrates that virtue can be taught, the other (89–96) that it cannot. This, however, is not the only way of interpreting the relation between the two arguments, nor is it the most plausible. The contradiction could be resolved by making a distinction between two types of possibility. To take an example, consider the difference between saying that an ambition is in principle achievable and that it can be achieved as things are, here and now. These are two very different kinds of possibility, the first can be called conceptual, the second empirical, and it may well be the case that something is possible in the first sense, but not in the second. This distinction makes good sense of the ending of the *Meno*. The argument of 87–9 that virtue is knowledge and hence teachable could be taken as a conceptual argument, because it involves a conceptual analysis of virtue and its relation to knowledge and goodness. The argument of 89–96 on the other hand should be taken as concluding that virtue is not teachable in the empirical sense; virtue may in principle be teachable, but as things currently stand in Athens and Thessaly (the two places mentioned in this passage), it cannot be taught. That it is an empirical conclusion is implied by the fact that many of the grounds adduced in its favour are matters of contingent fact. If the arguments are viewed in this light, then, there is no contradiction between them.[12]

Not only is this a possible interpretation, it also fits well with the way Socrates reacts in the aftermath of the two arguments. At the end of the argument that virtue is not teachable Meno wonders 'whether there are in fact no good men at all, or how they are produced when they do appear' (96d2–4). The first option, that there are no good men around (a somewhat pessimistic, not to say subversive, thought), would arise as a natural possibility if we thought that virtue could be taught but that, as things are, there are no teachers. And although the second option could mean 'since virtue is not even in principle teachable, how does it come?' it could also mean 'in addition to teaching, is there any other method by which it can be acquired?' And it is this second interpretation that Socrates goes on to take when he introduces his distinction between knowledge and true belief. He claims that they were wrong to insist earlier that virtue can *only*[13] be knowledge; it can also be true opinion. Anyone who has true opinions about something will be as useful as someone with knowledge. Virtue comes either by teaching (if it is knowledge), or by whatever method is appropriate to producing true opinion.

Thus Socrates and Meno see the task not as one of resolving an outright contradiction but of choosing between these two

---

[12] This line of interpretation is very close to that of Bluck (1961) 23–5.
[13] 96e2 (μόνον).

propositions: either there are no virtuous people as a matter of fact, or there must be in principle another way to become virtuous. Socrates appears to take the second option and argues that virtue can be either knowledge or true belief.[14] He then proceeds to discuss this distinction in more detail and, after pointing out that knowledge and true belief can be just as useful as each other, brings out the distinction by invoking an analogy. The problem with true opinions is that they are like the legendary statues of Daedalus which had a tendency to run away and were only truly valuable when tied down. Similarly, true opinions 'run away from a man's mind, so they are not worth much until you tether them by reasoning out the explanation' (98a2–4). After expounding this distinction between knowledge and true opinion, Socrates goes on to assess its implications for the question of whether virtue is teachable. He still insists that only knowledge can be taught, so that if there is virtue based on true opinion, it must come some other way. The nature of this other way emerges in the conclusion of the dialogue: such virtue comes by divine dispensation.

This conclusion presents us with a number of problems. First of all, it seems to be inconsistent with some of Socrates' remarks at the end of the slave boy experiment (85c6–d1):

So someone who does not know about something, whatever it may be that he doesn't know, has in himself true opinions on a subject without having knowledge ... At present these opinions, being newly aroused, have a dream-like quality. But if he is questioned on the same topics on many occasions and in many different ways, you can see that in the end he will have a knowledge on the subject as accurate as anybody's.

In the first sentence, 85c6–7, Socrates emphatically distinguishes knowing something from merely having a true belief, the very

---

[14] On this interpretation, therefore, Socrates still maintains that there is a kind of virtue equivalent to knowledge. This may seem to run against the text in a few places. At 89d5 Socrates suggests that what he is about to do in the following argument is to show that virtue is not knowledge, and when he refers back to this argument he says that what was established was that virtue was not knowledge (98e7–8; 99a7–8). Against this, however, we should note 96e2–3 and 98c8 where he says that it is not *only* knowledge that is useful but true opinion as well; 99a1–2 stresses again that there are *two* ways of guiding affairs rightly, a point supported by the claim that knowledge is a more valuable means of doing this than true opinion (98a6–8). All these texts show that virtue is not excluded from being knowledge. Rather, Socrates is saying that the kind of virtue that happens to be present in Athens is not knowledge but true opinion.

distinction, of course, that he will explicate later on. But the next sentence seems to contradict the conclusion of the *Meno* in not just one, but two ways. At the end of the dialogue, Socrates says that knowledge comes by teaching, and that true belief does not. In other words, knowledge and true belief must come by different ways. Now in 85c9–d1 he implies that the *same* process that led to the formation of true beliefs will lead also to knowledge. What is more, he also says in this sentence that this method is questioning, and throughout the experiment this has been opposed to teaching.[15]

Let us start with the second problem, that knowledge is said to come by questioning at 85c, but by teaching at the end of the dialogue. The best way of resolving the problem here is to distinguish one sense of teaching, where one simply instils opinions in someone else, from another, where one helps them to recollect, a kind of dialectical or 'maieutic' teaching. In the slave boy interview Socrates takes great pains to distinguish teaching from recollection but only because he wants to deny that he is teaching in the first sense; at the end of the dialogue, on the other hand, it is dialectical or maieutic teaching that is involved. Recollection and maieutic teaching are both indispensable for knowledge.[16]

But we still have the other problem, that at the end of the dialogue knowledge and true belief come by different ways whereas at 85c9–d1 they come by the same continuous process. Now there is no doubt that the boy has acquired true beliefs by questioning and dialectical recollection. So in the sense of 'teaching' at work in the conclusion of the dialogue, he has acquired true beliefs by teaching. So why is it that at the end of the dialogue only knowledge is said to be teachable? The best way of removing this contradiction lies in making a distinction between two types of true opinion, one formed by dialectical recollection the other not.[17] The

---

[15] See esp. 84d1–2.

[16] Socrates first introduces the maieutic sense of teaching into the dialogue at 87b8–c1 where he bids Meno not to quibble about words and treats the words 'recollectable' (ἀναμνηστόν) and 'teachable' (διδακτόν) interchangeably; thus 'knowledge is teachable' is equivalent to 'knowledge is recollectable'. Incidentally, we should take 'knowledge is recollectable' not merely to mean 'knowledge is something one can remember', but 'knowledge is something of which one can be reminded *by someone else*'. This sense implies that two people are involved and thus preserves some symmetry with 'teachable'. See Bluck (1961) 325–6.

[17] Someone who sees the need for two types of true belief is Canto-Sperber (1991) 91–3 and 104–5.

slave boy's true opinions are aroused in very special circumstances, those of careful dialectical supervision which proceeds sequentially (82e12). This does not exclude the possibility of there being other true opinions not so produced, and it is thoroughly implausible to suppose that the true opinions of the great men of Athens have been subjected to the elenchtic process. Their true opinions should therefore be placed in a different category from the slave boy's.[18]

There are two further problems which concern the claim that virtue based on true belief comes by divine dispensation. First, is Socrates sincere in claiming that those who have virtue by true opinion are the recipients of divine inspiration? It seems far more plausible to suppose that the conclusion of the *Meno* is ironic. After all, the people to whom this 'virtue' is dispensed include Themistocles and Pericles[19] and, since we know from *Gorgias* 515c4ff. that such people never ranked very high in Plato's estimation, the attribution of divine dispensation to them in the *Meno* is likely to be tongue-in-cheek. The main purpose behind Socrates' irony seems to be to stress – at several points – that those with mere true belief have no knowledge or understanding of what they are saying.[20] They hit upon the truth only in spite of themselves.

This is not the only reason for thinking that the conclusion of the *Meno* is heavily laced with irony. There has already been one ironic allusion to divine dispensation in the dialogue. In his conversation with Anytus, Socrates, with obvious irony, calls him a prophet for claiming to know that the sophists are not teachers of virtue without ever having encountered one. The Greek word Socrates uses for 'prophet' at 92c6 is *mantis*, and, when talking of the recipients of divine dispensation a little later on, he uses, among other terms, the Greek word *theo-mantis* (99c3). Furthermore, after Socrates has attributed 'divine dispensation' to the great men of Athens, Meno remarks that Anytus would take umbrage (99e2). This suggests that Meno, at least, is taking Socrates' remarks ironically.

[18] Such beliefs are very probably accompanied by a certain complacence; those who hold them are under the illusion that they have knowledge. The true beliefs that are recollected, on the other hand, come with a humbler attitude, the realisation that one is only at the beginning of a much longer process.

[19] This is clear from the conversation with Anytus and from the reference back to it at 99b5–9.

[20] 99c3–5; cf. 99e6–100a1.

But if the second half of the conclusion, that virtue comes by divine dispensation, is to be taken ironically, there is a further question to be asked. Is the virtue that Socrates attributes to the great men of Athens in fact genuine virtue, on a par with the virtue that is based on knowledge? So far we have been assuming that it is; that, in the conclusion of the dialogue, virtue is either knowledge or true opinion; and so is either imparted by teaching or 'divine dispensation' and that the virtue that happens to be present in Athens is of the second type. So there *is* virtue and there *are* good people in Athens but their virtue is not to be identified with any kind of knowledge. Remember how at 96d2–4 Meno asked 'whether there are in fact no good men at all, or how they are produced when they do appear', thus presenting Socrates with a choice between denying that there are good people around and finding an alternative means for virtue to be acquired. Socrates, it seems, has taken up the second option, thereby avoiding the depressing implications of the first. But now look at Socrates summing up the discussion at the end of the dialogue:

If all we have said in this discussion, and in the questions we have asked, [has] been right, virtue is acquired neither by nature nor by teaching. Whoever has it gets it by divine dispensation without understanding, unless he be the kind of statesman who can create another like himself. Should there be such a man, he would be among the living practically what Homer said Teiresias was among the dead, when he described him as the only one in the underworld who kept his wits – 'the others are mere flitting shades'. Where virtue is concerned such a man would be just like that, *a solid reality among shadows* (99e4–100a7)

The allusion to Teiresias in Hades, brief though it is, has important implications for the conclusion of the whole dialogue. The quotation itself seems to pick up a theme with which we are already familiar. Those who merely have virtue based on true belief are unstable and flit around (100a5). This recalls the impermanence of the statues of Daedalus. But the following sentence, with its allusion to shadows, introduces another way in which virtue based on true opinion is inferior. Such virtue is not genuine when compared with virtue based on knowledge. This in fact undermines the interpretation we may have been allowed to form so far, for although Socrates has deliberately led us to think that virtue can come in either of the two ways suggested and that virtue based on true opinion is none the less virtue, it turns out not to be the case after all. The Teiresias figure would be someone with genuine virtue; the rest only have some less substantial virtue or 'phantom' virtue in comparison. In other words, in response to Meno's query of 96d1–4 Socrates has not taken the second option after all, but the first, the subversive claim that there are indeed no *genuinely* good people around. By implication, he reserves his greatest insult to the great Athenian politicians right to the end. Earlier, at least, he seemed to allow them virtue if not the skill to impart or understand it; now he denies them the genuine article itself.

If this is the correct account of the conclusion of the dialogue, does it give us any more help in deciding whether D or K is the better interpretation of recollection in the *Meno*? The first half of the conclusion, that knowledge is 'teachable', i.e. can be produced by recollection, is compatible with both interpretations and so does not take us any further. The scope for disagreement comes with the second half, specifically over the question, which we have yet to answer, of how the true beliefs in question arise and of what lies behind the ironic claim that they come by 'divine dispensation'. The concluding pages of the dialogue are so indeterminate that it is difficult to answer this question with complete confidence. One could argue that these true beliefs are the result of partial recollection; this would be in line with K because it would show that recollection is not the prerogative of the philosophically earnest, but something in which non-philosophers, perhaps even anti-philosophers, engage. I wish to argue, however, that the true beliefs of these non-philosophers have an external origin that is quite independent of any process of recollection. On this line of interpretation Plato is already thinking of something that was to appear in the *Phaedo* and the *Republic*.[21] He envisages a second-best virtue that arises by conformity to a tradition, by reliance on hearsay or habituation. The opinions are thus instilled into people and not the result of dialectical teaching or recollection. Though one should be tentative here, there are some good reasons for allowing hearsay to play such a role in the *Meno*.

These can be found in an earlier passage, 97a9–b3, where Socrates uses an illustration to articulate the distinction between knowledge and true belief. Imagine someone who has been to a

---

[21] The connection between these different passages has been noticed by others: for instance, Taylor (1960) 144–5.

certain place, for example Larissa, and who can lead others there, and someone else who has never been there but has (presumably) been told the way. The first person has knowledge, the second mere true belief. The interest of this illustration is that it is the only point in this discussion which touches on the *formation* of true beliefs.

First of all, we need to settle one question. Are we being provided with an *example* of knowledge? If so, there is a problem looming because 'knowledge' of the road to Larissa would fail to meet the condition that knowledge be based on explanatory reasoning (98a3–4). The person who goes to Larissa does not go through any process of explanation and so, according to the third criterion, does not have any knowledge. A good solution would be to take the Larissa point not as an example of the difference between knowledge and true opinion, but as an analogy for it. This would avoid us having to say that for Plato there is such a thing as knowledge of unexplained facts and so escape the contradiction.[22] The point of the analogy would then be that knowledge must involve 'seeing' or working out a problem for oneself, rather than relying on someone else's authority.[23]

If one implication of the analogy is that true belief comes by hearsay, 'divine dispensation' ought therefore to embrace in its meaning the notion that those under its spell live on borrowed opinions, which might explain why they can neither teach nor defend what they believe. So now the conclusion of the dialogue is that knowledge and those true beliefs acquired *en route* to knowledge are opposed to another type of true belief, which is formed by hearsay. It is only the latter that we find in evidence at Athens, if at all.

The analogy of divine inspiration is in fact a very apt way to denigrate those who rely on hearsay. Such people hold their beliefs by proxy much like a prophet or a medium who is taken

---

[22] For this approach see Nehamas (1985) 27–8.

[23] This is a point that has already been made earlier in the dialogue when, in the course of the slave-boy demonstration, we are told that he does not just have to draw the knowledge from himself, but also *for himself* (85d6). Moreover, if Plato is taking knowledge as understanding, as his reference to explanatory reasoning suggests, the rejection of hearsay is a completely natural step to make. Coming to understand something in the synoptic way required is not something that can be done by someone else. We can only come to see the connections for ourselves. This point has been made by Burnyeat (1987) 21. See again Nehamas (1985) 27–9. See below pp. 253ff.

over by another force. Both groups are allowing someone else to speak through them.[24] What is more, Socrates has already used the notion of divine inspiration as a way of denigrating beliefs derived from hearsay. As we have seen, at 92c6 Socrates refers to Anytus ironically as a seer, a *mantis*. Interestingly enough, the comment that provokes this remark is Anytus' denial that the sophists could be teachers of virtue. Now, as far as Plato is concerned, of course, Anytus is quite right. The sophists could not in any way be considered teachers of virtue. But this is merely a true opinion; on his own admission, Anytus has never actually encountered the sophists and is relying on hearsay which prevents him from knowing anything about the sophists. So here we have a true belief based on hearsay being called the result of divine dispensation.

On the interpretation we are developing, therefore, we have an embryonic version of the Demaratus model in the *Meno*. Not only is the purpose of the theory in this dialogue limited to higher learning, but the double-origin theory suggested in the Demaratus analogy is beginning to emerge. The two different kinds of virtue, attained by two quite different methods, correspond to the two sources that feature in D. In terms of the analogy of Demaratus' wax tablet, the wood underneath stands for the latent resources that will provide knowledge, real virtue, or at least the superior type of true opinion; the surface wax accounts for all the rest, opinions true and false, derived from hearsay and tradition.

Now, in the introduction to this section (p. 21), we discussed a further feature of the analogy, the element of deceit. Demaratus' surface message, in our version of the story, was intended to mislead. In the next chapter, I shall be showing how this is an accurate interpretation of recollection in the *Phaedo* and how it portrays Plato as a deeply pessimistic philosopher. Just as in the story the surface message was intended to fool the Persians, the *Phaedo* treats the reports of the senses and of hearsay as in certain

---

[24] Taylor talks of 'ventriloquists, mediums, and cabinet ministers' (1960) 144, n. 1. See also *Ion* 534c7–d4 where Socrates points out that the prophet is merely someone through whom the god speaks.

At first sight it may seem strange that Socrates compares the Athenian politicians to prophets on the grounds that they have no understanding of what they say, but then invokes Teiresias as an analogy for someone who does have genuine understanding. I take it that Teiresias was a seer of a quite different order from those who have merely been possessed by a god. Unlike them, he did have a genuine understanding of what he was saying, as Homer's tribute to him implies.

respects deceptive. But things seem different in the *Meno*. Even if recollection is limited to higher learning and the true beliefs mentioned at the end of the *Meno* are formed by hearsay, it is unclear where deceit comes into the picture. The opinions at the end of the *Meno*, on which the alternative form of virtue is based, may come from an external source but they are still *true* opinions. Indeed, there seems something rather optimistic about the way Socrates introduces them at 96e7ff. True opinions, while they last, are said to be just as useful as knowledge. They may be only a second best, a substitute for knowledge, but for all that he seems reluctant to dismiss them out of hand.

Now although it would be unwise to claim that the element of deceit is present at the end of the *Meno*, such an optimistic interpretation of the type of virtue based on true belief would be misguided. For one thing, the virtues at the end of the *Meno*, apart from being impermanent, are also merely phantom virtues. At this stage in Plato's thought, it may be unclear exactly what makes these virtues insubstantial, mere shadows of the real virtue. The image of the shadows perhaps anticipates what is to come in the middle period with the comparison between forms and particulars so closely associated with the distinction between knowledge and opinion. But at least we should be wary of claiming that Plato is actually optimistic about the virtue formed independently of recollection.

There are also grounds for finding pessimism in Plato's outlook in the *Meno* in the reference to Teiresias. At 100a2–5 Socrates says that if a true statesman arrived he would be 'what Homer said Teiresias was among the dead, when he described him as the only one in the underworld who kept his wits – "the others are mere flitting shades"'. There is more to this allusion than first meets the eye, and it can be taken as an analogy for several things at once. Since Teiresias was a seer, divinely inspired, and blind, there is already a connection with recollection. Recollection is the divine part of us, as is made plain in the *Phaedo*, but also in the *Meno* by the religious tones in which the theory is introduced. What is also striking is the paradox of Teiresias who, though blind, could see so much more than anyone else. Similarly, someone who recollects turns away from the sensible world and may as well be blind, yet can see (mentally) things to which the uninitiated are blind. Teiresias can also be seen as a metaphor for

Socrates himself. Teiresias concealed his wisdom behind physical blindness; Socrates concealed his behind professions of ignorance and a satyr-like appearance. Furthermore, like Teiresias, he was sometimes inspired by a supernatural voice, a 'daimonion'.[25]

But perhaps the most interesting connection to be made is one between the comparison of the true statesman to Teiresias in the *Meno* and the philosopher-statesman in the cave allegory of *Republic* VII. Here Socrates depicts a group of people chained to their seats at the bottom of a cave. One of them manages to escape out of the cave and, with much difficulty, stumbles out towards the sunlight. If he were ever to return back down to the cave and attempt to force the prisoners to make the same journey, they would actually threaten to kill him.

In the course of the allegory, Plato compares the cave to the underworld;[26] and the solitary figure of the philosopher – the only one to have had a vision of the true reality – is reminiscent of Teiresias wandering among the shadows in Hades. Notice how the philosopher is even blinded when he first comes back down into the cave (516e3–17a4), and the source of his wisdom is divine (500c9). Another point of contact between these two analogies is the unpopularity of the true statesman. One of Teiresias' best known traits, at least to readers of Greek tragedy, is his tendency to make himself unpopular with politicians.[27] The reason for this is that he is able to see things that are strange and shocking to other people. The way Teiresias sees the world, the correct way, is utterly unlike that of his adversaries. This reinforces two connections I have already made: that between Teiresias and Socrates, who had a notorious propensity to say the wrong thing at the wrong time. That there should be a suggestion of this theme in the *Meno* is entirely appropriate, given the exchange between Socrates and Anytus with its dark overtones and innuendos of what is to come in the trial and execution.[28] But unpopularity is also the problem

---

[25] On Socrates' *daimonion* see *Apology* 40a4–6. On the misfit between Socrates' appearance and his intellect see Alcibiades' speech in the *Symposium* 215a6ff.

[26] 521c3. See also 516d5–6 (a quotation from Homer's depiction of the underworld in *Odyssey* XI 489–90).

[27] Teiresias' appearances in tragedy are marked by almost violent conflict with a leading political figure: with Oedipus in Sophocles' *Oedipus Rex* (316–462), Creon in the *Antigone* (987–1090) and Pentheus in Euripides' *Bacchae* (266–369).

[28] Apart from Anytus' warnings to Socrates in the *Meno* (94e3–5a1) we should also note Meno's rather sinister references to Socrates' wizardry at 80b4–7. It is worth emphasising the politically charged nature of the *Meno*. The inclusion of Anytus is

for the philosopher in the *Republic* who returns down to the cave.
What he has to say about the real world of forms seems at first
laughable and eventually so shocking that he is threatened with
death (517a4–6).

The reason I highlight this feature is that it fits in with the
revisionary element in D. It is part of this interpretation not
just that knowledge comes from a different source from opinion,
but that opinions are to be treated critically. Ultimately, the
philosopher who has recollected will see the world from an utterly
different perspective than he did before he had scraped away
the wax, even if some of his original opinions are preserved as
true. Not surprisingly, anyone who adopts so critical a stance may
be subject to the sort of treatment meted out to Teiresias, Socrates
and the philosopher who returns to the cave. If this is correct, the
ending of the *Meno* shows how the first appearance of recollection
is bound up with Plato's epistemological and political pessimism.

I said above that this interpretation makes the *Meno* anticipate
the account of inferior virtue in the *Phaedo* and the *Republic*,
and so it is worth taking a brief look at the relevant passages
in these dialogues. In a passage in the *Phaedo* that precedes
the actual recollection argument, Socrates draws a sharp contrast between the philosopher and the non-philosopher, especially
between their respective attitudes to death (64e8ff.). One way
in which they differ is that although they apparently talk of
the same virtues, for instance, courage and temperance, they
mean very different things by them. The popular conception
of temperance involves someone practising restraint over one
pleasure, but only because they really pursue some even greater
pleasure. Such people are really only 'temperate' because of intemperance. Similarly with courage: they only stand up to one danger
because they are afraid of even greater dangers. True philosophers, on the other hand, do not act for pleasure or fear, but

enough to ensure this, and the lengthy discussion of such figures as Pericles and
Thucydides reinforces the point. The dialogue concludes that none of these politicians
had any wisdom at all and that they were at best mere shadows of virtue. For all
of them, the intellectual hard labour of recollection is a political necessity. This also
explains the urgency of the earlier passage at 86b6–c2, the strongest claim of the whole
dialogue, where Socrates says that he would fight tooth and nail for the belief that
one should never give up inquiry. What is required for Athens, as for any other city,
is real knowledge. The improvement of the understanding is thus an essential for the
improvement of Athens. The worst thing to do would be to give up inquiry, i.e. give
up on the possibility of attaining virtue.

only for wisdom. That is the only currency in which they are prepared to deal.

There are two important things to notice about this distinction between different kinds of virtue. First, Socrates is emphatic that popular virtue is a counterfeit virtue. Whereas virtue based upon true belief is said in the *Meno* to be a mere shadow, these virtues are like shadow-paintings with nothing true or sound in them (69b6–8). This sounds like a development of the conclusion of the *Meno*. But it is a change in an even more pessimistic direction. The *Phaedo* presents the philosopher's virtues as a strong revision of popular views and, in stressing that we need to be purged of the popular approach to virtue before we can attain real virtue (69b8ff.), it fits well with the image of the Greeks scraping away the wax in the Demaratus analogy.

The second point is about the origin of the counterfeit virtues in the *Phaedo*. At 82a10–b3, discussing again the difference between the philosopher and the non-philosopher, Socrates talks of what happens to the souls of those who have failed to aspire to philosophy. The best of them are those who have practiced the pseudo-virtues of 68c5ff.;[29] their lot is to be reincarnated as disciplined animals, such as ants and bees. What is interesting is the description of them as

those who have practised popular and social goodness, 'temperance' and 'justice' so-called, developed from habit and training, but devoid of philosophy and intelligence . . .[30]

As in the *Meno* we are told that this kind of virtue comes 'without intelligence' (*nous*). Unlike the *Meno*, however, the *Phaedo* is more straightforward in telling us how such virtue does come. The method in question is practice (the method mentioned in the opening question of the *Meno* but subsequently ignored). The most plausible interpretation of this point is that the method of habituation is an essentially empirical process, and that in by-passing philosophy and *nous* it is also unconnected with our innate knowledge. The presence in the *Phaedo* of this theory

[29] I assume that the pseudo-virtues of 68c5ff. are the same as the demotic virtues of 82a10ff., especially given the similarity of language between 68c5–8 and 82b1.

[30] 82a11–b3: οἱ τὴν δημοτικὴν καὶ πολιτικὴν ἀρετὴν ἐπιτετηδευκότες, ἣν δὴ καλοῦσιν σωφροσύνην τε καὶ δικαιοσύνην, ἐξ ἔθους τε καὶ μελέτης γεγονυῖαν διὰ φιλοσοφίας τε καὶ νοῦ . . .

about the two types of virtue thus gives some confirmation of our interpretation of the *Meno*.

Finally, the topic of demotic virtue is also pursued in the *Republic*. In some passages it has a more enhanced status than in the previous two dialogues, presumably because it is discussed within the context of the ideal state. At 430a1–c6 Socrates talks of how the auxiliaries' courage is instilled. Their true opinion as to what is to be feared is made stable by something analogous to a dyeing process. At 430c3 the resulting virtue is described as 'civic' or 'political' virtue, which may be connected with *Phaedo* 82a11, thereby making the auxiliaries' courage less than real.[31] Similarly at *Rep.* 500d8 the guardian as craftsman is said to instil 'demotic' virtue into his subjects. The use of the word 'demotic' makes a reference to the *Phaedo* inevitable. The courage of the auxiliaries and the non-philosopher citizens generally is only political virtue and, like its counterparts in the *Meno* and the *Phaedo*, is imbued by an empirical process.[32]

This brings us to the end of our discussion of the *Meno*. We should note that our interpretation of the conclusion of the dialogue must remain tentative, like any other interpretation of this passage. Socrates gives us very few clues about what lies behind the notion of divine dispensation, and he explicitly warns Meno at the end of the provisional nature of their findings (100b4–6). But if we are right, we have seen how the idea of philosophy being discontinuous with ordinary ways of thinking is already present in the *Meno*. As we turn to the middle period, we shall see that this notion takes a firmer hold in Plato's thought and develops into a full-blown pessimism about common sense.

---

[31] For this connection see Adam (1963) 232.
[32] For a survey of demotic virtue in Plato see Archer Hind (1894) 149–55.

# CHAPTER 2

# Recollection in the middle period

Nothing in the *Meno* suggests that recollection is used to explain the emergence of our pre-philosophical judgements; furthermore, the conclusion of the dialogue shows the signs of a double-origin theory emerging in Plato's thought. In this chapter we shall argue for the Demaratus interpretation of recollection in the middle period, starting with the *Phaedo* in [1] before turning to the *Phaedrus* in [2] and finally looking at some relevant passages from the *Republic* in [3].

## [1] THE PHAEDO

Our focus of attention here will be on the famous recollection passage in the *Phaedo* 72e3–77a5. Socrates' eventual purpose in this argument is to prove the immortality of the soul; and his precise intention at this stage is to demonstrate that the soul must have existed before birth. Using the form of the equal as an example, Socrates claims that we have knowledge of the form, that we compare sensible equal objects with it, and that in order to make this comparison, we must already have knowledge of the form. He then tries to argue that we must have had knowledge of the form before we started to use our senses, and that the only time for this to have been is before birth; therefore the soul must have existed before birth. Many commentators have interpreted this passage as saying that recollection of the forms accounts for concept formation as well as the ability to compare forms and particulars.[1] For most of my discussion of the *Phaedo*

[1] It is now time to unmask some of the adherents of K in the *Phaedo*. The most articulate versions come from Cornford (1935) 108, Gulley (1954) 197ff. and (1962) 31ff., Ackrill (1973) 177–95 and Bostock (1986) 66ff.

I have said that K interprets recollection as explaining concept formation, but just

I shall focus upon two closely related questions: first, what is recollection intended to explain? Second, who actually recollects? This second question arises because Socrates frequently talks in the first person plural and it is important to determine whether he is referring only to his circle of philosopher-friends or to people in general. But both questions are so bound up with each other that I shall treat them in tandem. If Socrates turns out to be explaining only philosophical thought, the franchise of recollection will be very limited; and if there are occurrences of the pronoun 'we' that obviously have a wide reference, the explanandum in question is likely to be a general cognitive achievement. I hope to show that recollection is only involved in philosophical thinking, that the 'we' are the philosophically earnest and that there is a double-origin theory at work in the *Phaedo*. I shall end by discussing the way in which the theory of recollection is epistemologically pessimistic.

In our discussion of the *Phaedo* we shall be tackling some very difficult passages of argument, and so it is important not to lose sight of the larger issues at stake. Among other things, we are deciding between two ways of viewing the nature and role of philosophy. At one end of the scale, its role could be to start from partially understood concepts and beliefs and develop them into a more systematic theory; at the other, it could be to challenge them and make a decisive break with ordinary ways of thinking. One of the most important features of the *Phaedo* is that it presents a defence of Socrates and, in doing so, of philosophy itself; thus it is crucial not to mistake the nature of philosophy as Plato characterises it here. In my view, he is defending something every bit as revisionary as we find, for instance, in the *Republic*.

what is meant by 'concept formation' varies from one version of K to another. The most careful claims are made by Bostock who argues that recollection accounts for our ordinary and everyday grasp of meanings of those words, such as 'equal', of which there are no paradigm examples provided by sense perception; it should also be pointed out that Bostock gives a more linguistic slant to the issue than other commentators by talking about 'meanings of terms' rather than 'concepts'. At the other extreme, Gulley (1954) 198, n. 2 thinks that the form of the argument of the *Phaedo* 'almost' implies an unlimited range of forms. This approach is more typical of commentators on the *Phaedrus* where Plato is thought to be talking of the use of universals in language without implying any restriction whatever. Despite the differences between versions of K, I shall mount my attack on them as one body, because I am refuting interpretations which require recollection to explain any of our ordinary conceptual apparatus, however limited the range of concepts concerned.

I originally argued for D in Scott (1987). Independently, Fine (1992) 225, n. 41 and (1993) 137–8 has argued for similar restrictions on the scope of recollection.

Those who would have recollection at work in the earlier stages of learning distort Platonic philosophy by bringing it too close to the clarification of mundane concepts. So we are arguing here about more than the interpretation of a particular theory of learning; we are arguing about Plato's very conception of philosophy in a dialogue where that topic has a special urgency.

For most of this part I shall follow the actual course of the recollection argument of 72e3–77a5. After an introduction (72e3–73c10) containing back-references to the slave-boy demonstration in the *Meno*, Socrates sets out some general conditions for recollection (73c1–74a8). In the next two parts he focuses on two cognitive achievements: the first, that we have come to think of the form of equality from perceiving the particulars (74a9–d3), the second, that we compare the particulars to the form (74d4–75a4). This sets the stage for the crux of the argument, 74e9–75c6, where he argues that we could not have had such thoughts unless we had already known the form before we first used our senses, i.e. before birth. There is then a further stretch of argument to convince Simmias that we forget our knowledge of the form equal at birth and regain it by recollection (75d7–76d5). Socrates now thinks that he has shown that the soul must have pre-existed the body, and so brings the argument to a close, stressing, among other things, the importance of the existence of forms to the whole argument (76d7–77a5).

*General conditions for recollection* (73c1–74a8)

In this passage, Socrates sets out four conditions for recollection. If we are reminded of $x$ by $y$,

(i) we must have known $x$ beforehand (73c1–3),
(ii) we must not only recognise $y$ but also think of $x$ (73c6–8),
(iii) $x$ must not be the object of the same knowledge as $y$ but of another (73c8–9),
(iv) when $x$ resembles $y$, we must consider whether $y$ is lacking at all in relation to $x$ (74a5–7).

All these conditions, especially the third and fourth, are to play crucial roles in the ensuing argument. We shall come back to them later.

*We know what the equal is* (74a9–d3).

Socrates now secures Simmias' agreement that we know what the
equal is (74a9–b3):

'We say, don't we, that there is something *equal* – I don't mean a log
to a log, or a stone to a stone, or anything else of that sort, but some
further thing beyond all those, the equal itself: are we to say that there
is something or nothing?'
  'We are, by Zeus,' said Simmias; 'remarkably!'
  'And do we know what it is?'
  'Certainly.'

On K, Socrates is here talking about everyone's mundane grasp of
a universal concept which enables them to recognise particulars
as being equal, and underwrites their ability to use language. On
D, this is not a discussion of how we originally classified the sticks
and stones as equal, nor of how it is that we understand the term
'equal' in ordinary empirical judgements about particulars. The
fact that we talk of sticks and stones as being equal is simply
presupposed. Instead, Socrates focuses on the philosophical understanding of an entity very remote from most people's thoughts, the
form of equality.

An important clue as to which interpretation is correct can be
found in 74b1, in the way in which Simmias reacts to Socrates'
claim that we say 'there is something *equal*'. Simmias uses the
adverb 'remarkably' or 'amazingly' (*thaumastōs*). This is a phrase
very often watered down by translators into 'emphatically'. But this
is simply a mistranslation. Whatever Socrates is talking about, it is
an object of wonder (*thauma*), and this is hardly an appropriate way
to refer to the fact that sticks or stones are equal.

Now turn back to the sentence that provoked Simmias' excla-
mation in the first place. Socrates starts by specifying where his
interest lies: 'we say, don't we, that there is something equal'. This
is the form of equal, some further thing beyond all the particulars,
whose very being Simmias rightly acknowledges to be remarkable.
But in the middle of this sentence and very conveniently for us,
Socrates also tells us what he is not interested in: 'I don't mean a
log to a log, or a stone to a stone, or anything else of that sort . . .'
This expression is elliptical and, if filled out, would run: 'I don't
mean that we say that a stick is equal to a stick . . .'. This is the kind
of statement that Socrates dismisses as irrelevant to his argument,

and yet it is precisely in such statements that our humdrum grasp of the concepts and meanings is manifested. That Socrates is prepared to dismiss such statements so early in the argument is a good indication that recollection is not to be invoked to explain our ordinary grasp of 'equal'.

The idea that recollection is meant to explain concept formation, moreover, is not merely absent from the text, but is also the source of acute difficulties – difficulties that have been brought out by both Ackrill and Gulley.[2] The problem that Ackrill puts his finger upon concerns the third of the four conditions for recollection set out above.[3] Plato is right to point out that if we are to be reminded of $x$ by $y$, then we must have a recognition of $y$ that does not involve knowledge of $x$, otherwise we have the absurd result that in recognising $y$ we are already thinking of $x$, and so recollection of $x$ is impossible. But if we insist that Plato is using recollection to explain concept formation, if, that is, we need to have recollected the form equal in order to recognise the stick's equality, then we invite just that absurdity. In order to recognise the equal stick we already need to be thinking of the form, and so we cannot then go on to recollect it. If, on the other hand, we have not already recollected the form, then, on the assumption that recollection is meant to explain concept formation, we cannot recognise the equal stick as an equal stick, and so, in the absence of any associative bond,[4] it cannot serve as a stimulus for recollection. Either way, recollection of forms from sensible particulars will be impossible. In fact, we find ourselves impaled on a dilemma very much like the paradox in *Meno* 80e1–5, which is a cruel irony, because that was originally the very problem that recollection

---

[2] Gulley (1954) 197–8 paints himself into a corner by saying: 'What appears to be envisaged is an immediate transition from the sensible to the intelligible world, the argument relying on a contrast between sensation and a conceptual level of apprehension. Plato is apparently saying that the fact that we attain this conceptual level in describing what is given in sense-experience constitutes recollection of forms.' Gulley goes on to consider the claim at 74c7–9 that in being reminded of the form we are gaining *knowledge* of it, which he takes to imply that the immediate transition referred to above is one from mere sensation to philosophical knowledge of the forms; but, as he goes on to say: 'Plato never assumes elsewhere that the fact that we employ concepts to describe what we see is either a mark of knowledge of the forms, or in itself any reliable pointer.'

[3] Ackrill (1973) 183: 'There may be a lurking danger for Plato's programme. For if reminding is to explain concept-formation, can a pre-condition for reminding be recognition or something akin to it?'

[4] On the associative bond see 76a3–4.

was meant to solve. If, however, we do not say that reminding is meant to explain concept formation, all these problems disappear. Of course, recollection does explain concept formation of a very special kind, viz. our knowledge of Platonic forms, but not the formation of those concepts that we employ in ordinary thought.

According to D, the concepts that we need to say 'these sticks are equal' are formed by perception, and recollection has not as yet come into the picture. So not only does Plato not use recollection to explain our grasp of the equality of particulars, he actually gives his own empiricist explanation. The clearest evidence for this part of my interpretation comes not in the recollection passage itself, however, but in the 'affinity' argument of 78c10ff., and it is worth looking ahead to this passage for a moment. In this argument, Plato starts with the distinction between forms and particulars and applies a series of opposing characteristics to the two categories. The first pair is changing and unchanging (78d1–e5), the second perceptible and non-perceptible (or, more specifically, visible and non-visible). Plato asserts quite unequivocally that the particulars are perceived whereas the forms cannot be. So, to use the example of the form of equality that he cites in 78e1, this implies that the sticks, their equality included, are perceptible. This goes against K's assumption that the 'stickness' of the stick is perceptible but not its equality. K would therefore have to say that in this passage, Plato is being careless.

This move, however, is extremely implausible. If Plato had meant that particulars were in part perceptible and in part imperceptible, why would he not say so? It is exactly what he says about human beings. We are part body, part soul (79b1–2). We straddle the ontological divide that he is carefully building up. It would be extremely strange if he thought that particulars did the same, and yet said nothing at all about it. Furthermore, the symmetry on which so much of the argument depends would be at best thrown into jeopardy. It is far more plausible to assume that Plato means what he says. Particulars, their equality included, are perceptible.[5]

Finally, note that on K, we might have seen this passage, 74a9–d3, as beginning with an attempt to convince the ordinary

---

[5] Bedu-Addo (1991) 49, n. 35 holds that all people recollect to some degree, though their knowledge of forms is operative only subconsciously. However, apart from the fact that there is no mention in the text of any such subconscious operations, this

person of the existence of forms, whereas on my interpretation it assumes them straight off. But this should not be taken as a mark against D. For one thing, there is no reason to expect that Socrates is addressing ordinary people anyway. As early as 64c1–2, he set the esoteric tone of the dialogue by saying 'let us talk among ourselves, disregarding them [*sc.* the majority of people]'. Furthermore, in both that passage and in the recollection argument itself Socrates is talking to Simmias, and this brings out a crucial point. In the course of the earlier discussion (65d4–8), he swiftly gets *Simmias* to agree to the existence of forms – entities that are not to be grasped by sense-perception but by the soul on its own. Hence, at 74a9–c5, Socrates is not trying to convince an initiate of the existence of forms, but can assume Simmias' ready acceptance of it. What he goes on to do is to discuss the nature of forms in more detail and explore certain epistemological implications that will enable him to prove the pre-existence of the soul.

## *We have noticed the deficiency of the particulars to the form* (74d4–75a4)

This section is particularly embarrassing for K. Throughout it the interest lies not in classification, but in something very different, namely, the comparison between form and particulars. Socrates is not focusing on the fact that we use the terms 'equal', 'good', etc., nor is he restricting himself to the claim that we recognise that equal objects are, in certain contexts, unequal. He is taking all this for granted and saying that we refer these equals to another which is never unequal, which, of course, involves having the form before our mind. Once it is clear that comparison is what is at issue here, it is easy to see the absurdity of claiming that recollection is meant to explain mundane cognitive achievements made by everyone. Platonists may go around saying that sticks and stones

interpretation is ruled out by the claim in the affinity argument that perception is sufficient to account for our grasp of the equality of particulars.

Apart from the affinity argument, one text which shows that the equality, of particulars is perceptible is 75b6–7. Here he talks about comparing the equals from our sense perceptions to the form (εἰ ἐμέλλομεν τὰ ἐκ τῶν αἰσθήσεων ἴσα ἐκεῖσε ἀνοίσειν . . .). This implies that we do grasp the equality of the particulars from the senses and it is this sensible equality that we compare with the form. The point of the phrase is that whatever we are comparing to the form comes from the senses, and it makes little sense to say that we are comparing the stick *minus* its equality with the form. Rather, the stick is deficient to the form because there is something wrong with its equality; so its equality must be perceptible.

fall short of being like the form of equality but who else does? If we can avoid trivialising Plato's argument by attributing to him such assumptions, so much the better; and D allows us to do this.

Furthermore, there are some explicit remarks in this section of the argument that restrict the cognitive achievements in question to a small number of people. Remember again that in 74d4–75a3 Plato focuses on the comparison as his explanandum. Now at 74d9–e4 he describes this act from the point of view of the person making it:

> Then whenever anyone, on seeing a thing, thinks to himself, 'this thing that I now see seeks to be like another of the things that are, but falls short and cannot be like that object: it is inferior' do we agree that the man who thinks this must previously have known the object he says it resembles but falls short of?

As Ackrill has pointed out, what is remarkable about this sentence is its use of direct first-person speech.[6] The speaker who makes the comparison is quite clearly committed to the existence of forms that act as standards for the comparison.[7] It is equally clear from a later passage in the dialogue that the majority of people, the non-philosophers, take only the corporeal to be real (81b4–5). They reject the existence of Platonic forms and therefore cannot be those who are making the comparison described at 74d9–e4. That sentence can only apply to philosophers. Throughout this passage Plato is talking about the grasp of a form as a standard of comparison which is not some mundane cognitive achievement made by everyone but something quite remarkable and achieved, if at all, only by a few.

It is undeniable, then, that only a few people have compared forms and particulars. Once this is admitted, yet another argument in favour of D comes to light. At the beginning of the passage, Socrates set out four conditions for recollection. The last of these was that if one thing reminds us of another, and the two things are similar, we also compare one to the other (74a5–7). In other words, if I have been reminded of a form by a particular, I have also compared the two. Thus, if I have not compared the particular with

---

[6] Ackrill (1973) 194–5.

[7] The form is described by the speaker as being 'one of the things that are' (τι τῶν ὄντων) at 74d10.

the form, I have not been reminded of the form by the particular. But, as we have just made clear, most people have not made the comparison; therefore, most people have not been reminded of the form.

*We could not have compared the forms with the particulars unless we had already known the form before we first used our senses, i.e. before birth* (74e9–75c6)

Socrates has been building up his argument very carefully. By now, he has specified four conditions for recollection, and has drawn attention to two cognitive achievements – our knowledge of the form and our comparison between it and the particulars – that will form the basis of the argument for recollection. Given the implausibility, if not complete absurdity, of reading K into his description of these achievements, it seems that this interpretation has been squeezed out of the argument for good. Nevertheless, the next segment of the argument, 74e9–75c5, has given some encouragement to advocates of K. In this passage, Socrates starts out from the claim that we compare the form equal with the particulars (74e6–7) and then presents a very condensed argument to prove that we must have had knowledge of the form before birth. Here is the argument in full:

(1) Then we must previously have known the equal, before that time when we first, on seeing the equals, thought that all of them were striving to be like the equal but fell short of it.
(2) Yet we also agree on this: we haven't derived the thought of it, nor could we do so, from anywhere but seeing or touching or some other of the senses – I'm counting all these as the same.
(3) But of course it's from one's sense perceptions that one must think that all the things in the sense perceptions are striving for that which is equal, yet are inferior to it . . .
(4) Then it must surely have been before we began to see and hear and use the other senses that we got knowledge of the equal itself, of what it is, if we were going to refer the equals from our sense perceptions to it, supposing that all things are doing their best to be like it, but are inferior to it.
(5) Now we were seeing and hearing, and were possessed of our other senses, weren't we, just as soon as we were born?

(6) But we must, we're saying, have got our knowledge of the equal before these?

(7) Then it seems we must have got it before we were born.

Some commentators have seen in this argument evidence in favour of K.[8] In their view, the reference in (5) to what we have been doing since birth makes it sound as if recollection is meant to explain early learning after all. A closer look at this passage is needed.

In the previous section Socrates has said that we come to think of the form from the particulars and that this is recollection (73c13–74d2). He then focuses his attention on the judgement comparing the form equal and the particulars (74d4–e7), thus making way for the first step in the argument just quoted: we must have known the form before we first made that comparative judgement. The next move, (2), is to state that perception is a necessary condition for thinking of the form. We need not – and should not – take this as saying that perception *instils* knowledge of the form,[9] merely that use of the senses is a necessary condition for gaining knowledge, i.e. that to start the process off, we must have our memories jogged by sensible stimuli.[10] In (3) Socrates insists that it is the senses that prompted us to make the comparative judgement. It is at this point that the argument starts to become very condensed because by the next stage, (4), Socrates feels entitled to claim that we must have grasped the form before we ever used our senses. Once this is conceded it is easier to draw the conclusion, as he does between (5) and (7), that the form must have been learnt before birth. So what is it about (3) that does so much work? The assumption behind the argument is that any sense perception that prompted us to think of the form, the process referred to in (2), would *also* prompt us to make the comparison between form and particulars, the process referred to in (3); but if this perception prompted us to make the comparison we must, according to premise (1), have already grasped the form before having that perception. Crucial to this argument is the assumption

---

[8] Ackrill (1973) 192.

[9] This would clash with 65d11ff. and 82d9ff.

[10] Socrates is perhaps referring to the necessary role of sense perception at 83a6–7. For a convincing explanation of why Plato thinks that we are dependent on the senses in this way see Bedu-Addo (1991) 46–8.

that the *same* perception that put us in mind of the form would *also* put us in mind of the comparison and, given the prior knowledge condition implicit in (1), no perception could play both roles. So the moment of learning the form will always be pushed further back.

This seems to be the correct analysis of the argument.[11] As it stands, however, it is vulnerable to the objection that the perception that first prompted us to think of the form need not have been the same one that prompted us to make the comparison. Thus Plato does not allow for the possibility that, first, one perception merely jogs us to think of the form (2), and then, later, another perception prompts us to compare it with the particulars (3). Why, in other words, do the stages mentioned in (2) and (3) have to be simultaneous? The force of such an objection is difficult to deny, but it could never be a reason for rejecting this interpretation because Plato, as we have just seen, is clearly committed to the assumption that if one thing reminds us of another, and the two things are similar, we also think whether one is deficient to the other (74a5–7).[12]

How does this interpretation of the argument of 74e9–75c5 affect the decision between D and K? First, it should be clear that Plato is in no way committed to the extraordinary claim that everyone has been comparing equal particulars with the form since birth. (This claim would be doubly weird. Not only is it false that everyone makes the comparison, as we have already noted, but it is even more outrageous to say that they have been doing this since birth). The argument is making the much more subtle point that there could not be one perception that first put us in mind of the form and another later one that first put us in mind of the comparison. But when we were first prompted to make the comparison is not stipulated in this argument. To answer that question we need to turn back to the previous passage, 74d4–5a4, to examine the way in which he describes this comparison and the thinking of those who make it (74d9–e4). As we have just seen, this passage can only be

---

[11] I am indebted to Rowe (1993) 172–3 for this interpretation.

[12] It is, of course, a highly questionable assumption and it is unfortunate that Plato does not attempt to provide more support for it. Nevertheless, its presence in the text can hardly be denied.

A further problem for the argument of 74e9–75c5 arises from stage (2). Why are the senses necessary as a catalyst for recollection? Another possibility, one that Plato ignores, is that we grasp the form by rational intuition without any need for the senses. But see Bedu-Addo (1991) 46–8.

talking about a cognitive achievement occurring relatively late in a person's development, if it occurs at all.

### We forget our knowledge of the forms at birth and regain it by recollection (75d7–76d6)

Having now established that we did possess knowledge of the forms before birth, Socrates takes Simmias through an argument to decide whether we retain this knowledge consciously throughout our incarnate lives or whether we forget it at birth and recollect it later on. Simmias agrees to the second of these two options. Here is the point at which he does so:

'You don't think then, Simmias, that everyone knows those objects [sc. the forms]?'
  'By no means.'
  'Are they then being reminded of what they once learnt?'[13]
  'They must be.' (76c1–5)

At first sight the way Socrates states his conclusion in these lines, 'are they then being reminded of what they once learnt?' (76c4), suggests that everyone is in the process of being reminded of the forms, a claim that clearly rules out D in favour of K. But a more careful look at the argument of which 76c4–5 is the conclusion will show that these lines cannot be used as evidence against D.

As we have just seen, the point of the present argument is to help Simmias to decide between two alternatives. Socrates sets each of them out in 75d7–11 and e2–7 respectively and then at 76a4–7 repeats the choice facing Simmias as follows:

So, as I say, one of two things is true: either all of us were born knowing those objects [sc. the forms], and we know them throughout life; or those we speak of as 'learning' are simply being reminded later on, and learning would be recollection.

In the next few lines (76a9–b2) Socrates repeats to Simmias that he must make his choice.

---

[13] An alternative translation of this line would be 'Are they then reminded of what they once learnt?' This, however, would create a needless contradiction with an earlier passage. If Socrates and Simmias are now concluding that everyone recollects, they are contradicting what they have just decided, viz. that not everyone knows the forms. At 75e5–6 it has been stated that to recollect is to regain knowledge, so if everyone recollects, everyone knows, and this is just what has been denied.

When Socrates sums up the choice to Simmias at 76a4–7 his language is precise and clearly compatible with D. The first option is that we all have the knowledge at birth and retain it throughout our lives, the second that 'those we speak of as "learning"' recollect. The contrast between the phrase 'those we speak of as "learning"' in the second option and the word 'all' which qualifies the first person plural in the first option is quite marked and deliberate. So the choice that Simmias has to make is not between everyone retaining their knowledge throughout their lives and *everyone* recollecting it, but between everyone retaining it and *some people* recollecting it.[14]

What, then, has happened at 76c4? If there is to be any coherence to the argument as a whole, this line must still be referring to one of the options put to Simmias at 76a4–7. On my reading, it does, but Socrates is expressing himself in shorthand. We need to supply something like 'those we speak of as "learning"' as the subject of 'are being reminded'. Consider the consequences of not doing this. First, one would have to explain why Socrates has changed the relevant option without saying so. Second, one would have to explain away the fact that the actual argument given in favour of 76c4 supports not the reading where everyone recollects but only the one where those who learn recollect.[15] In short, the only way of giving this passage any coherence is to restrict the subject of the verb 'are being reminded' in 76c4, and such a restriction, of course, favours D.[16]

We have now examined the individual segments of the recollection argument. There are also some points to be made by looking over the argument as a whole. We can start with two further arguments against reading K into the passage.

The first relates to the way in which K needs the 'we' of this passage to refer predominantly to ordinary people. Although there are certain points at which the reference of the pronoun may have

---

[14] The option set out in 76a4–7 has already been mentioned in 75e2–7. Here the wording is compatible with K but also with D.

[15] Notice how in 76b1–2 Socrates also presents the second option in an abbreviated form. As this line comes immediately after the precise formulation in 76a4–7, it is even more implausible that he should have modified it without explanation.

[16] Hackforth (1955) 72, presumably aware of the mismatch between 76c4 and preceding argumentation, translates the line as '*Can* they then recollect what they once learnt?' (my italics).

been a matter of controversy, there are others where it must apply only to Socrates' circle. One such place is 75c10–d3 where Socrates says:

> our present argument concerns the beautiful itself, and the good itself, and just and holy, no less than the equal; in fact, as I say, it concerns everything on which we set this seal, *'what it is'*, in the questions we ask and in the answers we give.

This is clearly an allusion to the kind of dialectical question-and-answer sessions in which philosophers, rather than ordinary people, would engage. Another obvious example of Socrates' use of the first person plural to refer only to philosophers comes a little later at 76d8–e1, where he says that 'we' are always harping on the forms of beauty and goodness and comparing the sensible particulars to them.

If we try to do justice to the fact that in such places 'we' applies only to philosophers but also insist that in other places it applies to everyone, we have to make the referents of the pronoun veer without any warning between everyone and Platonists. This is a serious difficulty for K. D, on the other hand, allows no such unsignalled shifts in reference. True, at 76a5 'we' *does* apply to all men:

> either all of us were born knowing those objects [*sc.* the forms], and we know them throughout life; or those we speak of as 'learning' are simply being reminded later on, and learning would be recollection.

But this is quite acceptable on D's terms. The insertion of the word 'all' is very emphatic and is contrasted with 'those we speak of as "learning"' in what follows. These latter people are those who know, i.e. the 'we' of the previous passage (74b2). Plato has generalised the results of his argument to say that if some people recollect and have known before, there is no reason why everyone cannot have the knowledge latently, though there are several good reasons why not everyone recollects,[17] and this distinction is preserved in the emphatic contrast of subjects in 76a5–7.

The second problem for adherents of K is that, as well as requiring unsignalled shifts in the reference of 'we', they have to make the verb 'know' undergo an alarming change of meaning

---

[17] See, for example, 83d4ff.

in the course of the passage. At 74b2–3, in the passage already quoted on p. 56, it is affirmed with some enthusiasm that we know the equal:

'We say, don't we, that there is something *equal* – I don't mean a log to a log, or a stone to a stone, or anything else of that sort, but some further thing beyond all those, the equal itself: are we to say that there is something or nothing?'
    'We are, by Zeus,' said Simmias; 'remarkably!'
    'And do we know what it is?'
    'Certainly.'

At 76b5–c3, on the other hand, Simmias agrees that it is far from true that everyone has knowledge of the forms:

'If a man knows things, can he give an account of what he knows or not?'
    'Of course he can, Socrates.'
    'And do you think everyone can give an account of those objects [*sc.* the forms] we were discussing just now?'
    'I only wish they could,' said Simmias; 'but I'm afraid that, on the contrary, this time tomorrow there may no longer be any man who can do so properly.'
    'You don't think then, Simmias, that everyone knows those objects?'
    'By no means.'

The only way for K to deal with this is to say that at 74b2, 'know' means the ordinary knowledge of a concept, whereas at 76c1–2 it means proper philosophic knowledge of the definition. Without any warning, then, Plato makes the word undergo a considerable change of meaning.

D, on the other hand, can dispense with a shift in meaning of the word 'know' altogether, and so dissolve the problem completely.[18] When Simmias admits that he knows the equal, he means that he, like other Platonists, can give an account of a mathematical form, but does not concede any more than that. Then, at 75c7–d5,

---

[18] *Contra* Bostock (1986) 67–8. He concedes that 'know' changes from the mundane to the philosophical sense between 74b2 and 76b8, but thinks that this is the more economical way of dealing with the problem. If we restrict those who recollect to philosphers, he claims, 'there must actually be three levels of knowledge in play': proper philosophic knowledge, humdrum grasp of meanings, and a third intermediate kind which is the prerogative of philosophers, but falls short of a precise grasp of the definition (68). This argument, however, fails because, according to D, the passage makes no reference to our humdrum knowledge whatsoever. This sense of 'know' is not in play in the passage.

the argument is broadened to include all the forms, but it is not thereby implied that Simmias has knowledge of all of these, but simply that he engages in dialectical question-and-answer sessions about them (75d2–3).[19] That, in fact, is all that is needed to argue for recollection, just as in the *Meno* Socrates needs only to show that the slave boy has true beliefs (as opposed to knowledge, 85c6–7), but the argument for recollection is best introduced by citing the most successful case of this dialectical activity.

D, therefore, has none of the problems K has in keeping track of the pronoun 'we' or the word 'know' throughout the recollection passage. Nevertheless, while we are looking at the passage as a whole, we need to answer a couple of problems that do seem to arise on D. First, even if we grant that in the *Phaedo*, at least, K does not have much textual backing and in fact leads us into appalling difficulties, have we not, in replacing it with D, chosen a rather implausible theory? It seems to claim that all the concepts by which we classify our sense experience are empirically gained, while our grasp of the forms is recollected well after we have accumulated sense experience. But this seems puzzling. If we have these two *distinct* sources, how is it that both our empirical concept and our recollected knowledge are of 'equal'? There must be *some* connection.

There is, and it is certainly no coincidence for Plato that both the empirical concept and the recollected knowledge are of 'equal'. But the explanation for this is not that information 'leaks' from our innate source into our beliefs about particulars. The similarity between the empirical concept and the recollected knowledge stems from the similarity between the objects that are apprehended. In Plato's middle-period ontology there are two levels of entities, forms existing separately of the physical world, and particular instances of those forms. The particulars resemble the forms in a limited way, and this is no coincidence; they participate in the forms. If we apprehend the forms by recollection and the particulars by perception, there will indeed be a resemblance between the contents of recollection and perception, but that stems from the ontological link and not from a cognitive one.

---

[19] I am following Hackforth (1955) 76 here. Gallop (1975) 133 objects to this view because 'moral and mathematical forms are expressly said to be on a par (75c10–d2)', but the only way in which all the forms are put on a par at 75c10 is by being objects of dialectical argument, not of knowledge.

The similarity between our concepts is thus explained indirectly. It does not arise because our beliefs about particulars draw upon our innate grasp of forms, but because, unbeknown to most people, the particulars themselves participate in the forms. The following analogy may help. One person sees the original of painting in a museum; another sees a forgery. They have similar representations in their minds not because they have communicated with each other, but because there is a similarity between the objects themselves.

The second objection that we need to answer is this. On any interpretation of the recollection passage the overall course of the argument runs as follows. Everyone has in them knowledge of the forms; this knowledge was not acquired since birth but must have pre-existed birth; so the soul must have pre-existed the body. Then, with the help of the 'cyclical' argument, Socrates infers that the soul will continue to exist after it has lost its body. As in the *Phaedo* generally, Plato eventually wants to prove that all human souls are immortal, not merely the souls of philosophers. This raises a problem for an interpretation like D that imposes such restrictions on the numbers involved at the first stage of the argument. Will not this lack of universality persist all the way through to the conclusion so that Plato will have failed to prove that all souls are immortal? If, however, he were arguing that all people recollect to some degree, his argument would have the required generality.[20]

This objection can be met in two ways. First, the claim can hardly be that Plato has a better argument if we follow K rather than D. On D he takes a limited sample and generalises from it on the assumption that it is more plausible that all human beings are fundamentally of the same type than of two radically different types.[21] Let it be conceded that the argument of the *Phaedo* as it stands is, strictly speaking, invalid. If we follow the other interpretation and assume that Plato is proceeding from what everyone does, then the chances of him using a valid argument may at first look higher. But this advantage has been purchased at an absurd cost. The argument, even if *valid*, is based on a premise that is absurdly false and denied explicitly in the *Phaedo*, viz.

[20] For a statement of this objection see Gallop (1975) 120 and Bostock (1986) 67.

[21] It should be remembered that later, in *Phaedo* 81b1ff. (and even more in the charioteer myth of the *Phaedrus*), Plato goes to some lengths to explain why some people manifest their innate knowledge while others do not.

that everyone compares particulars to forms. Now, the moment advocates of K bow to the inevitable and concede that the number of those who compare forms and particulars is very restricted, they have to accept that the strict conclusion of the argument as a whole is similarly restricted. For, as we have seen, the claim that people compare forms and particulars is vital to the argument for recollection and pre-existence (74e9–75c6) and, if the number of people making this comparison is limited, so must the number involved in any conclusion validly inferred from the argument.

Second, the objection exaggerates the problems involved in restricting the scope of those who recollect; it considers it a great problem if Plato's inductive base is as narrow as D makes it. The objection only has force if it can show that Plato would have shared these worries. A brief look at the recollection passage in the *Meno* shows that this is not the case. In this dialogue, he attempts to prove the theory by taking one slave boy, showing him actually recollecting, and then assuming that if he can recollect, so can everyone else. He has no qualms about generalising from one case, and hardly expects us to respond, 'What a clever and interesting slave, I wonder if anyone else can do this.' A similar strategy is followed in the *Phaedo*. In the *Meno*, Socrates' argument depended upon the true opinions that the slave-boy acquired during the interview and the claim that these had not already been learnt in this lifetime; the *Phaedo* parallels this with the philosophers' knowledge of the equal and the claim that this was not derived purely from perception. In both dialogues these premises are used jointly to prove recollection for one or a small number of cases, from which Socrates then makes a tacit generalisation.

Now it might be suggested here that, although Socrates is not generalising from the widest sample in the *Meno*, he is doing so from the humblest sample which will do almost as well. Since someone of such humble origins can recollect, so too can anyone else. But nowhere in the *Meno* does Socrates actually argue in this way. What he does make use of is the fact that, because the slave boy has always been in Meno's household, they know that he cannot have already learnt geometry (85e3–6). It is not so much that he is a slave boy but that he is *Meno's* slave boy that matters, as it is this that ensures that the experiment is a controlled one.

Furthermore, the objection, with its scruples about generalising from a limited sample, is overlooking one of the most striking features of the *Meno* passage. Here there are no less than three generalising moves. The first, as we have seen, is from what the slave boy can do to what everyone can do. A second is from what can be done in geometry to what can be done in ethics. The original problem in the dialogue came from the threat of scepticism about moral discovery, and this Socrates tries to allay by showing that discovery is possible in geometry; he then generalises from geometry to cover all branches of learning (85e2–3). The third generalisation lies in his assumption that, because successful recollection is possible where the questioner knows the answers, it will be possible where the questioner does not – as will be the case in an ethical inquiry. In none of these cases does Plato show the slightest qualms about generalising. So the objector needs to explain why they are attributing such qualms to Plato in the *Phaedo*, especially at the cost of such absurdity.

It should be pointed out that there is a strategy common to both the *Meno* and the *Phaedo*, namely, that Plato is inferring not from the widest sample, but from the best sample. In the *Meno*, he takes one of the best disciplines available and generalises from that. In the *Phaedo*, he takes those who have made the best progress in inquiry and generalises from them.[22]

We have now established that recollection in the *Phaedo* is not used to explain mundane concept formation, which is to be accounted for empirically instead. Thus the two-source aspect of the Demaratus analogy fits the *Phaedo* well. Also, recollection is an activity confined to a few people only; most people, though they do indeed have the knowledge latently, do not manifest it. Before we leave this dialogue, we need to discuss the remaining issue implicit in the Demaratus analogy, namely the sense in which Plato's theory is pessimistic.

So far we might say our interpretation of the *Phaedo* is pessimistic in that far fewer people engage in recollection than some commentators have imagined. However, we have yet to show where the element of deception enters. True, most people rest content only with the information of the senses. But why should we say that they are *deceived* rather than merely missing out on something else? The analogy of Demaratus' tablet makes recollection out to be a deeply pessimistic doctrine. The surface message is actually deceptive and

[22] This type of strategy was to be used again by Aristotle in the *Politics* I 5, 1254a34ff.

in some way contradicts the message underneath. Is this right?

In fact, in stressing the element of deception, the analogy picks up on a point that is made in the *Phaedo* both before and after the recollection argument. Towards the beginning of the dialogue, Socrates explains to his companions why he is so confident in the face of death. This is because death is the separation of the soul from the body and the moment when the soul no longer relies upon input from the senses. This is a benefit because, as he says at 65b4–6, there is no truth, accuracy or clarity in the senses. The more the soul can separate itself from the bodily organs, the better its chances of attaining the truth. In this section, one part of the fault attributed to the senses, or more generally to the body, has to do with the fact that they distract the soul from intellectual activity; the other part stems from the fact that they fill it with images or fantasies,[23] and in a passage after the recollection argument, Plato, with added emphasis, returns to the idea that the senses actually mislead us.

From 82d9 onwards, he talks of the way in which philosophy takes over the soul and tries to release it from the prison of the body by showing the soul that 'inquiry through the eyes is full of deceit, and deceitful, too, is inquiry through the ears and other senses'. But what exactly is this deceit meant to involve? If the senses tell us that two sticks are on one occasion equal and on another unequal, Plato nowhere says that this sort of information is actually false. True, they do not tell us about the form equality, but that in itself is not deceit. However, Plato's point, developed at 83c5ff., is that bodily experiences, such as pleasures and pains, tempt us to 'take to be real whatever the body declares to be so' (83d4–6). Because of the vividness of these experiences, we are tempted to assume that only the corporeal can be real (81b4–6). This is the point at which the senses provide us with something that contradicts the correct metaphysic attained in recollection, and it is now easy to see how the Demaratus analogy does justice to the epistemology of the *Phaedo*. Those who attend to the surface message alone without having any inkling of the message underneath are, like the Persians in our story, simply deceived. Furthermore, the way in which the Greeks scrape away the wax to get down to the message underneath parallels a crucial feature in the *Phaedo*. What

[23] 66c3 (εἰδώλων).

is required for any successful inquiry is that we turn away from the perspective gained from sense perception. Philosophy is essentially discontinuous with this perspective. The other interpretation, K, mistakenly advocates not a rejection of the senses, but rather a synthesis between their message and our innate resources, and it is far from clear how, on this interpretation, the point about deception is to be understood.

## [2] THE *PHAEDRUS*

Those who interpret recollection as an explanation of concept formation have not confined their attention to the *Meno* and the *Phaedo*. There is another passage in which recollection plays an important part, the famous allegory in the *Phaedrus* (246a–257b) where Plato assimilates the experience of philosophy to the madness of love. The passage begins with the image of the soul as a winged charioteer drawn by two horses. In company with the gods, it follows a procession beyond the vault of the universe to attain a glimpse of true reality, a vision of the forms. While the souls of the gods achieve this with ease, ours do so with more difficulty (247b1–3). But such a vision is vital for the well-being of the soul and provides nourishment for its wings. Those that do attain a glimpse of the forms remain unscathed. But those that miss out on the vision may lose their wings and fall to earth (248c5–8). Here they are imprisoned in a mortal body like an oyster trapped in a shell, and in the process forget their vision of the forms. In the first incarnation after the fall, the soul must enter a human body. After its first incarnation it can choose to enter another human life or an animal one. If it chooses the latter, it can return to a human body in a future incarnation.

At this point, 249c4, Plato turns to his central topic, the nature of love, which he portrays as the highest kind of madness. This is explained partly by the contribution of the theory of recollection. A soul reincarnated as a human can, by coming into contact with a particular instance of beauty, begin to recollect its vision of the form of beauty. As it does so, as it comes to recognise the form of beauty dimly reflected in the particular, it is overcome by emotions of extraordinary power (250a6–b1). Such is the strength of these feelings that the person's whole life is turned upside-down and, in the lengths to which he will go to see his beloved and redeem his vision of the form, he appears completely mad to his fellow human beings. On recalling the form through the particular, the lover experiences pain, which Plato describes through the image of the wings of the soul regrowing, causing the kind of prickling and irritation that children have when they are first cutting their teeth (251c1–4).

Recollection is given a central role to play in the myth. But is it recollection as we have found it in the *Phaedo*, or is it as K interprets it? Throughout this passage, Plato associates recollection with an experience that feels extraordinary to the person who has it and that makes him appear a madman to the majority of people around him. In my view this tells strongly in favour of D. But there is a brief passage which many have thought to point to K. Just before he begins to describe the process of recollection, Plato talks of the choice of incarnation that face souls after their fall (249b1). After their first incarnation they may become animals. If they do this they can later be reincarnated as a human. But he adds that only a soul which has seen the forms can become a human. And it is when he spells out the reason for this that advocates of K prick up their ears:

For only the soul that has beheld truth may enter into this our human form: seeing that man must understand the language of forms, passing from a plurality of perceptions to a unity comprehended by reasoning; and such understanding is a recollection of those things which our souls saw before as they journeyed with their god, looking down upon things we now suppose to be, and gazing up to that which truly is. (249b5–c4)

Although there are a number of difficulties about the language used, difficulties that have provoked attempts to alter the text, most commentators interpret this passage in a way that clearly favours the K interpretation. Hackforth,[24] for instance, interprets the line of argument as follows:

Plato is careful to insist that the soul of an animal can pass into the body of a man only if the reverse transmigration has preceded (249b4). This

---

[24] Hackforth (1952) 91. See also Thompson (1868) 55 who says 'it is a law of human understanding that it can only act by way of generic notions ... sensibles are *per se* unintelligible'. One scholar who does not follow this line, remarkably enough, is Gulley (1954) 201, who, despite his reading of the *Phaedo*, does not take the *Phaedrus* passage as an attempt to explain the possibility of reasoning from sensation to conceptual apprehension. See also Irwin (1977) 173.

has of course already been said, or implied, at 248d1, but the reason for it is now given, namely that only souls which have seen true being in the supra-celestial procession can possess that power of conceptual thought which distinguishes man. If it were possible to imagine a soul starting its existence in an animal, its capacity of thinking when it passed into a man's body could not be accounted for.

On this interpretation, recollection, or its first stages, is invoked to explain the possibility of conceptual thought. And taking this sentence in this way does, it has to be admitted, make the argument of 249b–c a smooth one, and so we may be reluctant to interfere in such a way as to upset this.

Attractive as this interpretation seems, however, there are very strong grounds for rejecting it. As I have already indicated, one lies in the way Plato goes on to to describe recollection in the rest of the myth. K makes at least the earlier phase of recollection something routine and something experienced by every human being. As we shall now see, this flies in the face of much that he says about recollection elsewhere in the myth.

First of all, we should keep a firm grip on the way Plato characterises recollection. In recollecting, the lover undergoes a transition (250e2); the particular becomes the stimulus for a movement away towards the form. This shows how Plato conceives of recollection throughout the allegory as a matter of coming to see one thing through another. It also helps to explain the connection that Plato draws between recollection and the madness of love. It is because he sees so extraordinary an object through the particular that he is considered mad (249c8–d3):

Standing aside from the busy doings of mankind, and drawing nigh to the divine, he is rebuked by the multitude as being out of his wits, for they know not that he is possessed by a deity.

A few lines later the madness of the lover is explained by his attempt to make this transition to the form (249d4–e1). It is this kind of transition that keeps recollection far apart from anything mundane or routine.

The same point emerges from the connection between recollection and the regrowth of the wings. The act of recollection, of seeing the form in the particular, nourishes the shoots of the wings and helps them to grow again. But it also causes a strange feeling of pain (251b1–c5):

by reason of the stream of beauty entering through his eyes there comes a warmth, whereby his soul's plumage is fostered; and with that warmth the roots of the wings are melted, which for long had been so hardened and closed up that nothing could grow; then as the nourishment is poured in, the stump of the wing swells and hastens to grow from the root over the whole substance of the soul: for aforetime the whole soul was furnished with wings. Meanwhile she throbs with ferment in every part, and even as a teething child feels an aching and a pain in its gums when a tooth has just come through, so does the soul of him who is beginning to grow his wings feel a ferment and a painful irritation.

Plato associates recollection, even in its earliest stages, with the extraordinary feeling of the regrowth of the wings. Again, there is no stage of recollection that is represented as routine.

By means of these associations between recollection, the madness of love and the regrowth of the wings Plato sets the person who recollects apart from the many. This amounts to a clear-cut distinction between two kinds of people, the lover and the non-lover, a distinction that Plato retains throughout the allegory. Here he is talking about the non-lover at 249e4:

but to be put in mind [of the forms] by the things here is not easy for every soul; some, when they had the vision, had it but for a moment; some, when they had fallen to earth were unfortunate enough to be corrupted by evil associations, with the result that they forgot the holy objects of their vision.

Notice that when Socrates talks of those who have forgotten by falling into the wrong company, there is no suggestion that they can remember anything at all. On the other hand, they are perfectly well able to classify particulars under concepts. In other words, the knowledge that they have forgotten has nothing to do with the wherewithal for human intelligence in general to function.

Plato describes the non-lover in more detail at 250e1–5:

Now he whose vision of the mystery is long past, or whose purity has been sullied, cannot pass swiftly hence to see absolute beauty, when he beholds that which is called beautiful here; wherefore he looks upon it with no reverence, and surrendering to pleasure he tries to go after the fashion of a four-footed beast and to beget children . . .

When such people view a beautiful object, they do not see it as a likeness of the original at all, and so treat it with no respect. The real lover, on the other hand, treats the sensibles as reminders of the vision, not as objects of desire in themselves.[25] When he recollects, he feels an emotional tug, provoked by the divine associations of the form, and his whole attitude is conditioned by this. The non-lover, however, experiences none of this, but acts like an animal (250e4–5) – i.e., *as if he had never seen the form*. There is an emotional dimension that is lacking in the case of the non-lover, because the memory of the forms is playing no role in his life at all. Yet, since there is nothing to say that he cannot classify an object as beautiful, the memory of the forms is not invoked to explain such mundane acts of recognition.

So recollection, recognising the form through the particular, is seen in the passage as a transition which inevitably involves an extraordinary emotional experience and sets one person apart from the many. Because the wings begin to grow from the very start of the recollective process, all stages of recollection will be accompanied by this experience. Thus, the *Phaedrus* fits very well with D – except for the sentence at 249b6–c1. K's account of this, initially attractive as it is, presents us with an anomaly in the wider context of the myth. We need, therefore, to take a closer look at the passage. The crucial sentence ran:

man must understand the language of forms, passing from a plurality of perceptions to a unity comprehended by reasoning.[26]

Socrates then goes on to identify this cognitive achievement with the process of recollection.

There are a number of questions to be asked about this sentence. First, what level of cognition is implied by the word 'understand'

---

[25] Compare 249c7.

[26] δεῖ γὰρ ἄνθρωπον συνιέναι κατ' εἶδος λεγόμενον, ἐκ πολλῶν ἰὸν αἰσθήσεων εἰς ἓν λογισμῷ συναιρούμενον. The Greek is so difficult that it has led some commentators to emend the text in three places, despite a consensus of manuscripts. For a more detailed survey of the problems see Verdenius (1955) 280. Fortunately, the problems involved do not greatly affect our issue. (1) λεγόμενον on its own has been deemed impossible without either τό before, or τι after, which led Heindorf to insert τό. (2) ἰόν has provoked objections because it is surely the person, not the form, which goes to the unity, hence Badham's change to ἰόντ'. But Verdenius (1955) 280 argues that we can make sense of the text as it stands without either emendation: λεγόμενον = λόγος, and, in this usage, no article is needed, for it is quite admissible to talk of the λόγος (= the man) going to the form. So a more literal translation might be 'a man must understand an account according to a form ...', but I have kept Hackforth's more elegant phrase, 'the language of forms', which, on its own, does not prejudice the issue between D and K either way. (3) συναιρούμενον has been changed to συναιρουμένων by those who translate the verb as 'collect' and then point out that it is not the form that is collected together, but the sense perceptions. We can avoid this change if we take

(*sunienai*)? It could mean 'understand something said' in a casual sense (hence the commentators' point about generic terms essential to language and rational thought). Alternatively, we can take it as understanding of a more advanced kind (i.e., having knowledge of) an account or definition according to a Platonic form, something quite different from an innocent generic concept. So far there seems to be nothing to push us either way; the language leaves it open.

Things begin to tilt in favour of D when we come to the word translated as 'reasoning' (*logismos*). This is a word that means 'calculation' (often in a mathematical sense), implying a deliberate, perhaps laborious activity, whereas the generalising process to which, according to K, the text is referring is automatic. Furthermore, in the same part of the sentence, Plato talks about a movement away from many sense perceptions to the form. Now K takes this to refer to the way in which we move from raw sense data to the generic terms by which we understand them. But Plato's language corresponds much more closely to D, according to which we move away from sensible appearances in this world, leaving them behind, and go on to contemplate the form on its own. From what has emerged from our analysis of the overall context, this is clearly the point of the passage as a whole. What K is advocating, however, is not a departure from one to the other, but rather a synthesis of the two which is necessary to generate empirical understanding.

One proponent of K, Hackforth, refers us to *Republic* 476a for a parallel usage of this language of 'going to the form'. Yet if we look at that passage we do indeed find a parallel, but not one which helps K. At *Republic* 476b10–11, Socrates says that those who would be able to go[27] to the beautiful itself would be few, and he says this to contrast the philosophers with people who do not acknowledge the form at all. At 476a4–7 he has just stated in no uncertain terms the distinction between the one form and the many particulars, which are also called appearances (thus recalling the reference to

the word as passive, meaning 'comprehended', and to say that the form, 'the one', is grasped by reasoning is quite familiar to readers of middle-period Plato. (We should, *contra* Gulley (1954) 200–1, resist the temptation to read 'collection' into this passage. This new turn in Plato's dialectic is only announced later on at 265d. Furthermore, συναιρέω is not part of Plato's terminology for this procedure; it is not used anywhere else in his works.)

[27] Note that he uses the same verb as in *Phaedrus* 249b7 (ἰέναι).

perception at *Phaedrus* 249b7–c1). So this section of the *Republic* is certainly an excellent parallel for the *Phaedrus* passage, according to D at least. In both cases, the philosopher moves away from the many objects of sense perception to the one form which is apprehended by reasoning.

What is emerging is that the crucial sentence fits better with D than with K when examined internally. But if we now take it to be referring to the way a philosopher moves away from particulars to forms, how are we are to understand the claim that humans *must* make this transition? On K, where Plato was talking about reasoning according to universals, the word 'must' had a descriptive sense: 'it is a fact of human nature that we have rational thought'. But if we take the word 'must' descriptively, and yet interpret the rest of the sentence as an account of distinctively philosophical reasoning, we end up with a blatant falsehood. It is not a fact of human nature that everyone makes the transition to the forms as a philosopher does. This problem, however, is easily solved. We take the word 'must' in a prescriptive sense: human beings *ought* to go to the form, whether we actually do or not. It is our epistemological (and hence moral) duty. This notion should already be familiar to us from the *Meno*. At the end of the slave boy demonstration, Socrates emphasises our epistemological duty to continue to inquire:

one thing I am ready to fight for as long as I can, in word and act: that is, that we shall be better, braver and more active if we believe we must[28] look for what we don't know than if we believe there is no point inquiring because what we don't know we can never discover. (86b7–c2)

Another parallel, this time from a very similar context to that of the *Phaedrus*, comes in Diotima's speech about the ascent to the form of beauty in the *Symposium*, 210a4ff. Here she talks of the different stages in the movement away from particulars to the form, and at each one says how we *must* make the ascent.[29]

If the crucial sentence of 249b6–c1 refers to the duty that human beings have to ascend from particulars to forms, we are left with one final question: how is it supposed to fit into the surrounding pattern of argument? According to K, the order of argument ran as

[28] Again, there is an important similarity of language. The word for 'must' in this line, 86b8, is the same as in *Phaedrus* 249b6 (δεῖ).
[29] From 210a4 to e1 there is a string of verbs governed by 'must' (δεῖ) in 210a4.

follows: all human beings reason according to universals; because this cognitive achievement involves recollection of the forms, a soul that has never seen the forms cannot enter a human form. On D, we do still have an argument, though a different one: human beings have an obligation to make a philosophical transition to the form; this involves recollecting the forms, and so a soul that has never seen the forms cannot enter a human form. In other words, unlike animals, human beings have the obligation to become philosophers, and – if 'ought' implies 'can' – only a soul which has seen the forms can do this and so have this obligation.

The Demaratus interpretation turns out to fit with Plato's treatment of recollection in the *Phaedrus* after all. The type of argument that K reads into 249b5–c4 initially seemed plausible, but the language of the crucial sentence actually favours D, and an argument can still be extracted on this reading. If we then recall that the context of the myth as a whole favours D, the matter is settled. The *Phaedrus*, in fact, seems to treat the theory of recollection much as the *Phaedo* does, tying it down firmly to the separation of copy and model that is one strand in the middle-period theory of forms.

## [3] THE REPUBLIC

This concludes my defence of the Demaratus interpretation of recollection. In chapter 1 I took a cautious line, showing that in the *Meno* Plato was not concerned with early learning as his explanandum and that towards the end of the dialogue a two-source theory emerges with an external account of the formation of true beliefs. In this chapter I have attributed a more determinate version of D to the *Phaedo*. Plato is excluding ordinary learning from the scope of recollection, has an empiricist story about how we form the materials of ordinary thought and holds a depressing view of most people as bound fast to the deceptive organs of bodily sensation. The *Phaedrus* at first seemed to pose a threat to any attempt to limit the scope of recollection to higher learning, but we have now seen that this threat was illusory.

I have confined myself to Plato's theory of recollection, though in fact this is by no means his only contribution to the theory of learning. There are other epistemologically weighty dialogues, notably the *Republic* and the *Theaetetus*, which have important things to say on this topic but which make no mention of recollection. A thorough treatment of Plato's theory of learning would have to discuss the relevant passages from these dialogues. As I said in the general introduction, however, this book does not have encyclopaedic ambitions and so I shall not attempt to broaden my scope beyond the theory of recollection. Nevertheless, let me finish by showing how some of the issues we have seen associated with recollection are maintained or developed in the *Republic* and the *Theaetetus*.

In my account of recollection in the *Phaedo* and the *Phaedrus* I have contrasted two very different interpretations of the contribution that the senses make to conceptual thought. K allows the senses only a very meagre input. If we are to form the judgement, 'those objects are equal' or perhaps even 'those objects are horses',[30] we need, among other things, the notions of equality and horse. But Plato allegedly thinks that sense perception cannot give us these notions, and so we must derive them from elsewhere. Thus, in proposing the theory of recollection, Plato is meant to be presenting us with a thesis about ordinary cognitive development. On my interpretation, things are very different. Plato is an empiricist when it comes to explaining how ordinary concepts are formed and no process of recollection is involved in the development of them. Thus, the senses are rather generously endowed since they are able to give us opinions about how things are in the world and even about what is or is not real (*Phaedo* 83d6). Furthermore, it is precisely because of this self-sufficiency that they are able to deceive us. In support of this view it is worth repeating that whereas there are texts talking about the deceptiveness of the

---

[30] A further problem that some versions of K would have to tackle is that of the range of forms. If the *Phaedrus* is meant to explain the use of universals in language we need forms corresponding to all universal terms, hair, mud and dirt included. One advantage of embracing D is that we avoid tying down recollection to this particular crux. We should note that the only parallel text that K could appeal to for its range of forms in the *Phaedrus* is the notorious sentence at *Republic* X 596a5–7: 'Do you want us to start looking in our usual way? We are accustomed to assuming a form in each case for the many particulars to which we give the same name' (Βούλει οὖν ἐνθένδε ἀρξώμεθα ἐπισκοποῦντες, ἐκ τῆς εἰωθυίας μεθόδου; εἶδος γάρ πού τι ἕν ἕκαστον εἰώθαμεν τίθεσθαι περὶ ἕκαστα τὰ πολλά, οἶς ταὐτὸν ὄνομα ἐπιφέρομεν). However, it is not clear that this is the correct translation of the sentence, as Smith (1917) has argued. On linguistic, if not philosophical, grounds he claims the following is more likely: 'We are accustomed to assuming a single form for the many particulars; to these we give the same name [as the form]'; this translation does not commit Plato to a vast range of forms. At the very least, Smith's arguments cast considerable doubt upon the usual claims made for this sentence.

senses, there are none in the *Phaedo* or the *Phaedrus* about how we
would be unable to think at all with only the senses to aid us. K is
reading problems into these dialogues that are simply not there.

Now the idea that we can form concepts and thoughts relying
merely on the senses and without drawing on the soul's own
resources is a point made clearly in the *Republic* as well. There
are two passages to note. The first comes in book v, 474b3ff.,
a passage which we have already cited in our discussion of the
*Phaedrus*. Socrates has just introduced the claim that the rulers
of the ideal state ought to be philosophers. He then attempts to
define the philosopher more carefully and in the course of doing
so distinguishes the philosopher from the 'lovers of sights and
sounds', people who immerse themselves in the particulars and
take delight in attending every kind of performance and festival
they can. The philosopher, on the other hand, pursues knowledge
of the form of beauty itself. At 476a9–c1 Socrates develops the
distinction between the two types:

on the one side are those whom you just called lovers of spectacles and
lovers of crafts and practical men, on the other side are those whom
we are discussing, and whom alone one would call philosophers. . . . The
lovers of sights and sounds, I said, like beautiful sounds and colours and
shapes, and all the objects fashioned from them, but their thought is
unable to see and welcome the nature of Beauty itself. . . . Those who
can reach Beauty itself and see it in itself would be only a few, would
they not?[31]

Up to this point one could interpret these lines as saying that the
lovers of sights and sounds do have some inkling of the form of
beauty which enables them to recognise the beautiful particulars
as beautiful. Their problem is that they have not yet attained a full
understanding of the form.

The next few lines, however, rule out such an interpretation
(476c2–4):

As for the man who believes in beautiful things but not in the existence
of beauty itself, nor is able to follow one who leads him to the knowledge
of it, do you not think that his life is a dream rather than a reality?[32]

---

[31] Trans. Grube (1981).
[32] At first sight this passage, by claiming that the lovers of sights and sounds *cannot* even
attain knowledge of the forms, seems to go beyond even the pessimism of the *Phaedo*.
However, Plato need not be taken as denying that such people have the knowledge
deep within them; he is claiming that it is buried so deeply in them that their chances
of recovering it in this incarnation are nil. This should be related to the suggestion

The point about the lovers of sights and sounds is not that they have some partial understanding of the form of beauty but that they would deny its existence altogether. Knowledge of it, partial or otherwise, plays no role in their thinking about beautiful objects at all. In other words, the way the lovers of sights and sounds deny the existence of forms is very similar to the way ordinary people in the *Phaedo* are said to think that only the corporeal can exist (81b4–5).

The second passage, *Republic* VII 523a5ff., is a direct discussion of the adequacy or inadequacy of sense perception. Socrates holds up to his interlocutor three fingers, the middle finger being smaller than one and larger than the other. He claims that the senses are reliable when they tell us that it is a finger, because they do not at the same time indicate that it is not a finger, whereas with certain other properties, such as largeness and smallness, that is just what they do. So, in the case of the judgement 'this is a finger', Plato allows the senses the same self-sufficiency he granted them in the *Phaedo*, and when he goes on to talk of the inadequacy of perception he does not say that it cannot tell us that the finger is large, but that it tells us that it is both large and small. It can only confuse us because it does have at its disposal, as it were, all the concepts banned by the K interpretation. Thus in allowing the senses to make confused judgements Plato is in fact being very generous to them. Their inadequacy consists in their being cognitively unsound rather than cognitively sterile.

It is interesting to note that this view of the contribution of the senses common to both the *Phaedo* and the *Republic* is actually retracted by Plato later when he came to write the *Theaetetus*, in which he gives an account of the inadequacy of perception that is very much like the type that K tries to read into the earlier dialogues. The passage in question is his analysis of judgement at *Theaetetus* 184b8ff. There he makes a distinction between what the mind perceives on its own, and what it perceives by means of the senses, and he argues that certain properties such as hardness are the prerogative of certain individual senses, whereas beauty, similarity, being and some other forms are perceived by the mind on its own. What is involved here is precisely an analysis of

of *Phaedo* 83d4–e3 that once the body has perverted the soul into a purely corporeal view of things, there is little hope of any conversion to philosophy. The knowledge is still there, but the perversion in one particular incarnation is irreversible.

thoughts such as 'this object is beautiful or useful', or simply, 'this object is', from which Plato concludes that at least one component must be contributed quite independently of the senses, that is, by the activity of the mind on its own.[33] It is not that the senses are unreliable, but that they are incapable of being used to grasp certain properties.

This passage in the *Theaetetus* is a significant stage in Plato's development. It represents a rejection of a view of the senses that runs throughout the middle period,[34] a view that is an essential part of D. In recanting his generosity towards sense perception and removing from it even the ability to provide unreliable information Plato moved towards a new set of considerations similar to those that K is importing back into recollection. This is an anachronism, however, because recollection is firmly tied to the middle-period ontology and epistemology.

There is another respect in which the epistemology of the *Phaedo* is, on my interpretation, now remarkably close to that of the *Republic*. In Plutarch's analogy, the Persian readers of the wax tablet, having no inkling of the message underneath, were deceived into believing the message on top. In applying this to recollection I have claimed that, in Plato's view, most people did not even begin to recollect but instead accepted the information of the senses, thereby forming a distorted picture of reality. In the *Phaedo* the senses are unequivocally said to deceive us. This type of epistemological pessimism comes out just as strongly in the *Republic*, especially in the story of the prisoners in the cave in book VII. We have already made a connection between the conclusion of the *Meno* and the cave allegory at the end of chapter 1, and where the *Phaedo* is concerned, the connection is just as tight. The prisoners sit staring at a wall at the bottom of a cave; behind

---

[33] 185e1. Admittedly, when talking of the inadequacy of the senses at *Phaedo* 83a1ff., Plato had differentiated between the mind investigating with the senses and doing so on its own (83b1). Very similar terminology is used at this point in the *Theaetetus*. Nevertheless, the differences between the two passages are stark. When the *Theaetetus* makes the distinction, it does so for cases of ordinary empirical judgements, so that in the same judgement there could be a sensible and a mental component. In the *Phaedo*, however, the distinction parallels the division between the physical world and the forms, so that when the mind investigates on its own, it has left the world of changing objects behind. In the *Theaetetus* such a departure is not necessary to the distinction. Thus while in the *Phaedo* Plato is pejorative about the use of the senses, in the *Theaetetus* there are no such overtones.

[34] Plato's *volte-face* on this issue has been discussed by Burnyeat (1976) 29–52.

them burns a fire and between them and the fire some puppets are moved about. The result is that all they see are shadows and they take these to be realities. One of the prisoners manages to escape and, turning round to the fire, is initially dazzled by the light. After he becomes used to it he realises that all he believed to be real was in fact a charade. The process is repeated again as he ascends out of the cave towards the sunlight. At each stage of his ascent he is dazzled by the increasing brightness before coming to realise that what before he took to be reality was but a sham or a reflection.

This is a brilliant parable for the way philosophical discoveries were for Plato startling revisions of ordinary ways of thinking. The pain experienced by the prison dweller at each level of his ascent illustrates just how wide the gap is between what Aristotle was to call 'the more familiar to us' and 'the more familiar in nature'. As we saw at the end of chapter 1, this pessimistic view is further underscored by Plato's description of what happens when he returns to the cave and tells the remaining prisoners of the illusion under which they are living. They respond with mockery and, eventually, violence. If my interpretation of recollection is correct, the cave parable of *Republic* VII is developing a line of thought strongly reminiscent of the *Phaedo*. The gap that the *Republic* portrays between the perspective of the prison dweller and the one who has escaped is very similar to that between the ordinary person of the *Phaedo* who has not begun to recollect – the counterpart of the Persian readers of Demaratus' letter – and the philosopher who has begun to recollect and see the world in a very different way. In proposing the D interpretation, therefore, I am showing that the pessimism of book VII of the *Republic*, and with it the revisionist conception of philosophy, are already clearly present in the *Phaedo*.

Finally, a twist in the tale. Once we have felt the full force of Plato's pessimism about the pre-philosophical state, we can begin to appreciate his enormous optimism about the ability of human understanding to transform itself. Plato was not a sceptic. In his view, if we now happen to be imprisoned in the mundane perspective, we are not condemned to remain so. And the greater the inadequacy of that perspective, the more remarkable is the power of philosophy to transform it.

# *Aristotelian experience*

# Introduction

The next four chapters will consider Aristotle's theory of learning. We begin in chapter 3 by determining his attitude to innatism and then, in chapters 4–6, look at his theory specifically in the light of our revised understanding of Platonic recollection. This revised view of Plato's theory raises two particularly relevant questions. The first concerns the distinction between ordinary and higher levels of learning. We have just seen how Plato's theory was directed exclusively at higher learning and that although he did have an empiricist account of ordinary learning he showed no interest in developing it. Now, there can be no doubt that in the post-Aristotelian era, Epicurus and the Stoics had a strong interest in the formation of ordinary concepts. This leaves an important question-mark hanging over Aristotle himself. Was it he who introduced the topic to philosophy, or do we have to wait for Epicurus to put it on the agenda?

We shall tackle this issue in chapter 4. One of the most famous passages in Aristotle's works is the last chapter of the *Posterior Analytics*, which explains how we grasp the universal by progressing from perception, memory and experience. There is, however, a controversy about the interpretation of this passage, a controversy that shows striking parallels to the debate about Platonic recollection. Is Aristotle here trying to explain ordinary concept formation, or is he talking about the discovery of scientific first principles, or both? Chronologically, Aristotle stands between Plato's indifference to questions about ordinary learning and the Hellenistic fascination with them; this therefore gives the controversy about this passage added importance.

The other salient issue for this section arises from the fact that Plato takes so dismissive an attitude to ordinary ways of thinking. By contrast, Aristotle optimistically declares: 'men have a sufficient natural instinct for what is true, and usually do arrive at the truth' (*Rhetoric* I 1, 1355a15–17). But is the contrast so clear-cut? In his ethical works, for instance, Aristotle often castigates common opinion, and subjects it to what might appear quite startling revision. So is this alleged difference between Plato and Aristotle, like so many others, one that begins to disappear on closer inspection? We shall deal with this issue at some length in chapters 5–6. My strategy will be to treat scientific and moral discovery separately, in chapters 5 and 6 respectively. This is because Aristotle, in marked opposition to Plato, emphatically distinguishes moral from scientific expertise.[1] Although we shall eventually conclude that Aristotle does have a similar account of discovery to cover both science and ethics, it would be a mistake to presuppose this from the start.

Before we go any further, however, a remark needs to be made about the relevant texts. Aristotle, as far as we know, never wrote a whole treatise on discovery or learning as such. He did write a treatise on the nature of scientific knowledge, the *Posterior Analytics*, but this has surprisingly little in it about discovery. Our other evidence for his views on scientific discovery comes from occasional chapters in various other works. Often these chapters are written as the introductions to works – the opening chapters of the *Physics* and the *Metaphysics* fall into this category. As far as moral epistemology is concerned, he never devoted an entire work to it, let alone to moral discovery. The *Nicomachean* and *Eudemian Ethics* do have a number of introductory or digressionary passages explicitly devoted to method, learning and discovery. Often, however, the best way of proceeding is to uncover the views on discovery implicit in his discussions of first-order ethical topics such as happiness or virtue. So, whereas in the previous chapters we could concentrate on relatively compact and self-contained texts, in this section we shall have to range quite widely to piece together an epistemological jigsaw puzzle.[2]

[1] In his ethical works, he frequently warns his readers about the dangers of expecting moral knowledge to have the kind of exactness or precision of mathematics or theoretical science. See *N. E.* I 3 *passim* and 7, 1098a20ff. Also, much of the emphasis of *N. E.* VI is on bringing out the difference between the types of knowledge involved in science and moral insight, *phronēsis*. (Throughout chapters 3–6 I shall retain the term *phronēsis* when referring to moral insight.)

[2] For the purposes of quotation in this section, I shall use, with occasional modifications, the Revised Oxford Translation = Barnes (1984), except for the *Posterior Analytics*, where I shall use Barnes (1993).

CHAPTER 3

# The rejection of innatism

## [1] VARIETIES OF INNATISM

Aristotle is often seen as an empiricist and as someone who thought that at birth the mind is like a *tabula rasa*, a blank slate. That he rejected Plato's theory of recollection is clear enough; whether he rejected all other forms of innateness and likened the mind to a *tabula rasa* is another question. In this chapter, I shall discuss his reasons for rejecting recollection and attempt to answer this further question. As I suggested in the general introduction, however, we have to prepare the philosophical ground carefully before we can determine his position on the innateness issue. In particular, we need a clearer idea of what forms of innatism there may be other than recollection, and also of how to understand the contrast between innatism and empiricism.

We are now considering what it means to say that something is innate to the mind, whereas in the previous two chapters we discussed what level of cognition might be explained by an appeal to innateness. Another set of distinctions that could be made is between the innateness of ideas (or concepts), beliefs and knowledge.[1] Although in some contexts these distinctions are important, in this chapter I shall focus solely on the question of what it is for an item to be innate to the mind whether the item in question is an idea, a belief or knowledge.

According to Plato's variety of innatism, there are items of knowledge in the mind at birth that have also been there in a precarnate state. I now wish to distinguish two other types of innatism which do not assume the pre-existence of the soul. The first could be called a theory of latent knowledge, the second dispositional innatism.[2]

---

[1] This threefold distinction should not be confused with the distinction of levels. It is possible to talk of concepts, beliefs and knowledge at either level. I shall discuss the distinction between the innateness of ideas, beliefs and knowledge on pp. 188–90 below.

[2] On the different varieties of innatism see Barnes (1972), Savile (1972), Hacking (1975) ch. 6 and Jolley (1984) ch. 9.

The theory of latent knowledge was held by Leibniz and could be described as being like Plato's theory, but pared of pre-existence. Knowledge lies within us waiting to be aroused by the stimulus of experience. That we are not aware of such knowledge, nor ever have been, does not mean that we do not have it latently. Leibniz agreed with Plato that learning is really a process of making something already there in the soul explicit, but did not allow this to imply that we must have been aware of these truths before.[3] Arguing against the view that for an item of knowledge to be in the soul we must have been aware of it he asks:

Must a self-knowing substance have, straight away, actual knowledge of everything that belongs to its nature? Cannot – and should not – a substance like our soul have various properties and states which could not all be thought about straight away or all at once?[4]

In addition to the theory of latent knowledge there is another variety, dispositional innatism, which will be especially important for our purposes. Historically, this theory has often been associated with the innateness of ideas and was espoused by Descartes and some of the Cambridge Platonists in the seventeenth century.[5] They held that the mind is innately disposed to form a certain set of ideas, whatever it happens to experience. It is not, however, equipped with the ideas themselves at birth. To illustrate this type of innateness, Descartes talked of ideas being innate to us as certain diseases are innate to some families.[6] In using the analogy he emphasised that the infants of such families do not possess the disease in their mothers' wombs but merely have a certain propensity to contract them. Similarly, babies are not actually born in possession of their innate ideas, but only with the dispositions to form them.

---

[3] Leibniz recognises his relationship to Platonic recollection at *New Essays*, Preface, I i and I iii = Remnant and Bennett (1982) 52, 78–9 and 106. See also *Discourse on Metaphysics* 26 = Parkinson (1973) 36.

[4] *New Essays I i = Remnant and Bennett (1982)* 78.

[5] Among the Cambridge Platonists, More and Cudworth embraced dispositionalism and often took some care to reject claims that we are born with any actual ideas. See, for instance, More (1662) 17 = Patrides (1969) 223. Descartes made similar qualifications to innatism. See next note.

[6] Haldane and Ross (1911) I 442. He also uses the example of innate generosity.

This theory is different from a theory of latent ideas because, as we have just seen, it is not the ideas themselves that are innate but the dispositions to form them. But if the ideas are not innate, what is the difference between dispositionalism and empiricism? According to the empiricism of Locke, for instance, human beings are equipped with no more than bare cognitive capacities. What we learn is a question of whatever we happen to experience. According to dispositional innatism, on the other hand, we may ostensibly start out with a blank tablet (just as the child in Descartes's analogy is truly healthy), and we do rely on our perceptions to learn, but we are of such a nature as to favour the formation of a certain group of ideas or beliefs as opposed to others, such as the idea of God. The essential point is that the mind is so structured as to form certain ideas and beliefs, whatever it may happen to encounter in experience; there is therefore a limiting factor that derives from the nature of the mind itself and is not dependent upon experience.

The distinction between dispositional innateness and empiricism was also clarified by Leibniz. Although he espoused the theory of latent knowledge and ideas, he also embraced the theory of innate dispositions. In his dispositionalist moods he dismisses the image of the blank tablet because it allows anything to be written on it. His tablet would be such as to favour a certain message. He also talks of the mind having special affinities, dispositions, aptitudes and pre-formations, as well as potentialities and tendencies,[7] all of which he opposes to a bare passive faculty.[8]

If we now focus upon the dispositional variety of innatism, we might understand the contrast between innatism and empiricism as follows. To be an empiricist is to assert that at birth there are no predispositions to form particular ideas or beliefs. Here the metaphor of the *tabula rasa* seems very apt. But this is in fact a very extreme theory, and it is possible to be an empiricist without dispensing with innate dispositions altogether. Let me

---

[7] *New Essays*, Preface and I i = Remnant and Bennett (1982) 52 and 80; see also 86.

[8] The way in which Leibniz seems to set these two types of innatism side by side has been discussed by Savile (1972) 117–19 and Jolley (1984) 171–9. For an interpretation that claims that for Leibniz dispositionalism in fact reduces to implicit or unconscious knowledge see Broad (1975) 134–5 and Jolley (1988) 86–7.

give an instance of this which comes to light from looking at the Locke–Leibniz debate. So far we have represented Lockean empiricism as a position that rejects anything but bare faculties. But Locke himself does in one place emend this:

Nature, I confess, has put into Man a desire of Happiness, and an aversion to Misery: These are indeed innate practical Principles, which (as practical Principles ought) do continue constantly to operate and influence all our Actions, without ceasing: These may be observ'd in all Persons and all Ages, steady and universal; but these are Inclinations of the Appetite to good, not Impressions of truth on the Understanding. I deny not, that there are natural tendencies printed on the Minds of Men; and that from the very first instances of Sense and Perception, there are some things, that are grateful and others unwelcome to them; ... But this makes nothing for innate Characters on the Mind, which are to be Principles of Knowledge ... (*Essay* I iii 3)

Here Locke acknowledges innate dispositions towards behaviour and so seems to move away from the image of the blank slate. But he still wants to insist that, although there may be inborn tugs of appetite, there are still no inborn intellectual tugs towards certain notions or beliefs. In reply, however, Leibniz argues that Locke has now sided with the innatists:

PHILALETHES [speaking for Locke]. Nature has put into man a desire for happiness and an aversion to misery; these are indeed innate practical principles which (as principles ought) do continue constantly to influence all our actions; but these are inclinations of the soul to good, not impressions of some truth that are engraved on the understanding.

THEOPHILUS. I am delighted, Sir, to find that you do after all acknowledge innate truths as I will shortly maintain. The principle agrees well enough with the one I have just pointed out which leads us to pursue joy and avoid sorrow. For happiness is nothing but lasting joy. However, what we incline to is not strictly speaking happiness but rather joy, i.e. something in the present; it is reason that leads to the future and to what lasts. Now an inclination that is expressed in the understanding becomes a precept or practical truth; and if the inclination is innate then so also is the truth – there being nothing in the soul that is not expressed in the understanding ... 9

---

9 *New Essays* I ii = Remnant and Bennett (1982) 90.

Leibniz seems prepared to say that when an innate tug of appetite becomes expressed as an idea, that idea should be called innate; because of this tug of appetite, we are bound to form certain ideas whatever the circumstances in which we live. All human beings of their own nature feel pleasure and pain, so you can be assured that wherever they live and whatever happens to them they will have the notions of pleasure and pain. Now imagine if Locke had conceded the truth of this to Leibniz. His next move might be to say that innatism so construed is a rather trivial thesis. What would make an innatist case interesting would be if, for instance, the belief in the existence of God were innate just as the notion of pleasure is. So the real debate is not about whether there is any innate endowment at all – that is a rather uncontroversial point – but about the size and richness of this endowment.

This example shows that the distinction between innatism and empiricism can be construed as a matter of degree. A radical or extreme empiricist might deny that there are any innate predispositions. But there can be a less extreme version of empiricism which does not eshew all innate predispositions entirely, though it does make only a very restricted appeal to them. Only in the case of radical empiricism is the image of the *tabula rasa* apt.

## [2] ARISTOTLE ON SCIENTIFIC DISCOVERY

We can now turn to the question of whether Aristotle allows any form of innatism in his account of scientific discovery. First, a brief word about Aristotle's conception of scientific understanding. The objects that fall under the domain of a particular Aristotelian science, be they natural objects or abstracted (i.e. mathematical) objects, all have essences or forms. A biologist might be concerned with a certain species, for example man, whose essence includes being a social animal. For Aristotle, the form or essence is explanatory of other features of the species in question. So, for instance, its ability to communicate is necessary given that it is to be social; its having a tongue is then necessary given its need to communicate. The various characteristics that are found in men are to be traced back to the essence, and thereby explained. Aristotle thus divides the properties of an object into those which are essential, and those which follow from it having the essence it has. Properties of this latter type are called 'necessary accidents'.[10]

To understand any feature of the object, therefore, involves being able to demonstrate how that feature follows from the essence of the object. Understanding is explanatory and explanation proceeds, ultimately, in terms of essences.[11] These essences thus act as first principles in an Aristotelian demonstrative science. But if having scientific understanding of a proposition always involves explaining it in terms of another, we cannot have scientific understanding of the principles themselves. As the most explanatory propositions, they are themselves incapable of explanation. Thus if principles are to be knowable, there must be another kind of knowledge apart from scientific understanding. Aristotle accepts this line of reasoning, posits a form of knowledge distinct from scientific understanding, reserves it for principles and terms it *nous*.[12]

On Aristotle's account, the principles of a science include the definitions stating the essences of the kind in question.[13] Therefore, as for Plato, the discovery of definitions is a topic demanding Aristotle's attention. But it is only in the second book of the *Posterior Analytics*, particularly in the final chapter, that Aristotle explicitly discusses the subject. He begins by posing a problem about the discovery of first principles (99b25–32). First, he asks whether knowledge of such principles could arise without already being

---

[10] καθ' αὑτὰ συμβεβηκότα *An. Po.* I 6, 75a18–9.

[11] For two excellent discussions of Aristotle's account of scientific understanding see Kosman (1973) and Burnyeat (1981).

In this brief synopsis of Aristotle's theory of scientific understanding I am omitting any mention of the syllogism. In the *Posterior Analytics*, Aristotle held that scientific understanding not only involved demonstrating the explanatory relations between propositions but also exhibiting them in the syllogistic format. There are numerous problems surrounding the role of syllogistic in Aristotle's theory of science, but they do not affect the point being made in this chapter. On the problems involved here see Barnes (1975) and (1981).

[12] For this line of argument see *An. Po.* II 19, 100b12 and *N.E.* VI 6, 1141a7. In *N.E.* VI 7 he discusses a synthesis of scientific understanding and *nous* which he terms 'wisdom' (*sophia*).

Throughout chapters 3–6, I shall retain the Greek word *nous* when referring to knowledge of first principles. (The standard translations, e.g. 'intuition' or 'intellect', can be more misleading than helpful.)

[13] Some of Aristotle's clearest statements that definitions are principles can be found at *An. Po.* I 3, 72b24, II 3, 90b24 and II 13, 96b21–5. See also I 2, 72a21 and I 33, 89a18.

present. This proposal is quickly dismissed because it apparently contravenes the principle laid down at the opening of the *Posterior Analytics* – 'All teaching and all learning of an intellectual kind proceed from pre-existent knowledge' (71a1–2). Knowledge, it seems, cannot simply come out of nowhere.

It is at this point that Aristotle turns to consider the question of innateness. Having rejected the idea that the states of knowledge come from nothing he turns to the other extreme and considers what is clearly a reference to Platonic recollection. Are the states of knowledge 'present in us without being noticed'? This too is dismissed: 'It is absurd to suppose that we possess such states; for we should possess pieces of knowledge more exact than demonstration without it being noticed.'[14] Aristotle has now constructed a dilemma. Knowledge cannot come into being from nothing nor can it be there already. To solve the dilemma he then goes on to find a middle ground between the two alternatives:

We must therefore possess some sort of capacity – but not one which will be more valuable than these states in respect of exactness. And this is clearly true of all animals: for they too have a connate discriminatory faculty, which is called perception. (99b32–5)

He develops this solution by saying that perception instils the universal. It does so by leaving behind memories which, grouped together as experience, provide the conditions for the knowledge of principles. We shall be discussing this account in more detail in chapters 4 and 5 below, but here we need to concentrate on his rejection of Platonic recollection. There are two questions: first, why does Aristotle reject the theory, and second, in doing so does he leave himself room to espouse any other kind of innatism?

What Aristotle objects to in Plato's theory is the idea that the most precise knowledge should be 'present in us without being noticed'. But this is unclear: without being noticed by whom? Is he referring to the person who allegedly has the knowledge or to bystanders? These options yield two very different interpretations. Barnes takes the latter option and has Aristotle make a very

[14] For the same point see *Met.* I 9, 992b33–3a2.

straightforward objection. Babies and infants are clearly not perceived to have such high-grade knowledge.[15] Barnes then admits
that this would invite from the innatist the standard rejoinder
that the knowledge is latent and needs some kind of catalyst
to awaken it. At this point Aristotle's text leaves us without
an answer, but Barnes suggests that he 'would doubtless have
accepted Locke's answer to this reaction. It reduces innatism
to the uncontroversial hypothesis that human infants have certain innate cognitive *capacities* the exercise of which waits upon
experience.'

On the other interpretation of Aristotle's objection, what he
finds absurd is the idea that the presence of the innate knowledge
escapes the notice of the person who has it. This would mean
that Aristotle's target is already a theory of latent knowledge.
What he finds absurd is the notion of our having such knowledge
unbeknown to ourselves. This interpretation is more plausible if
only on grounds of charity. It puts Aristotle already further along
in the argument; in the first interpretation all he does is to raise
a rather facile objection which can be readily dismissed by the
innatist.

If this is the correct interpretation, it is unclear what arguments
Aristotle would use in support of his assertion. The one point he
could not use is Locke's attack on latent knowledge. Here is
the passage where Locke makes the point to which Barnes is
alluding:

It seeming to me a near Contradiction to say that there are Truths
imprinted upon the Soul which it perceives or understands not; imprint-
ing, if it signify anything being nothing else but the making certain
Truths to be perceived. For to imprint anything on the Mind without the
Mind's perceiving it seems to me hardly intelligible ... No Proposition
can be said to be in the Mind which it never yet knew; which it was
never conscious of. For if any one may; then, by the same Reason, all
Propositions that are true, and the Mind is capable ever of assenting
to, may be said to be in the Mind and to be imprinted: Since if any one
can be said to be in the Mind, which it never yet knew, it must be only
because it is capable of knowing it; and so the Mind is of all Truths it
shall ever know. ... So that if the Capacity of knowing be the natural

Impression contended for, all the Truths a Man ever comes to know, will, by this Account, be, every one of them, innate; and this great Point will amount to no more, but only to a very improper way of speaking; . . . (*Essay* I ii 5)

There are two problems with this argument. First, Locke uses as a *premise* the claim that for a proposition to be in a mind at a certain time the mind must be conscious of that proposition at that time, or at least must have been conscious of it at some previous time. Thus Locke does not *argue* against the possibility of latent knowledge, but merely assumes it to be impossible. The second problem is that even if one agrees with Locke's premise, the whole passage leaves the theory of *recollection* intact. Locke places two alternative conditions for a proposition being in the mind at a certain time: either the mind must be conscious of that proposition at that time, or *must have been conscious of it at some previous time.* But according to the theory of recollection we have indeed been aware of certain items of knowledge previously, so this second condition has been met.[16]

Lockean arguments cannot therefore be used to bolster Aristotle's rejection of recollection in *An. Po.* II 19 and it should by now be clear that Aristotle is relying more on intuition than argument in this passage. There is, however, one more important point about Aristotle's rejection of recollection to note. When we first encounter Aristotle's description of Plato's theory as 'absurd' we might think this natural enough. After all, even those sympathetic to Plato have thought certain aspects of the theory bizarre. Leibniz had much to praise in Plato's theory but recoiled from the association of his theory with reincarnation and recollection.[17] And among modern commentators who have thought it worthwhile to write at some length on the theory, Gregory Vlastos talked of it as 'that

[16] Locke himself appreciated that a theory of recollection would slip through the net of I ii 5 and so in a later edition added a further argument to catch it (*Essay* I iv 20). The argument is that in recollection we are always aware that we are recollecting, whereas we do not think we are recollecting when we learn. Hence learning cannot be recollection. In reply, Leibniz rightly points out that not all recollection need be conscious: see *New Essays on Human Understanding*, I iii = Remnant and Bennett (1982) 106–7. For an account of memory that dispenses with awareness of recollection see Martin and Deutcher (1966).

[17] For references see n. 3 above.

wildest of Plato's metaphysical flights'.[18] But, curiously enough, Aristotle does not dismiss Plato's theory as absurd because of its links with reincarnation or its metaphysical extravagance. What he objects to is something quite distinct, namely, the suggestion that the most precise kind of knowledge might be latent within us.

But if Aristotle rejects the theory of recollection for this reason, it does not follow that he has rejected all other varieties of innatism. For instance, he could still allow anything less than the most precise kind of knowledge to be latent at birth. Furthermore, there is nothing in his remarks to rule out the possibility of innate dispositions. In fact, such dispositions seem similar to his own notion of potentiality. If we talk in Aristotelian terms about an acorn having the potentiality to grow into an oak-tree we are not talking about some bare capacity to grow in any way at all, but a predisposition to develop in a very specific way given certain appropriate external conditions. So far from refuting this kind of innatism Aristotle could easily have made use of such innate dispositions in his own account of cognitive development. We might have innate dispositions to group items of our experience into the correct natural kinds, thus giving ourselves the appropriate starting-point for further inquiries into the essences of those kinds.

Aristotelian as the notion of dispositional innateness might seem, however, there is very little evidence that he did adopt it. In *An. Po.* II 19 itself, after rejecting Plato's theory he gives his own account in which perception, memory and experience make all the running. If he had wished to invoke the idea of innate dispositions he would surely have made some mention of them here. In general, he is keen to stress the work of perception in the learning process. This is well known – and explains the attribution of empiricism and of the *tabula rasa* theory to Aristotle. So even if nothing in Aristotle's general theory rules out dispositional innatism, he does not seem willing to endorse it either.

But there are some qualifications to be made here. First, there is one innate disposition that he clearly does endorse. At the very beginning of the *Metaphysics* he says that all human beings by nature desire to know (980a21). Thus we all have an inborn predisposition to wish to learn. This in itself does not mean we have any

[18] (1983) 56.

dispositions to get things right. Perhaps this further point is what lies behind the optimistic sentence from the *Rhetoric*: 'men have a sufficient natural instinct for what is true, and usually do arrive at the truth' (I 1, 1355a15–17). This may imply a predisposition to believe true propositions rather than false ones. Had Aristotle developed or even mentioned this in his epistemological writings, we would be able to talk far more confidently about a commitment to some form of dispositional innateness on his part.[19] However, he keeps silent on this issue and almost always chooses to emphasise the role of experience over any innate features of the mind. So my conclusion is that although he does allow some kind of innate learning-readiness, he gives the greatest burden of the explanation to experience. To ascribe to the *tabula rasa* theory is too crude, but he is, in the more cautious sense I have outlined, an empiricist about scientific discovery.

[3] MORAL LEARNING

This is not as yet to rule out any appeals to innateness in Aristotle's account of moral learning. His views on this subject are complicated by the fact that in the fully virtuous person two general conditions have to be met: the person must have excellence of character (moral virtue), and the intellectual excellence concerned with action, *phronēsis*. The distinction between the intellectual and moral components of the completely good person stems from a distinction between two parts of the soul, rational and non-rational, made at *N.E.* 1 13, 1102a25ff. The rational part is that with which we think and, if all goes well, attain the truth; the non-rational is especially associated with our desires and emotions. Intellectual virtues thus belong to the rational part of the soul, moral virtues to the non-rational (1103a3–10). The intellectual virtue of *phronēsis* guides the non-rational part or, as he puts it more picturesquely, gives commands for the other to obey, like a father to a son;[20] for example, in the exercise of courage the non-rational part of

---

[19] Wardy (1990) 236–8 has suggested that Aristotle may be developing some such account in *Physics* VII 3.

[20] 1102b31ff. Because the 'non-rational' part of the soul is able to respond to the commands of reason it can be said to participate in reason in a sense and is quite distinct from the nutritive part of the soul which cannot respond to reason at all.

the soul has to feel the particular degree of fear or confidence as determined by *phronēsis*. Although these two kinds of virtue are distinct, it is not possible to have one without the other (1144b30–2). Moral virtue without *phronēsis* would lack the guidance necessary for feeling and doing the right things; *phronēsis* would be unattainable in the absence of sound moral character because the presence of excessive desires, for instance, would distort one's practical judgement and view of the good.

If there are two aspects to the good life there will be two components to moral education: the education of the practical intellect, and the training of the non-rational part of the soul, a kind of character formation. Aristotle's preliminary remarks in *N.E.* II 1[21] suggest a preference for empiricism in both kinds of development:

> Intellectual virtue in the main owes both its birth and growth to teaching (for which reason it requires both experience and time), while moral virtue comes about as a result of habit. . . . (*N.E.* II 1, 1103a15–17)

Aristotle defers his discussion of the intellectual virtues until *N.E.* VI, so his discussion of moral education in II 1–4 is focused on character formation and the acquisition of moral virtue. One of the most important things to be achieved in this process is that the learner comes to do and feel the right things both as a matter of disposition and with pleasure (or, at least, not without pleasure). Someone who manages to do the right thing but only after a painful internal conflict is not fully virtuous. The process of moral education, the formation of moral virtue, consists in habituation, a process of bringing someone to take pleasure in virtuous acts by repetition. This Aristotle thinks 'makes all the difference' in moral education (1103b23–5). At the beginning of such a process we do not even have any natural inclinations towards virtue, merely the capacity to become virtuous (1103a19–26). Thus, since habituation 'makes all the difference' we could, given the appropriate upbringing, just as well become morally vicious as virtuous. On this line

---

[21] It is clear from the way he discusses the question both here and earlier in I 9, 1099b9–11 that the opening question of the *Meno* is in the background. The same goes for X 9, esp. 1179b20–1.

of thought we are at birth, morally speaking, blank tablets. All he seems to allow us in the way of natural endowment is the capacity to receive virtue, which might mean the capacity to enjoy doing virtuous acts given the right upbringing.

But if this is the correct account of Aristotle's position in *N.E.* II 1, it is not the whole story. Later on in the same book, when setting out the doctrine of the mean, Aristotle claims that we are innately predisposed towards one of the two extremes.[22] For instance, of the extremes relative to temperance, we are more inclined to intemperance (II 8, 1109a14–16). Later, in the course of his discussion of generosity, he claims that most people have a greater natural disposition to meanness than to the other of the two extremes relative to generosity, extravagance (IV 1, 1121b14–16). Related to our natural predisposition towards intemperance is his belief that the human species has a natural affinity with pleasure; hence its importance for ethics and in particular for the question of moral upbringing.[23] In this case, we find Aristotle committing himself to an innate disposition of the kind that even Locke admitted and that Leibniz subsequently tried to exploit.

For Aristotle, then, elements of our characters may be innate. But none of the examples mentioned so far seems particularly conducive towards our successful moral development. As well as predispositions to vice, however, Aristotle does raise the possibility of innate dispositions to some of the virtues:

all men think that each type of character belongs to its possessors in some sense by nature; for from the very moment of birth we are just or fitted for self-control or brave or have the other moral qualities . . . (*N.E.* VI 13, 1144b4–6)

What is envisaged is a form of innate virtue, 'natural virtue',[24] although, as he goes on to stress, such a state, in the absence of *phronēsis*, would not count as genuine virtue and could just as

---

[22] II 8, 1109a13–16. In II 9, 1109b1–3 he says that people vary in their natural tendencies.

[23] See II 8, 1109a14–15 and X 1, 1172a19–20.

[24] Compare the way in which Descartes talked of certain families who might have an innate predisposition towards generosity. See Haldane and Ross (1911) I 442.

well lead us astray. Someone, for instance, with natural 'courage'
is very likely to go beyond courage to the excess of the mean,
rashness. This shows that Aristotle does admit the existence here
of innate dispositions to certain types of behaviour, but he gives
the dispositions no role to play in moral education, and even talks
of the dangers they pose for acquiring virtue proper.

Even if Aristotle had given character-innateness a greater role
to play in his theory, our interests lie with cognitive learning, and
it remains to be seen whether he allows innateness any place in the
development of *phronēsis*. At one point, in the course of a discussion
of voluntary action, he considers the suggestion that moral insight
is innate (III 5, 1114b5–12). He sets out an argument purporting to
show that evil action is involuntary:[25]

> the aiming at the end is not self-chosen but one must be born with an
> eye, as it were, by which to judge rightly and choose what is truly good,
> and he is well-endowed by nature who is well endowed with this. For it
> is what is greatest and most noble, and what we cannot get or learn from
> another, but must have just such as it was when given us at birth, and to
> be well and nobly endowed with this will be complete and true natural
> endowment.

On this argument, moral insight is assumed to be innate and not
developed by our own efforts; consequently, our view of the goals
of life, and so ultimately the kind of people that we are, will
be determined innately. So if a person commits evil acts, it is
simply because they were not endowed by nature with the correct
moral insight, and so their wrong-doing is involuntary. Aristotle's
rejection of this proposal is brisk. He takes it as an argument to
show that wrong action, rather than right action, is determined
by nature and so involuntary (1114b3–4). But as he goes on to
point out, the proposal implies that right action will be equally
involuntary (b12–3), and this, apparently, is not something that
his opponent is prepared to accept.

This is the only point in the *Nicomachean Ethics* where Aristotle
explicitly rejects innatism as an explanation of the development
of moral insight. Nevertheless, whenever he talks about moral

---

[25] I would like to thank David Coleman for pointing out to me the significance of
this passage.

learning he shows no signs of departing from empiricism. The explanation for this lies in the connection Aristotle makes between *phronēsis* and the perception of particulars. We have already mentioned the role that *phronēsis* plays in determining what counts as an instance of a virtue in any particular case.[26] In the course of making this point, Aristotle even talks of *phronēsis* as a kind of perception:

But up to what point and to what extent a man must deviate before he becomes blameworthy it is not easy to determine by reasoning (*logos*), any more than anything else that is perceived by the senses; such things depend on particular facts and the decision rests with perception. (II 9, 1109b20–3)[27]

But unlike most other kinds of perception, *phronēsis* is a faculty that is developed only with experience and use. In VI 8 he says that it 'is concerned not only with universals but with particulars, which become familiar from experience, for it is length of time that gives experience' (1142a14–16).

As this last quotation shows, however, *phronēsis* is not only connected with particulars, but involves a more general conception of the good life as well; it supplies the universal premise in practical deliberation.[28] Here too, its development is accounted for empirically. Moral universals derive from particulars and, 'and of these therefore we must have perception . . .' (VI 11, 1143b4–5). A little later on in the same chapter he advises us to 'attend to the undemonstrated sayings and opinions of experienced and older people or people of practical wisdom not less than to demonstrations; for because experience has given them an eye they see aright'.

---

[26] See above pp. 101–2. This is a point foreshadowed in *N.E.* II 6, 1107a1–2; in VI 1, 1138b20 the insight which detects the mean is called 'right reason' and this is then identified with *phronēsis* in VI 13, 1144b21–8.

[27] See also IV 5, 1126b2–4 and VI 7, 1141b15.

[28] VI 5, 1140a25–8 and VI 7, 1141b14–15. On the role of *phronēsis* see Sorabji (1980) 205ff. It seems clear that the intellect has a variety of roles to play in living virtuously. Whether all of these roles or only some should be attributed to *phronēsis* is somewhat controversial, but it is not necessary to argue the point here. What we need to establish is whether or not innateness is used to explain the acquisition of the intellectual virtues involved in practice.

So in the *Nicomachean Ethics*, Aristotle gives no place to innatism in the cognitive aspect of moral learning, although he does allow in passing for the possibility of innate character traits. Instead, all his explicit claims put the emphasis on experience. This continues to play the central role in the last chapter of the work, where the question of moral education is once again raised. Here, Aristotle treats the role of teaching with great caution and, taking a lead from *Meno* 91a6ff., he points out the fact that whereas the practitioners (the politicians) fail to teach, the professed teachers (the sophists) fail to practice virtue. In the end, he gives the greatest emphasis to experience. In particular, he criticises the practice of the sophists of getting people to learn constitutions and sets of laws by heart. Only to someone with experience will such things be of any use. This echoes Plato's own opposition to the use of hearsay in teaching in the *Meno*, the crucial difference being that whereas for Plato any opinions must be checked against our innate knowledge, for Aristotle they are checked against the fruits of experience.

# CHAPTER 4

# *Levels of learning*

In this chapter, I shall turn to the question of what level of learning Aristotle was trying to explain, and shall argue that, like Plato, he had little interest in developing an account of ordinary learning. Let me start, however, with two qualifications to this view. First, as in the previous chapter, the focus of this discussion is on cognitive learning. As Plato had done in the *Republic*, Aristotle does show an interest in the early stages of character formation, the education of the non-rational part of the soul. This was made clear in the previous chapter. What I am claiming, however, is that he shows little interest in articulating the earliest stages of cognitive development.

Second, I am only saying that Aristotle does not develop any detailed account of ordinary cognitive learning. I am not saying that he was *completely* silent on the issue or that we cannot get some clues as to how he would have tackled it. The point is that he did not make it an important problem in his epistemology. There are indeed hints scattered around some works like the *De Anima* about how our first concepts of universals are derived from particulars. Our earliest sense perceptions leave behind images, which can become memories. For the next stage we could take a leaf out of the *De Memoria*. At 450a1–15 Aristotle describes a process of contemplating the image of a triangle, but in such a way that one does not see it as having any particular size, and attending to only general characteristics. A similar process of abstraction could apply to images of e.g. man. No doubt this is all true, but my claim is that in the extant works Aristotle makes no serious attempt to articulate this in any detail.

Now many scholars would take issue with this and point to the passage we have examined in the previous chapter, *Posterior Analytics* II 19, as an account of exactly the sort of learning in which I have claimed Aristotle is not interested. After rejecting Platonic recollection Aristotle gives his own account of cognitive development which proceeds through a number of stages, starting with perception, then memory and experience. A claim frequently made is that Aristotle is here talking about the process by which we first form universal notions. The interpretation that I wish to defend is quite different. Aristotle is talking of the way in which a scientist would make observations, record and collate them, and then extract an understanding of first principles, thus reaching the terminus of scientific achievement.

The stage-by-stage account of cognitive development that Aristotle gives in *An. Po.* II 19 has been called a 'genetic' account of learning and is in fact presented in three versions, each more detailed than its predecessor.[1] Although Aristotle suggests that each clarifies its predecessor the third is notoriously difficult to interpret. I shall start by considering the first two and once we have decided whether these are about ordinary learning, higher learning or both, we shall turn to the final version.

In the first version he tells us that while all animals have sensation only a few have the power to retain their sense images. Among the animals that can achieve this there is a further division between those that can derive reason (*logos*) out of the retention of sense images and those that cannot.

The second version is a little more detailed:

Thus from perception there comes memory, as we call it, and from memory (when it occurs often in connection with the same item), experience; for memories which are many in number form a single experience. And from experience, or from all the universal which has come to rest in the soul (the one apart from the many, i.e. whatever is one and the same in all these items) there comes a principle of skill or of understanding . . . (100a3–8)

Aristotle compares this process to a battle in which a retreating army can reform by one man making a stand, which allows the next to do the same, and so on until the original formation is regained. It is an inverted domino effect, and just as the ability of each man to make a stand depends upon his predecessor's having

---

[1] The first runs from 99b34, the second from 100a3, and the third from 100a15 to 100b3.

done the same, each stage in the cognitive development depends on the materials supplied its predecessor.

It is not surprising that a number of commentators have been tempted to read these versions of the genetic account as descriptions of ordinary concept formation. Much of the language of the first account and expressions in the second such as 'one experience that comes from many memories', 'the whole universal that has settled in the the mind', and 'the one apart from the many' seem to point to the formation of ordinary concepts. If so, we are being given an account that explains how successive images leave as their residue a general notion that enables us to group items in experience together in classes.[2] Aristotle is not, however, explaining the discovery of general scientific principles. To give an example, this is the phase of intellectual development in which Aristotle is supposed to be interested:[3]

1  *X* sees a swan
2  *X* retains the memory image of a swan
3  *X* retains the images of several swans
4  *X* forms a concept of swan

rather than:

1  *X* sees that this swan is white
2  *X* remembers that this swan is white
3  *X* remembers that this swan and that swan are white
4  *X* understands that all swans are white

If the account that *An. Po.* II 19 gives is meant to cover the first of these sequences it begins to look very similar to the account of learning given by the Stoics:

When a man is born, the Stoics say, he has the commanding part of his soul like a piece of paper ready for writing upon. On this he inscribes each one of his conceptions. The first method of inscription is through the senses. For by perceiving something, e.g. white, they have a memory of it when it has departed. And when many memories of a similar kind have occurred we then say we have experience. For the plurality of similar impressions is experience. Some conceptions arise naturally in the aforesaid ways and undesignedly, others through our

[2] For this view see le Blond (1970) 134 and (1979) 64–5 with n. 8 and 73–4.
[3] The examples are from Barnes (1993) 271.

own instruction and attention. The latter are called 'conceptions' only, the former are called 'prolepses' as well. Reason, for which we are called rational, is said to be completed from our prolepses during our first seven years.[4]

This passage unambiguously confines itself to the earliest phases of learning. Should we read Aristotle in the same way?

An obvious reason against doing so is the immediate context of *An. Po.* II 19. The whole point of the chapter is to explain how we get knowledge of first principles, a type of knowledge that Aristotle describes as being more precise even than demonstration (99b27). How, therefore, could Aristotle, having formulated the purpose of the chapter with such clarity, then proceed to give an account that falls so far short of fulfilling that purpose? On the strength of this consideration alone, one might simply reject the 'Stoicised' interpretation of *An. Po.* II 19. But some commentators have found the temptation to adopt it so strong that while conceding that Aristotle's overall purpose is to explain scientific discovery, they nevertheless find him giving a Stoicised account to fulfil this purpose. The net result of such interpretations will be the accusation that Aristotle is confused between two sequences. Whereas this chapter ought to be yielding an account about the development of scientific concepts, corresponding to definitions of essences, we are only given a story about ordinary concept formation. Aristotle may have set out to explain the discovery of principles, but if he is content to do this with an account of vulgar concept formation, as the language of the chapter suggests, he must have been confused as between the vulgar concept and the scientific.[5]

The claim that Aristotle could have been confused in this way

---

[4] Aëtius, *Plac.* IV 11 = *Stoicorum Veterum Fragmenta (SVF)* II 83, lines 13–23, trans. Long and Sedley (1987) I 238 modified.

[5] It is important to realise what the problem is not. Some scholars have been worried that Aristotle seems to waver between giving us an account of how we form *concepts*, and one about how we discover general principles. The *principles* which ought to be under discussion are surely propositional in form, yet much of the language in the chapter seems to suggest concept formation. Ross (1949) 675 thinks that it would be possible to argue that concept formation and the discovery of first principles are inseparably intertwined, but Aristotle would have needed to provide such an argument explicitly, and so Ross concludes that he means to claim that these distinct processes are alike only in being inductive. Both Hamlyn and Barnes also argue that the use of a concept carries with it the ability to understand propositions about that concept, but do not think that Aristotle needed to be explicit on this point (Hamlyn (1976) 178; Barnes (1993) 271). So Barnes, for instance, defuses the puzzle on the grounds that 'the conceptual sequence terminates in something that is either a propositional

is, for all this, highly implausible. If anyone made and used the distinction between the vulgar and the scientific, it was Aristotle. For what else is the distinction between the more knowable to us and the more knowable in nature? Indeed *An. Po.* II 19 itself recalls the distinction; the stages that mark the route towards *nous* are said to be 'less knowing' than the end result (100a10–11). That he should invoke this terminology shows how well aware he is that the point of the initial dilemma is precisely to challenge us to give an explanation of how we progress from the more knowable to us to the more knowable in nature. So if an interpretation of this chapter results in a charge of such an un-Aristotelian equivocation that is a good reason for rejecting it.

There is also a more specific reason for rejecting the interpretation. The word Aristotle uses to refer to the third stage in the genetic account, the stage where many memories are collected together, is 'experience' (*empeiria*). Now in the Stoic account of concept formation, to which *An. Po.* II 19 is in effect being assimilated, the same word is used, and because this stage is explicitly said to come before the age of seven, the age of reason, we can infer that, for the Stoics, experience is a pre-rational phase in a child's cognitive history. But to give this word the same sense in Aristotle would be extremely strange. The word *empeiria* is not common in his works, but on the other occasions where he does use it it has a clearly post-rational sense, referring to the collected observations of an aspiring scientist. One occurrence of the word comes from a passage very closely parallel to *An. Po.* II 19, *Met.* I 1, where Aristotle says that sensation is common to all animals, memory only to some; a small number have experience, and men alone use reasoning and skill. Memory derives from sensation, and experience in its turn derives from memory; many memories of the same thing produce one experience, and then from experience come understanding and skill. Experience differs from understanding or skill in that it does not grasp the explanation. It grasps the 'that', not the 'because' (981a28–9) and so cannot claim to be wisdom (*sophia*).

principle or at least immediately yields one', and so Aristotle might have regarded the difference between the two sequences as a 'trifling pedantry'. Kahn (1981) 395–7 has also argued that the alleged gap between concept and proposition is a pseudo-problem, but goes on to say that this is not the end of our difficulties, for in place of the old gap appears a new one, between the vulgar concept and the scientific.

At 981a7–9 Aristotle gives us an example of what counts as experience:

For to have a judgement that when Callias was ill of this disease this did him good, and similarly in the case of Socrates and in many individual cases, is a matter of experience.

Clearly he is thinking of a kind of doctor who, although short on universal explanations, has a good record of individual cases. This is a very different sense of experience from the Stoic account.

We find a similar point, this time using an astronomical example, in a passage of the *Prior Analytics*. In I 30, talking about the principles of a science, he says that it is the task of experience (*empeiria*) to provide the principles of each science (46a18); he then says that once the appearances (*phainomena*) have been adequately grasped the demonstrations (which depend upon the principles) are discovered. He illustrates this with the case of astronomy, but says that it applies to every kind of science and technical expertise. It seems most implausible to suggest that by experience Aristotle here means anything else but the observations of empirical observers. He could hardly be celebrating the achievements of the under-sevens. And in the passages from his treatise, *On the Heavens*, where he mentions the appearances from which astronomy starts, he is undoubtedly talking about the collected data of a seasoned observer.[6]

For these reasons we should read *An. Po.* II 19 not as an account of ordinary learning, but of the way in which a scientist proceeds by making individual observations, recording ('memory') and collating them ('experience') towards the discovery of the essences of objects that fall within their discipline. But if this is so, what are we to make of the phrases that have tempted commentators to read the chapter as an account of ordinary learning? In the first version of the genetic account, for instance, Aristotle talks of the final stage as the achievement of 'reason' (*logos*) out of perception and memory. Some interpreters immediately assume that the word *logos* must be taken in a Stoic sense which would indeed make this passage into an account of ordinary learning. But this version of the genetic account is extremely vague and there is nothing forcing us to make this interpretation of it. Instead

[6] II 13, 293a23ff. and III 7, 306a5ff.

of taking *logos* as 'reason' or 'rationality', we could translate it as 'account' or 'rationale' (referring to the systematising power of creatures with experience) or even 'definition', which is to be the culmination of the process.

In the second version, what has tempted many to think that Aristotle, like the Stoics, is talking about the formation of our ordinary general concepts is the sentence 'from experience, or from *all the universal which has come to rest in the soul (the one apart from the many, i.e. whatever is one and the same in all these items)* there comes a principle of skill or of understanding.' Nevertheless, the words in italics could be explained by appealing to *An. Pr.* I 30 which, as we have seen, is the only other place in the *Analytics* where experience (*empeiria*) is mentioned. In talking of experience as the prerequisite for the discovery of principles and demonstrations, Aristotle adds a condition for its functioning in this way:

For if none of the true attributes of things had been omitted in the survey, we should be able to discover the proof and demonstrate everything that admitted of proof, and to make that clear, whose nature does not admit of proof. (46a24–7)

The same point could be being made in *An. Po.* II 19. It is the job of scientific experience to 'grasp the whole', i.e. to compile a complete catalogue of the things that are said universally of, for instance, man; but this leaves us with the task of understanding why these things are said universally of man, which is a further stage in the process, the attainment of *nous*.[7]

I said above that Aristotle gives three versions of the genetic account, and it should now be clear that there is no reason to read an account of ordinary learning into the first two. But this still leaves a question-mark hanging over the third:

Let us say again what we have just said but not said clearly. When one of the undifferentiated items makes a stand there is a primitive

[7] In this interpretation I have been taking the conjunction 'or' (ἤ) of 100a6 epexegetically so that the the the words 'from all the universal . . .' (100a6–8) reiterate 'from experience' (100a6). An alternative reading which would also make these lines an account of higher learning has been suggested by McKirahan (1992) 243. On his view the 'or' is progressive: 'the principle of science comes from experience, *or rather* from the universal in the soul'; for McKirahan, 'the universal at rest in the soul is a stage intermediate between experience and scientific knowledge'. It is a stage in which one grasps the universals and has gone beyond mere experience of particulars; but one has not yet understood these universals as principles, i.e. how they explain other propositions in the science.

universal in the soul; for although you perceive particulars, perception is of universals – e.g. of man, not of Callias the man. Next a stand is made among these items, until something partless and universal makes a stand. E.g. such-and-such an animal makes a stand, until animal does; and with animal a stand is made in the same way.[8]

The exact meaning of these lines is obscure but, as with the two previous versions of the genetic account, there is nothing which compels us to read it as an account of ordinary learning. The first problem to confront us is the meaning of the phrase 'one of the undifferentiated things'. Some of the commentators who are looking out for an account of ordinary concept formation at this point take this phrase as referring to a raw sensation that has not yet been differentiated as belonging to a certain kind.[9] But it seems very unlikely that one sensation can on its own be responsible for concept formation. There must be repeated perceptions.[10] To avoid this difficulty we should take 'undifferentiated' to refer not to a particular that is the same in species as other particulars, but to the *infima species*. This sense of the word occurs elsewhere in the *Posterior Analytics*[11] and it serves to distinguish the *infima species*, e.g. man, from the *genus*, e.g. animal, a distinction made explicitly in our passage at 100b2–3 where Aristotle talks of a progression from 'such and such an animal makes a stand until animal does'.

If this is the correct sense of 'undifferentiated' in *An. Po.* II 19 the point is that in the process of cognitive development we reach the *genus* only after we have already reached the *infima species*. Admittedly, this could be interpreted as an account of ordinary learning: when we first form our concepts we start with the more

---

[8] 100a14–b3: ὃ δ' ἐλέχθη μὲν πάλαι, οὐ σαφῶς δὲ ἐλέχθη, πάλιν εἴπωμεν. στάντος γὰρ τῶν ἀδιαφόρων ἑνός, πρῶτον μὲν ἐν τῇ ψυχῇ καθόλου (καὶ γὰρ αἰσθάνεται μὲν τὸ καθ' ἕκαστον, ἡ δ' αἴσθησις τοῦ καθόλου ἐστίν, οἷον ἀνθρώπου, ἀλλ' οὐ Καλλίου ἀνθρώπου)· πάλιν ἐν τούτοις ἵσταται ἕως ἂν τὰ ἀμερῆ στῇ καὶ τὰ καθόλου, οἷον τοιονδὶ ζῷον, καὶ ἐν τούτῳ ὡσαύτως.

[9] Hamlyn (1976) 179; see Tredennick (1960) 259, note d.

[10] 100a4–5. This has been pointed out by Lesher (1973) 61, n. 42.

[11] The term 'undifferentiated' (ἀδιάφορος) can mean either individuals that are the same in species or the species themselves. For the first sense see *An. Po.* II 13, 97b7–8. Later on in the same chapter, however, at 97b31, the word is used to mean *infima species*. On this see Barnes (1993) 249. (In 97b31 Aristotle talks of ἀδιάφορα referring back to καθ' ἕκαστον in b28 which is said to be easier to define than the καθόλου. The distinction between καθ' ἕκαστον and καθόλου can, for Aristotle, be taken in two ways, either as the distinction between individual and species or between two types of form, specific and general. In this context individuals cannot be meant because it is impossible to define them. So if the καθ' ἕκαστον of b28 refer to the *infima species* the ἀδιάφορα of 97b31 will follow suit.)

specific. But a different interpretation, one that makes these lines an account of higher learning, is also possible. Aristotle is clarifying the final phases of scientific discovery and is focusing on someone who has now collected a large range of observations and who is advancing to the point of formulating definitions. Aristotle's claim is that in this final process of development the definitions of the more specific universals are discovered before the more general.

What is attractive about this interpretation is that it echoes a line of thought that has appeared in the *Posterior Analytics* at II 13, 97b7–15:

We should look at what are similar and undifferentiated, and seek, first, what they all have that is the same; next, we should do this again for other things which are of the same genus as the first set and of the same species as one another but of a different species from those. And when we have grasped what all these have that is the same, and similarly for the others, then we must again inquire if what we have grasped have anything that is the same – until we come to a single account: for this will be the definition of the object. And if we come not to one but to two or more accounts, it is clear that what we are seeking is not a single thing but several.

Aristotle has completed his discussion of definition by division and now sets out the following method of definition: we should begin by taking a number of individuals that are similar in species (i.e. *infima species*) and then we ask what it is that they have in common; we then proceed to another group of individuals that are similar but in a different (*infima*) species and do the same. This is repeated for as many species as there are, and, at the end of it, we go back and ask what all these species have in common, the answer to which will be a definition of the genus. If there is nothing in common between the species then we shall know that the term we were seeking to define is homonymous. Aristotle goes on to give an example of this procedure, using pride (*megalopsuchia*) as the definiendum (97b15–25). As it turns out, the two species – inability to endure insult, and indifference to fortune – have nothing in common, so the definiendum is ambiguous. A little later on, he advises us to start from the *infima species* rather than the *genus*, as homonymies are more easily detected in this way (97b28–31).

This section of II 13 provides a very good parallel to the third version of the genetic account, where we also move from the *infima species* to the *genus*. In neither chapter is Aristotle talking about the very first moment when the notion of 'man' or 'animal' came into our heads, but about how a scientist eventually articulates these ordinary concepts into definitions.[12] That II 19 should be referring back to II 13 is an attractive hypothesis anyway. If the avowed aim of II 19 is to explain how we discover essences it ought to pick up some of the earlier chapters that are concerned with that very subject, and II 13, which discusses the search after definitions, is just such a passage.[13]

The overall aim of *An. Po.* II 19, like its companion piece, *Met.* I 1, is to explain how we attain knowledge of the first principles of a science. Its context should make it clear that it is an account of higher learning, whatever temptations individual expressions in the chapter may give us to suppose otherwise. Aristotle provides three versions of the genetic account and everything he says in the first two is best interpreted as an account of how a scientist starts by making, recording and then collating observations, prior to formulating definitions. The third version clarifies the final stages of the discovery in which first principles, i.e. definitions, are finally articulated, and it does so by drawing upon an earlier chapter of the book according to which one must first define the specific universals and then work up to more general, thereby reaching the terminus of scientific discovery.

Once it is conceded that neither *An. Po.* II 19 nor *Met.* I 1 are accounts of ordinary learning, anyone looking for Aristotle's views on the subject soon runs out of places to look. For, apart from some tantalising hints in the psychological treatises, Aristotle has little to say about the matter, and it seems that, like Plato,

---

[12] Notice how in the procedure recommended in *An. Po.* II 13, we already know in a sense what we are looking for; we have already made the grouping according to species and genus; what we are going on to do is to pick out the essential common property or, as Barnes (1993) 248 puts it, to justify the classification that we have already made. On this see below, pp. 120–29.

[13] A connection between *An. Po.* II 13, 97b7ff. and II 19, 100a14ff. has been noticed by Waitz (1844–6) 431 and Tricot (1962) 245. Brunschwig (1981) 84–6, however, claims that we should be wary of making a connection between II 13 and 19, because the first is a passage about method (written by Aristotle the dialectician), the second about genetic psychology (written by Aristotle the naturalist). This is a useful *caveat*, but it should not be taken so far that one cannot see any likeness at all between the two passages. If the method to follow is to proceed from the less to the more general, then an account of how the universal is discovered will follow the same pattern, as Brunschwig seems to admit ('... la méthode prescrite par le dialecticien imite la trajectoire décrite par le naturaliste' 86).

he was interested primarily in higher learning. The interest in ordinary learning had to wait until the Hellenistic age. Why this should have been we shall discuss at the end of section III.

# CHAPTER 5

# Discovery and continuity in science

If Aristotle set out to explain more or less the same phase of intellectual development as Plato, the explanation that he gave was very different. In chapter 3 we remarked on one such difference in Aristotle's theory, namely his total rejection of innateness. In this chapter and the next we shall focus on his strikingly un-Platonic optimism about the continuity between the more knowable to us and the more knowable in nature. We shall do this separately for science and ethics, but it will be clear by the end of the next chapter that there are remarkable similarities between his treatment of the two domains.

In the scientific case, the distinction between the more knowable to us and the more knowable in nature is one between a view of the world as presented to us in sense perception and the perspective in which natural phenomena are set in their true explanatory ordering. That the more knowable to us is associated with perception is clear from *Physics* I 1, 184a16–25, *Topics* VI 4, 141b10, and *An. Po.* I 2, 72a1–5 where Aristotle talks of a continuum beginning with the prior for us and ending with the prior in nature, with perception at one end and, at the other, the grasp of first principles. So the distinction between the more knowable to us and the more knowable in nature overlaps with the other distinctions we have seen at work in the last two chapters: the distinction between the cognitive states of perception (or experience) and scientific understanding (or *nous*), and distinction between the corresponding objects of those states – between the fact and the explanation (or the essence).[1]

To show how Aristotle considers the more knowable to us as good preparation for progressing to the more knowable in nature,

[1] For the grasp of the fact as better known to us see *N.E.* I 4, 1095b2–7. See also *An. Po.* I 13, esp. 78a27–8. For a concise discussion of this distinction see Mansion (1979).

I shall discuss four texts, starting again with *Posterior Analytics* II 19 and its companion piece, *Metaphysics* I 1, then going on to *Physics* I 1 and *Posterior Analytics* II 8. I discuss them in this order because the continuity between the more knowable to us and the more knowable in nature becomes more marked as we go along.[2]

## [1] POSTERIOR ANALYTICS II 19 AND METAPHYSICS *i* 1

In charting the progress from perception *via* memory and experience to wisdom and the grasp of first principles, both these chapters are thereby charting the movement from the knowable to us to the knowable in nature. More specifically, as we have seen, Aristotle proposes in *Posterior Analytics* II 19 that perception as a capacity (*dunamis*) provides a way out of the dilemma with which he opens: we cannot acquire first principles without any pre-existing knowledge nor, on the other hand, can such knowledge already be in us without our awareness (99b26–30). He spends most of the rest of the chapter claiming that perception, having started the process off, in turn gives rise to the next stages that eventually culminate in *nous*. But there seems to be an obvious objection here. If perception is only a capacity it is not yet knowledge; *nous* may come into being from a pre-existent *capacity*, but it still needs to be shown that it comes into being from pre-existing *knowledge*. However bizarre Aristotle may have found Platonic recollection, at least that theory could could not be accused of violating the principle that all learning derives from pre-existing knowledge. As if aware of this, Aristotle does let slip an interesting remark at 99b37–9: the lowest kind of animals have no knowledge apart from perception.[3] What catches the eye here is the claim that perception, even at the lowest level, can count as a kind of knowledge, and if perception, even more memory and experience. Perception is therefore a kind of pre-existent knowledge.

But this is still only a start. Knowledge has to be derived from pre-existing knowledge, but not any pre-existing knowledge; there must surely be some requirement that this knowledge is relevant

---

[2] For another attempt to understand Aristotle's conception of discovery by studying these texts synoptically, see Bolton (1976), (1987) and (1991). I am thoroughly sympathetic to his approach, even though we differ on some of the details about how the interconnections are to be made.

[3] οὐκ ἔστι τούτοις γνῶσις ἔξω τοῦ αἰσθάνεσθαι.

to what it pre-exists. In *An. Po.* II 19, however, Aristotle does not really explain in what way each stage is relevant to its successor and ultimately to knowledge of first principles, *nous*. He seems keener to point out the differences between the stages than to explain what it is about each that paves the way for the next.[4] The same seems to be true of the parallel account in *Met.* I 1. Here he lays special emphasis on demonstrating that the stage that immediately precedes wisdom, experience, is distinct from wisdom. He talks of this distinction as the difference between understanding the 'that' and the 'why', or a distinction between the activity of gathering the factual observations and explaining them scientifically. But we need to say more about these two stages other than that they differ in this respect; we need an account of the relation between the starting points and the results of the discovery, the more knowable to us and the more knowable in nature, and of how the one can lead us to the other.

## [2] PHYSICS I 1

Another place to look for such an account is *Physics* I 1, where Aristotle characterises and illustrates the journey from the more knowable to us to the more knowable in nature.[5] In the first paragraph he states that where any discipline has first principles it is only by grasping these that one can attain genuine understanding (184a10–14). He then introduces the distinction between the more knowable to us and the more knowable in nature by saying that the path of discovery will be from one to the other:

Plainly, therefore, in the science of nature too our first task will be to try to determine what relates to its principles. The natural way of doing this is to start from the things which are more knowable and clear to us and to proceed towards those which are more clear and knowable by nature; for the same things are not knowable to us and knowable without qualification. So we must follow this method and advance from what is

---

[4] Some interpreters have thought that Aristotle is giving just such an explanation in the parenthesis of *An. Po.* II 19, 100a16–b1: 'for although you perceive particulars, perception is of universals – e.g. of man, not of Callias the man'. The suggestion of these commentators is that even in perception we grasp the essence dimly. For a discussion of these lines and of this interpretation, see the appendix to this section, pp. 152–6.

[5] In my discussion of *Phys.* I 1, I am indebted to some of the results of Wieland (1970) 84ff. and (1975) 128–32.

more obscure by nature, but clearer to us, to what is more clear and more knowable by nature. (184a14–21)

So far this all fits in well with what we already know from the *Posterior Analytics* about the distinction between the more knowable to us and the more knowable in nature, but it does not tell us any more. In the last paragraph of the chapter, however, Aristotle goes on to characterise the nature of the two perspectives in more detail. His first characterisation of things clearer or more knowable to us is that they are undiscriminated or blurred;[6] in proceeding towards things more knowable in nature one becomes familiar with their elements by making distinctions. In the next sentence he says something that in many translations looks extremely perplexing. Here it is as rendered in the Revised Oxford Translation:[7]

> Thus we must advance from universals to particulars; for it is a whole that is more knowable to sense perception, and the universal is a kind of whole, comprehending many things within it, like parts.

What is troubling in this sentence is that Aristotle uses two expressions, *katholou* and *kath' hekaston*, that normally invoke a contrast between general and specific, a contrast that can sometimes be taken as between genus and species, sometimes between species and individual. If we assume that either of these contrasts is at work in these lines our interpretation both of this chapter and others would disintegrate into chaos. Aristotle would be saying here that the general is what is more knowable by perception which would lead to obvious contradictions with other texts. He would also be saying that we proceed from the general to the particular, but this jars with texts such as *An. Po.* II 13 and 19.[8]

Whatever contrast is implied in these words it cannot be between general and particular or between genus and species. Fortunately, Aristotle does give some clarification by saying that what he is talking about is 'a kind of whole, comprehending many things within it, like parts'. In moving from the more knowable to us we move away from a kind of cognition in which a number of elements have been compounded and await differentiation. This

---

[6] 184a22 (συγκεχυμένα).

[7] 184a23–6: διὸ ἐκ τῶν καθόλου ἐπὶ τὰ καθ᾽ ἕκαστα δεῖ προϊέναι· τὸ γὰρ ὅλον κατὰ τὴν αἴσθησιν γνωριμώτερον, τὸ δὲ καθόλου ὅλον τί ἐστι· πολλὰ γὰρ περιλαμβάνει ὡς μέρη τὸ καθόλου.

[8] II 13, 97b7ff. and II 19, 100a15ff. See pp. 115–6 above. Cf. also *An. Po.* I 18 *passim*.

has been well explained by Wieland⁹ who argues that if this is
what is meant by the first side of the contrast (the *katholou*), then
the other (the *kath' hekaston*) is merely the opposite. So the route
from the more knowable to us to the more knowable in nature
involves separating a jumbled-up whole into its constituents. This
would also explain why Aristotle has just called the perspective of
the more knowable to us 'undiscriminated' or 'blurred' (184a21).
In all this, Aristotle is talking about the way we move from a
pre-technical, undiscriminated concept towards a more articulated
state of understanding.

But this raises a crucial question. When Aristotle describes the
more familiar to us, the pre-scientific concept as 'blurred' how
pejorative is he meaning to be? Is he dismissing such concepts
as 'confused', as some translations imply? Interestingly enough,
the word that I have translated as 'undiscriminated' or 'blurred'¹⁰
had been used in just this way by Plato in a passage that we
have already discussed, *Republic* VII 524c4, where he disparages
the information provided by the senses.¹¹ Holding up three fingers
to his interlocutor, Socrates says that the senses tell us that the
same finger is both large and small, and that if this was all we had
to go by we might end up thinking large and small were the same
thing. This would be a disastrous confusion, and it is up to the soul
independently of the senses to decide that small and large are two
distinct things. In this context we have an obvious confusion on our
hands, a confusion, in fact, of opposites.

Does Aristotle mean to dismiss the pre-technical perspective as
'confused'? The best way of answering this question is to look at
the two examples he gives of blurred or 'confused' concepts in
this chapter. One of his examples is of children who go round
at first calling all men father, and all women mother; later they
distinguish the two (184b12–4). The whole here is a mixture of
the forms man and father (these are the parts); the two are
in fact related as species and sub-species, whereas the children
treat 'father' as if it were co-extensive with 'man'. What they
will do is to come to distinguish the two and so learn about

---

⁹ (1970) 91, n. 7. For a useful discussion of 184a23–6 along similar lines see Owens (1971);
see also Mansion (1979) 165–6.
¹⁰ συγκεχυμένα, 184a22.
¹¹ See p. 83 above.

both of them. Now, because the original whole does not properly reflect the way the real world is organised, one might say that the child's concept is 'confused', but even here their mistake is less of a blunder than the confusion that Plato attributes to the senses in the *Republic*. There the two things that are mixed up are opposites, whereas in Aristotle's example they are at least related more closely and, as a result, he has more confidence that the child's concept of 'father' can in time develop into the right one.[12]

In the other of the two examples, Aristotle is being less pejorative again. The example focuses upon the difference between a word and its definition (184a26ff.). The word that awaits definition signifies something undifferentiated; the analysis breaks this whole into the elements which would in this case be the elements of the definition (the *genus* and *differentiae*). Now, Aristotle is not saying here that the parts that make up this whole are wrongly grouped together (as in the child example). The word 'circle' in our ordinary use is a legitimate whole; in using the word and in differentiating the world according to it we are roughly right in mapping out reality. So, in this example, Aristotle's talk of a blurred concept is less pejorative than in the second example, and much less so than in the Platonic context. All he means here is that the elements of the whole are not yet broken down.[13]

What both these examples show is that the route from the more knowable to us to the more knowable in nature is a continuous one, in which we never leave the realm of knowledge (*gnōsis*), and there

---

[12] In case this passage is used as evidence of a strong interest in early learning on Aristotle's part, remember that he treats the example not as the explanandum but as the explanans. It is a phenomenon with which we are already supposed to be familiar and which can therefore be used to explain inquiry into first principles, i.e. higher learning.

The phenomenon that Aristotle cites is still attracting interest. It has recently been treated as a semantic error on the part of children between the ages of about 1.5 to 2. Apart from the examples Aristotle cites there are many others, e.g. children calling horses, lions and cats 'dog', or cars, coaches and trucks all 'truck'. Their fault is to over-extend the word beyond its more limited meaning. This does not mean, however, that they are conceptually confused. Some recent experiments show that children who over-extend one of these words in speech production nevertheless have no difficulty grasping them correctly in comprehension. See, for example, Fremgen and Fay (1980).

[13] For a more detailed but broadly similar account of the two examples see Owens (1971) 468–72.

is no abrupt cut-off between knowledge and ignorance, such that we graduate to a new level just at the end.[14] The epistemological journey consists in the articulation of something already grasped. We start with what is compounded and proceed by disentangling it and analysing it into first principles.[15] So in this chapter Aristotle is not saying that the path of discovery is from universal to particular, or from genus to species, but from a concept which embraces a number of elements in an unarticulated way to a more articulated level of understanding – for instance, from the hazy notion of circle to its definition.

Another crucial feature of the blurred or compound concepts is that they are better known in perception (184a24–5). But at first sight this seems to jar with a comment about the more knowable distinction in *An. Po.* I 2, 72a1–5 where, having said that the more knowable to us is nearer to perception, he adds that it is nearest to the particulars. This, of course, is quite in keeping with his general views on the tight association of perception and particulars. Thus, in the *Analytics* passage, the journey from the more knowable to us to the more knowable in nature is from particulars to the general. We have just rejected a reading of *Phys.* I 1 according to which the very opposite was happening, but even on our present interpretation, as the circle example suggests, we move from one sort of general concept to another, and particulars do not seem to have come into the picture.

Nevertheless, these two passages do fit together. The point in *An. Po.* I 2 is that we do not perceive universal explanations and *Phys.* I 1 can be read as agreeing with this because it implies that what is more knowable in nature (i.e. the elements and principles, and hence the explanation) is further from perception. As far as the perception of particulars is concerned, we should not assume that because particulars are what we perceive, we perceive them merely as particulars, i.e., we perceive them in all their particularity. *An. Po.* I 2 need only be saying that whereas the objects of our 'more knowable' cognitive states are universal explanatory essences, the objects of our perception are particulars.

---

[14] This is why it is appropriate for Aristotle to use the expression, 'the more *knowable* to us'; even at the start of an inquiry, our cognitive state can be described in terms of knowledge (γνῶσις).

[15] See Wieland (1975) 131.

But this does not mean that when I perceive Socrates and when I perceive Callias I see them as two entirely different things. If this were so, we would need tremendous powers of discrimination to see every single individual as purely that individual, if we did not actually go mad in the process. *An. Po.* I 2 should not be interpreted as saying how we represent the particulars that are the objects of our perception.

*Phys.* I 1, on the other hand, should be read in just this way. We perceive particulars as members of certain roughly understood groups. We see the world in bundles – the child's mistaken concept of father-man goes hand in hand with the perception of certain individuals as father-men. Likewise our understanding of the word 'circle' is part and parcel of our perceiving certain objects as circles. I suggested above that we should align the more knowable to us with knowledge of the 'that', as opposed to the 'because' or essence. I would now extend this by associating knowledge of the 'that' with the hazy concepts of *Phys.* I 1. Thus the use of a hazy concept is involved in the judgements, 'this is a circle' (perception) and 'there are circles' (experience), whereas the articulated understanding of the parts that make up the whole is involved in, or constitutes our knowledge of the essence of the circle, and so all explanations concerned with circles.

## [3] POSTERIOR ANALYTICS II 8

Our overall question was how the more knowable to us provides the relevant pre-existent knowledge for the acquisition of first principles, i.e. the movement towards the more knowable in nature. Neither *An. Po.* II 19 nor *Met.* I 1 yielded much of an answer, but *Phys.* I 1 has given us something more promising. Perception is enriched by a concept that is already an unrefined version of the scientific concept. The concepts are in a sense the same; the vulgar concept maps the world out into roughly the same groups as the scientific. Given this useful starting-point, we can go on to justify our grouping by analysing the structure of these concepts and articulating what we already know.

But perhaps this is not enough. How do we go about this articulation? If the whole includes a number of parts to be differentiated, how do we know which are the right parts to take hold of? To answer these questions we need to turn back to *An. Po.* II, to a passage in chapter 8:

Just as we seek the reason why when we grasp the fact (sometimes indeed these two things become plain at the same time – but it is not possible to get to know the reason why *before* the fact) in the same way we plainly cannot grasp what it is to be something without grasping that it exists; for we cannot know what something is when we do not know whether it exists. But as to whether it exists, sometimes we grasp this incidentally, and sometimes by grasping something of the object itself – e.g. of thunder that it is a sort of noise in the clouds; and of an eclipse that it is a sort of privation of light; and of man that it is a sort of animal; of soul that it is something which moves itself.

When we know incidentally that something exists, necessarily we have no grasp on what it is; for we do not even know that it exists, and to seek what something is without grasping that it exists is to seek nothing. But when we grasp something of the object, the business is easier. Hence in so far as we grasp that it exists, to that extent we also have some grasp on what it is. (93a16–29)

The first few lines of this passage, 93a16–20, pick up a theme that has already been established in *An. Po.* II. There are four things to look for: that something is, why it is, if it is, what it is (89b24–5). Aristotle explicitly identifies knowing the second and fourth of these, the cause and the essence, in *An. Po.* II 2.[16] We can only understand why an object has a certain attribute when we have grasped the object's essence, as, according to Aristotle's theory of demonstration, we have to be able to show that the attribute in question belongs to the object by virtue of its essence. Although

---

[16] 90a14–5 and 31–4.

[17] When Aristotle first mentions this distinction at II 1, 89b23–4, it looks as if the words 'if' (εἰ) and 'that' (ὅτι) are carrying the burden of the distinction. In fact the difference between the two is between knowing that a thing exists (ἔστιν ἁπλῶς), and knowing that it has a certain property (ἔστιν ἐπὶ μέρους), e.g. that the moon exists, and that it is eclipsed (II 2, 89b38–90a5). This should not be taken as a difference between a substance existing and its having certain properties, because both night (90a5) and eclipse (93b3) feature as examples of things that exist, and neither of them are substances. On this see Mansion (1976) 165–6.

93a37–b3 shows that in II 8, at least, Aristotle is not making anything of the distinction between knowing if something exists and knowing if it has a certain property. From the same syllogism, he concludes that we know that the moon is eclipsed but not why, and that we know that there is an eclipse but not what an eclipse is. If Aristotle is treating the difference between knowing whether something exists and knowing whether it has a certain property superficially in this chapter, then the problem set up in 93a18ff. could be applied either to an inquiry that sets out from the knowledge that there is an eclipse (or, perhaps, that there are such things as eclipses), or from the knowledge that the moon is eclipsed.

he does not make an explicit identification between the first and the third, he treats them in tandem and in II 8 itself makes the distinction between them appear superficial.[17]

When it comes to discovering the essence (for example, of man) we must already know that men exist and then we can go on to ask what their essence is. Thus the pre-existent knowledge that makes our learning of the definition and so of the proper explanation possible is the knowledge of the fact. This is the same point made in the account of discovery in *An. Po.* II 19 and *Met.* I 1. Knowledge of first principles or essences derives from the purely factual knowledge involved in perception and experience. But then Aristotle raises a problem about inquiring into the essence on the basis of the fact alone. How can we know that something is if we do not know what it is? If we do not know what it is at all, we cannot know that it is – except incidentally. We are seeking nothing.

The whiff of the *Meno* is in the air.[18] Aristotle is toying with the objection that what he thought would be the starting-point of an inquiry into the essence cannot after all act as pre-existing knowledge because it does not constitute a grasp of the object. Without knowing the essence of the object in question we do not in fact know that it is, so we do not know what we are inquiring into. Aristotle's solution here is to say that we must already have a partial understanding of what the object is in order to know that it is non-incidentally. The point is repeated in II 10, 93b32–5.[19]

So we can grasp the fact in two ways, 'properly' and 'incidentally'. In the first case, knowing that a thing is involves grasping 'something of the thing itself' (93a22). Aristotle is not precise about what he means by this expression, though he does go on to give a series of examples some, but not all, of which suggest knowing already the genus to which the object belongs. One interpretation of these lines is that the part of the essence is some essential feature of the object. Unless we represent an object to ourselves under a description that would feature in the essence, we have no real grasp of the object, only an incidental one. Thus the proper definition of thunder is 'a noise in the clouds due to quenching of fire'; the partial definition is 'a certain type of

---

[18] The connection between *An. Po.* II 8 and Meno's paradox has been brought out by Bolton (1976) 516.

[19] Compare the problem implicit in the *Meno* about using examples as starting-points in the search for definitions.

noise in the clouds'; and an example of an incidental grasp of
the fact, which omits any reference to the essence, might be
'thunder is the thing that frightens Callias'. This interpretation
seems right, except that it needs a qualification. Sometimes the
non-accidental grasp of the 'that' will not be of a predicate that
features in the essence itself, but will be a 'necessary accident'
of the object. It counts as a non-accidental grasp because it
is directly explicable by the essence. This interpretation allows
for the fact that in the examples of non-accidental knowledge
Aristotle includes knowing that the soul is a self-mover (93a24)
which is not an essential feature of a soul, but a necessary
accident.[20]

This passage is of great importance as it goes some way towards
bridging a divide that has so far played an important part in
Aristotle's theory. We saw how in *Met.* I 1, for instance, there
seemed to be a clear-cut division of labour between experience[21]
which grasps the 'that', and wisdom, which grasps the 'because'.
But in the passage from *An. Po.* II 8 we are told that a proper
grasp of the 'that' is already partially a grasp of the essence (and
so of the explanation). It is because of this that the grasp of the
fact, the more knowable to us, is a reliable starting-point for the
discovery of first principles.

Does the point made in *An. Po.* II 8 go beyond that made in
*Phys.* I 1? Both passages show a way in which the starting-point
contributes towards the discovery. *Phys.* I 1 talks of a pre-scientific
concept that accounts for our roughly correct ordering of the world,
but awaits analysis into its logical elements. In *An. Po.* II 8, on the
other hand, this analysis has already started to take place, even
in the knowledge of the 'that', i.e., in having this knowledge in a
non-incidental way, we have implicitly picked out one of the parts
or elements that featured in *Phys.* I 1.

Although the two passages are making different points, they
do nevertheless complement each other very well. According to
*Phys.* I 1, what lies behind judgements that there are circles is

---

[20] *Topics* 120b21–6, *De Anima* 408a30ff. For the suggestion that the partial knowledge of
the definition will be the grasp of at least one of the predicates that feature in the
essence of something see Barnes (1993) 218–19. For the qualification about necessary
accidents see Bolton (1987) 133–42, esp. note 27.

[21] I take it that knowing that the objects of a certain kind exist is the work of experience,
*empeiria*, as we have already encountered in *An. Pr.* I 30, *An. Po* II 19 and *Met.* I 1. On
this see Ackrill (1981) 377.

a concept that embraces a number of undifferentiated parts. So this passage is in effect saying that in moving from a judgement of a thing's existence to its essence we move from an unanalysed whole to its constituents. But *An. Po.* II 8 goes beyond this by saying that even to grasp this compounded concept in a way that will be useful for an inquiry into first principles one needs to have some idea of one or more of its parts already. Thus we may have the hazy concept of 'man' but, unless we know that one of its parts is animal, it will be of little use. In fact, our knowledge of one of the parts goes to explain our success in applying the hazy concept to objects around us. It is difficult to see how someone who only had incidental knowledge of something could have been consistently successful in picking out instances of that thing. So *An. Po.* II 8 can be used to expand the point of *Phys.* I 1.

## [4] LEARNING AS NATURAL CHANGE – METAPHYSICS IX 8

We have seen how in *An. Po.* II 19 Aristotle is concerned to show that the learning of first principles is a process that starts from some knowledge, even if that knowledge is a humble thing like perception. But that left us asking how the pre-existent knowledge would act as the appropriate material for the knowledge that marks the end of the process. In *Phys.* I 1 we found Aristotle providing some sort of answer to this question. In a confused or articulate way we have the knowledge when we start. *An. Po.* II 8 took this further by saying that in possessing the pre-existent knowledge the learner already has part of the end-state knowledge.

What we have seen, then, is the way in which a contrast is initially drawn between the more knowable to us and the more knowable in nature and, in some contexts, great emphasis is placed on the difference between the two sides of the contrast. *Met.* I 1 and *An. Po.* II 19 are good examples of this. In *Phys.* I 1 and *An. Po.* II 8, however, Aristotle wants to modify this to bring out the continuity between the two cognitive levels. It should not be difficult to see why. The more he emphasises the differences between the knowable to us and the knowable in nature the more difficult it becomes to explain how we are able to move from one to the other.

But there is also a peculiarly Aristotelian reason for bringing out this continuity. Underlying his views about learning are much more general views about natural development. We should not forget that for Aristotle learning and discovery are forms – paradigmatic forms – of change and growth. A sign of this is that his very extensive writings on the subject of change are peppered with illustrations involving teaching and learning, whether it be learning music, building, mathematics or grammar.[22] If learning is to be seen as a distinctively Aristotelian kind of change, we should expect to see how his standard metaphysical apparatus applies to it.

When something comes into being it must come to be out of something, and Aristotle says that the matter pre-exists the change. In what way will this apply to learning? In *An. Po.* II 19, Aristotle is trying to show how the process of acquiring first principles conforms to the condition set in the opening of the *Posterior Analytics*, 'all teaching and learning derives from pre-existing knowledge'. Now this condition seems to be a specific epistemological application of the Eleatic precept that something cannot come out of nothing. Aristotle accepts this precept and accommodates it in at least two ways, one of which is his claim that something comes to be out of matter which pre-exists the change. So the opening fanfare of the *Posterior Analytics* could thus be seen as demanding that learning, like any other change, requires a 'that out of which', a 'material cause'.[23] The genetic account of *An. Po.* II 19 could be seen as a more elaborate application of this principle. Indeed Aristotle's language very much suggests this in the way that each stage in the genesis of *nous* 'comes to be' out of its predecessor. The language of 'becoming' occurs frequently in this chapter[24] and is standard terminology is his account of the material cause.

The other way Aristotle tries to accommodate the Eleatic precept is to invoke the distinction between potentiality and actuality. When someone learns they start out only potentially

---

[22] See, for example, *Phys.* I 7 (becoming musical – 189b34ff.), *Met.* IX 8 (learning to play the lyre – 1049b 31ff.), *Met.* IX 3. (learning the craft of house-building – 1046b33ff.), and *An.* II 5 (learning grammar and geometry – 417a21ff.). See also *Phys.* III 3, 202a31ff.

[23] Compare *Phys.* II 3, 195a18–19, where the premises of an argument are seen as the matter out of which the conclusion comes. (Grasping the premises of an argument was used as an example of pre-existent knowledge in *An. Po.* I 1, 71a5ff.)

[24] See 100a2ff.

knowing and then move towards a state of actual knowledge. So in this case, someone who grasps the more knowable to us actually, grasps the more knowable in nature potentially. Once the learning process is complete and the change is made they will grasp the more knowable in nature actually. Now we have already had a suggestion of this in *An. Po.* II 19 where perception which constitutes the pre-existent knowledge for *nous* is also called a potentiality (99b32–3). There is, however, rather more to say than this. In this case, the potentiality for grasping the more knowable in nature temporally pre-exists the actuality, just as in general one might think that potentiality pre-exists actuality in time. But Aristotle does not think this is quite accurate as an account of the temporal relationship between actuality and potentiality.

In his discussion of the relationship between the two in *Met.* IX 8, Aristotle defends the claim that in certain respects the actual is chronologically prior to the potential.[25] For instance, an actual man brings a potential man into actual existence. So in the case of learning he would say that learners may know potentially but they need a teacher to convert this potentiality into actuality.

So far,[26] he has only said that the actual is prior in species, e.g. the father is prior to his son, but he then goes on to make a stronger claim which will be of considerable interest to us. In some cases the actual can be prior even in the individual. The example he gives of this comes from learning:

it is thought to be impossible to be a builder if one has built nothing or a harpist if one has never played the harp; for he who learns to play the harp learns to play by playing it, and all other learners do similarly. And thence arose the sophistic argument that one who does not know a science will be doing that which is the object of the science; for he who is learning it does not know it. But since, of that which is coming to be, some part must have come to be, and, of that which, in general, is changing, some part must have changed (this is shown in the treatise on movement) he who is learning must, it would seem, grasp some part of the knowledge. It is surely clear, then, in this way, that the actuality is in this sense also, viz. in the order of becoming and of time, prior to the potentiality. (*Met.* IX 8, 1049b29–50a2)

---

[25] *Met.* IX 8, 1049b17–50a3.  [26] I.e. from 1049b17 to 27.

In the sophistic argument to which he refers, we have a version of *Meno*'s paradox. Someone learning to play the harp must play the harp in order to learn, but to play the harp they must already have the knowledge they hope to acquire. The resolution of the sophism consists in saying that the actualisation of the potential, and therefore learning, depends on the existence of prior actuality even within the same individual. His conclusion is that the learner must have some of the knowledge that he is trying to attain (1050a1–2).

The reference to partial knowledge in this chapter recalls Aristotle's claim in *An. Po.* II 8 that to inquire into a definition one must already have grasped some part of the essence (93a22),[27] and we can now see that the more knowable to us, as we have been examining it, is an obvious case of the partial knowledge mentioned in *Met.* IX 8. The point of *An. Po.* II 8 is that the learning is only possible on the condition that the prior knowledge already involves something of the more knowable in nature itself. This shows quite graphically how Aristotle's metaphysics is the source of the methodological claims that we have been exploring.

Aristotle's tendency to break down the polarities he sets up in some texts can now be seen in the following light. Like Plato he wants to distinguish clearly between the starting- and the finishing-points.[28] He does this with considerable clarity, inventing new terminology for the purpose. Yet he also sees learning as a paradigmatic form of natural change and, given the conditions he has established elsewhere for the possibility of change, must now explain how learning, as the transition between two stages so sharply distinguished from each other, can take place. In the face of this, he remains true to his analysis of change (in particular to the demand for an appropriate prior actuality), and accordingly modifies his conception of the more knowable to us. The result is the conceptually enriched perceptions of *Phys.* I 1 and, even more, the partial knowledge of *An. Po.* II 8. This conception of partial knowledge in perception enables Aristotle to resist the Platonic notion of a discontinuity between the perceptual perspective and scientific or philosophical understanding.

[27] Compare the phrase 'grasp some part of the knowledge' (ἔχειν τι τῆς ἐπιστήμης, *Met.* IX 8, 1050a1) with 'when we grasp something of the object' (ἔχοντές τι αὐτοῦ τοῦ πράγματος, *An. Po.* II 8, 93a22).

[28] For Aristotle's awareness of his debt to Plato for this distinction see *N.E.* I 4, 1095a30–b1.

CHAPTER 6

# Discovery and continuity in ethics

[1] TRANSITION FROM SCIENCE TO ETHICS:
ARISTOTLE'S APPEARANCES

When Aristotle talked of the path of discovery in the first chapter
of the *Physics* he had in mind a smooth and gradual transition
from the perspective of perception to the attainment of first
principles and not, as Plato had done, a journey of almost fright-
ening disorientation. But so far we have only been considering
Aristotle's views on scientific discovery, whereas our treatment
of Plato was at least as much concerned with ethical discovery.
It was, after all, ethical discovery that originally gave rise to
the problem in the *Meno*. The purpose of this chapter is to
see how far these conclusions about Aristotle's account of scientific discovery can be applied to ethics.[1] *Phys.* I 1 says at the
outset that its account of discovery will apply to all inquiries
in which there are first principles. But does he really mean to
include ethics?

I have already suggested that we should not be too eager to
find a tidy fit between scientific and ethical discovery given the
repeated warnings in the *Nicomachean Ethics* against ignoring the
differences between the two.[2] On the other hand, one *prima facie*
reason for expecting to find something common to both areas is
that he sometimes uses the same terminology when talking about
discovery both in science and ethics. The distinction between the
more knowable to us and the more knowable in nature, which we
found pervasive in scientific contexts, crops up in his ethical works

---

[1] An excellent account of Aristotle's ethical method can be found in Barnes (1980); for
studies which bring together Aristotle's views on method in both ethics and science
see Nussbaum (1986) ch. 8 and Irwin (1988) ch. 2.
[2] *N.E.* I 3, 1094b11–28; 7, 1098a20ff.
[3] See e.g. *N.E.* I 4, 1095b2–4.

as well.3 But the common term that has attracted the most interest
is the term *phainomenon*, which I shall translate as 'appearance'. We
have already met this term in a scientific context at *An. Pr.* I 30,
46a17–22:

> it is the business of experience to give the principles which belong
> to each subject. I mean for example that astronomical experience
> supplies the principles of astronomical science; for once the appearances
> were adequately apprehended, the demonstrations of astronomy were
> discovered. Similarly with any other art or science.

In this passage Aristotle treats the appearances as the constituents
of experience. An individual appearance is more or less the same as
a perception and constitutes a grasp of the fact. In other words, the
appearances fall into the category of the more knowable to us.

What has interested scholars is the way in which the same term
appears in discussions of ethical method, notably in this passage of
the *Nicomachean Ethics* (VII 1, 1145b2–7):

> We must, as in all other cases, set the appearances before us and, after
> first discussing the difficulties go on to prove, if possible, the truth of
> all the reputable opinions about these affections or, failing this, of the
> greater number and the most authoritative; for if we both resolve the
> difficulties and leave the reputable opinions undisturbed, we shall have
> proved the case sufficiently.

Here Aristotle seems to treat the word 'appearance' interchangeably with 'reputable opinion' (*endoxon*) which, as we are told in the
*Topics*, is an opinion 'accepted by everyone or by the majority or by
the wise – i.e. by all, or by the majority, or by the most notable and
reputable of them' (I 1, 100b21–3).

At first sight one might be unimpressed by the fact that Aristotle
uses the term 'appearance' in both science and ethics. When used
in scientific contexts, it might be said, the term simply refers to a
sense observation. Aristotle is proposing that we set out the observations of sense and then go on to elaborate theories to explain
them, making sure that we always preserve them, i.e. that the
theories fit the facts, not the other way around. On the other hand,
in the ethical context we are enjoined to set out prevalent or reputable opinions and to try to make them consistent with each other.4
There are in fact two points lurking here. The first is that

---

4 The 'endoxic' method of *N.E.* VII 1 is not confined to ethics but also applies to
philosophy of science, e.g. to inquiries into time, movement and space.

Aristotle may be using the term 'appearance' in radically different ways, the second that he may be advocating two quite different methods of treating appearances. As to the first point, if we assume that the 'perceptual' appearances, for instance of biology and astronomy, are the raw data of sense, free from theories or 'conceptual schemes' we shall indeed see an enormous difference in Aristotle's accounts of scientific and ethical discovery. Our previous discussion, however, should make us very reluctant to find too harsh a distinction between perceptions and concepts in Aristotle's epistemology. We have seen that the combined accounts of *An. Po.* II 8 and *Phys.* I 1 present the perceptual appearances not straightforwardly as factual observations, but involving an unarticulated concept of the essence. This substantially reduces the gulf between the perceptual and conceptual appearances.[5]

The other difference I mentioned was one of method. In *N.E.* VII 1 the method being recommended involves taking stock of the reputable opinions and then establishing agreement among them. In science, on the other hand, it involves collecting observations and then producing theories to explain them. There is no denying the difference here. Nevertheless, these differences in method do not eradicate all similarities in the underlying epistemology. I want to suggest that in both ethics and science the movement from the more knowable to us and the more knowable in nature is a progression from a state where a vague or hazy concept is grasped to one in which the concept is more clearly articulated.

That the recommendations of *Phys.* I 1 do apply at least in some measure to ethics is supported by a passage from *Eudemian Ethics* I 6:

About all these matters we must try to get conviction by arguments, using the appearances (*phainomena*) as evidence and illustration. It would be best that all should clearly concur with what we are going to say, but if that is unattainable, then that all should in some way at least concur. And this if converted they will do, for everyone has some contribution to make to the truth, and with this as a starting-point we must give some proof of these matters. For by advancing from true but unclear judgements one

---

[5] For an interpretation that sees a sharp divide between the 'endoxic' and observational methods see Owen (1975) 113–4. My interpretation is in some respects similar to Nussbaum (1986) 244–5 who took Owen to task by arguing that the term *phainomenon* never has the sense of a 'hard' theory-free observation, but always means something enriched by a scheme of beliefs.

will arrive at clear ones, always exchanging the usual blurred statement for what is more knowable.[6]

This passage is a kind of hybrid between *N.E.* VII 1 and *Phys.* I 1. In the process of making the appearances consistent with one another we 'go forward'[7] towards the more knowable (*sc.* in nature) and this represents an improvement in clarity over what was originally blurred.[8] So just as in science, the ethical appearance involves a blurred concept and the progress towards the more knowable in nature will be one of articulation and refinement.

In the *E.E.* Aristotle goes slightly beyond what he says in the *N.E.* In the *Nicomachean* passage he announces his intention to save all the appearances or, failing that, most of them; in the *Eudemian* passage he intends to save *all* the appearances if not as they stand then once they have been appropriately modified. We can obtain at least some kind of consensus if we change the opinions in some way. As the next sentences talk of refinement and articulation of appearances, we can assume that this is the kind of conversion Aristotle has in mind. He is not converting people in the sense of changing their view to something diametrically opposed, but modifying it. I said above that the *Eudemian* passage is a hybrid of *Phys.* I 1 and *N.E.* VII 1; in fact, the articulation method of the *Phys.* I 1 is being used to show how the agreement aim of the *N.E.* VII 1 is to be attained. The articulation method of *E.E.* I 6 (and *Phys.* I 1) is used to produce the consensus required in the method of *N.E.* VII 1.[9] This becomes clearer when we remember that the

---

[6] 1216b26–36: πειρατέον δὲ περὶ πάντων τούτων ζητεῖν τὴν πίστιν διὰ τῶν λόγων, μαρτυρίοις καὶ παραδείγμασι χρώμενον τοῖς φαινομένοις. κράτιστον μὲν γὰρ πάντας ἀνθρώπους φαίνεσθαι συνομολογοῦντας τοῖς ῥηθησομένοις, εἰ δὲ μή, τρόπον γέ τινα πάντας, ὅπερ μεταβιβαζόμενοι ποιήσουσιν. ἔχει γὰρ ἕκαστος οἰκεῖόν τι πρὸς τὴν ἀλήθειαν, ἐξ ὧν ἀναγκαῖον δεικνύναι πως περὶ αὐτῶν. ἐκ γὰρ τῶν ἀληθῶς μὲν λεγομένων οὐ σαφῶς δέ, προϊοῦσιν ἔσται καὶ τὸ σαφῶς, μεταλαμβάνουσιν ἀεὶ τὰ γνωριμώτερα τῶν εἰωθότων λέγεσθαι συγκεχυμένως. The text here is problematic, though none of the crucial words for our purposes are under threat.

[7] Compare *Phys.* I 1, 184a24. See also *N.E.* IV 1, 1121a9–10.

[8] In Greek, there is an interesting similarity between the claim here that 'everyone has some contribution to make to the truth' (ἔχει γὰρ ἕκαστος οἰκεῖόν τι πρὸς τὴν ἀλήθειαν, 1216b30–1) and the point of *An. Po.* II 8 that in knowing that something exists we 'have some grasp on what it is' (ὡς ἔχομεν ὅτι ἔστιν, οὕτως ἔχομεν καὶ πρὸς τὸ τί ἔστιν, 93a28–9). Like the concept implicit in experience and in the grasp of the fact, an appearance gains its epistemological value from the fact that it is meant to be a reliable starting-point in an inquiry, a piece of knowledge that can be refined and developed.

[9] For this point see Stewart (1892) II 120–1 and Burnet (1900) xli.

refinement method is not only to be seen as establishing some kind of consensus among the different views, but also as extracting the nugget of truth in each of them. When a reputable opinion is initially set down, it can seem simply false. But what Aristotle is interested in doing is bringing out how in one sense the opinion is false, in another true. To do this he has to produce a refined version of the opinion, which could be accepted as true. Once he has done this he can go on to bring out the agreement between the appearances. As soon as they have been modified so as to come out true they can no longer conflict with one another.

The co-operation between the refinement and agreement methods can be be seen at work in a number of places in both the *Eudemian* and *Nicomachean Ethics*. Some of the best examples of this symbiosis are to be found in the discussion of friendship in *N.E.* VII–IX, where disagreements are cited and then resolved by the refinement of the opinions concerned. For example, in *N.E.* VIII 1 Aristotle raises an old dispute about whether friendship is between likes or unlikes (1155a32–b8). It is resolved by his distinction between the different kinds of friendship: virtue, pleasure and utility friendship.[10] Aristotle uses the distinction between utility and virtue friendship to settle the dispute in question. Virtue friendship is between likes (1156b7–8), indeed the friend is another self (1170b6–7), whereas utility friendship needs to be based on unlikes (otherwise the parties cannot be of any use to each other – 1159b12–15). IX 8 is devoted to another disagreement: is self-love a good or a bad thing? Aristotle settles the dispute by distinguishing different senses of 'self'. If it is the appetitive self that is in question, the love is bad; if the rational self, it is good.[11] A third example is the disagreement in IX 9, 1169b2ff. about whether a happy person will need friends. As in the first example, the distinction between types of friendship is used. The happy person will need virtue friendships but not those of pleasure or utility (1169b22ff.). In all these cases Aristotle quite self-consciously uses differentiation to bring opinions into agreement with each other

---

[10] The primary kind of friendship is found where two people love one another for their virtue (VIII 4, 1157a30–1); friendship of pleasure occurs where two people become friends because of the pleasure that they give each other, and friendship of utility where they become friends out of mutual utility.

[11] This example is cited by Stewart (1892) II 121.

and, in the last case, explicitly wants to unearth the element of truth in the appearances.[12]

*N.E.* VIII–IX is particularly rich in examples of Aristotle's method being put into practice, but the appeal to and refinement of appearances has already been at work in the chapters on moral virtue, III 6–IV 9, which show the two complementary aspects of the method of the *Physics* at work. On the one hand, he frequently appeals to views generally held and so treats the more knowable to us as an adequate starting point in inquiry. On the other hand, there is also much differentiation in action. Our ordinary ways of thinking and of speaking, though roughly correct, often fuse together different (but related) notions. Aristotle is at pains to discriminate them and consistently shows a preoccupation with clarifying and articulating the blurred concepts of the more knowable to us.

To list all the examples would be unnecessary, but they seem to fall into general types: sometimes a virtue is confused with the vice or extreme that lies closer to it. In *N.E.* II 8 we were warned that where the mean lies closer to one of its extremes, a similarity will appear between the virtue and that specific vice. He cites generosity/extravagance and courage/rashness as examples (1108b30–2). He sees the rash person as a pretender to courage whose pretence must be unmasked. But in addition to being confused with vices, virtues can have similarities to each other and so tempt us towards homonymy. Both the pairs, generosity and magnificence, and magnanimity (*megalopsuchia*) and love of honour fall into this category.[13] Another class of blurred concepts comes

---

[12] See IX 9, 1169b22–3. One particularly strong reason Aristotle has for wanting to find some kind of consensus lies in his belief that 'men have a sufficient natural instinct for what is true, and usually do arrive at the truth' (*Rhetoric* I 1, 1355a15–7). Now, someone could object to this optimism by pointing to the widespread occurrence of disagreement. (See e.g. Socrates in the *Euthyphro* 7b7–d7.) Where there is disagreement only one party (at best) can be right, so the presence of disagreement is surely a good sign that error is considerably more common than Aristotle supposes. So it is essential for Aristotle to show that, underlying this disagreement, is some more basic kind of consensus. That is, although we might at first be struck by the disparity of opinions, on closer examination, we can see how they can be made to cohere. If we are successful in detecting this agreement we can resist the conclusion that a large number of people are radically in error.

[13] Vices can also be confused with each other. Cf. *N.E.* IV 1, 1119b30–34, where he talks of the way in which we sometimes mix up prodigality and self-indulgence (and *akrasia*). In doing this we are 'weaving together' (συμπλέκοντες) the different states; this recalls the way the pre-scientific concept of *Phys.* I 1 is a 'pouring-together' (συγκεχυμένον, 184a22) of different elements. The metaphor of weaving is used in a very similar context in *N.E.* VII 13, 1153b14–15.

to light in the discussion of incontinence (*akrasia*). Both this and its opposite, continence (*enkrateia*), need to be distinguished from the virtue of self-control and its opposite (1145a36–b2); continence also needs to be distinguished from obstinacy in the same way as courage from rashness (1151b4–17).

On this view, then, Aristotle canvasses and attempts to accommodate the views not only of the wise but also of non-philosophers engaged in practical affairs and of 'the many'.[14] This now brings us to the central point of this chapter. If Aristotle allows the majority, if not all, of the prevalent opinions to play a substantive role in determining the outcome of an inquiry, his assessment of the more familiar to us in ethics will be every bit as optimistic as it was in science. This will then give us as clear a contrast between Plato and Aristotle as we could wish – not merely between their different conceptions of discovery but also between their ways of understanding the project implicit in ethical philosophy itself. For Plato it must involve the challenging and rejection of the appearances, for Aristotle their refinement and distillation.

But, plausible as this contrast may appear, we should not be too quick to accept it. The central topic of the *Nicomachean Ethics* is the nature of the good which he identifies with happiness (*eudaimonia*, I 4, 1095a18–20). In the first book, when opening his discussion of the topic, Aristotle does indeed consult opinions over a very wide spectrum. Yet the last book appears to give considerable, if not exclusive, emphasis to the activity of intellectual contemplation. It seems at first sight difficult to see how such an approach could be said to be saving any of the appearances other than those of a handful of remote and ineffectual dons. This disquieting fact suggests two ways of undermining the conclusion we have reached. First, one could ask whether Aristotle does aim to accommodate all the appearances in the way just set out; perhaps he really intends to revise other people's opinions just as he sees fit. But even if he does genuinely

---

[14] Aristotle's commitment to accommodating something of the views of the many is clear in the *N.E.* See I 4 where he says we only need to consult opinions that are reasonable and most prevalent (1095a29–30); see also I 8 for a declaration of intention to listen to the many because it is improbable that these 'should be entirely mistaken but rather that they should be right in at least one respect . . .' (1098b27–9).

For a helpful survey of *consensus omnium* arguments in Aristotle, and in ancient philosophy more generally, see Oehler (1969) 234–71, esp. 237–41.

attempt to accommodate himself to all the appearances, the place given to intellectual contemplation in book X still raises a second question, namely whether this attempt is at all successful.

To tackle these questions we need to study his account of happiness in more detail and to compare the two discussions of happiness in books I and X of the *N.E.* The first book starts out true to the method by setting out some appearances about happiness. The question is to what extent these appearances are 'saved' in the answer eventually given in book X. Now we should bear in mind that just what answer he actually gives in book X is notoriously controversial. *Prima facie* Aristotle seems to say that happiness consists in the exercise of just one activity pursued for its own sake, intellectual contemplation. A large number of commentators now reject this and think instead that Aristotle advocates a life which includes all the moral virtues practised for their own sakes, alongside the activity of contemplation. This is often known as the 'inclusive' conception of happiness, whereas the former has been called the 'monolithic' conception. Now to decide which of these two is right would be too large a task here.[15] But it would also be unnecessary. In what follows it should become clear that the problem at issue – in what way book X can be said to accommodate all the opinions – arises on either interpretation. But I shall postpone treatment of book X for the moment and start with an examination of the appearances that Aristotle sets out in the first book.

## [2] DISCOVERY AND HAPPINESS IN THE *NICOMACHEAN ETHICS*

Aristotle attempts to narrow down the nature of the good at the beginning of *N.E.* I 4:

Verbally there is general agreement; for both the general run of men and people of superior refinement say that it is happiness ... but with regard to what happiness is they differ and the many do not give the same account as the wise. For the former think it is some plain and obvious thing, like pleasure, wealth or honour ... (1095a17–23)

The next chapter goes on to list the three most prominent opinions. The many think that happiness is pleasure; the 'more refined'

---

[15] The literature on this issue is enormous. Particularly influential have been Ackrill (1980) and Cooper (1975), esp ch. 3. The most extensive treatment of the problem is Kraut (1989).

– those of a more active disposition – identify it with honour; and the third candidate, mentioned only to be postponed, is contemplation.[16] In the previous chapter, we were told that honour and pleasure are both 'obvious' things (1095a22–3), which suggests that the first two appearances of I 5 are more knowable to us and hence more easily comprehensible. This already points to a similarity with Aristotle's account of scientific discovery in which the grasp of the 'that' given in perception is also more easily accessible, the perspective that we naturally have of the world given our nature as the sort of creatures that we are.[17] But our real interest lies in whether he attempts to give these opinions any role in the inquiry and, if he does, whether he has any success in doing so. At first sight what Aristotle says in the rest of *N.E.* I 5 suggests a negative answer to the first question. He refers to the many's preference for pleasure as bestial and the identification of happiness as honour as 'too superficial'. We need to see whether this is the last word on these appearances, starting with the case of pleasure.

A clear indication that the pleasure appearance is going to do some work in the *N.E.* comes as early as I 8. After setting out the appearances in I 5, he pauses in the next chapter to reject the candidate of his Platonist friends and then gives his own account of happiness in I 7. The conclusion of this argument is that happiness consists in the activity of the rational soul in accordance with virtue. In I 8 he returns to the appearances saying that we should not just judge our results by inspecting the argument itself, but also check it against 'what is said':

The characteristics that are looked for in happiness seem also, all of them, to belong to what we have defined happiness as being. For some identify happiness with virtue, some with practical wisdom, others with a kind of philosophical wisdom, others with these or one of these accompanied by pleasure or not without pleasure; while others include

---

[16] I 5 conforms rather well to the account of the reputable opinions (*endoxa*) in the *Topics* I 1, 100b21–3. There the list is one of greater exclusiveness: 'Those opinions are reputable (*endoxa*) which are 'accepted by everyone or by the majority or by the wise – i.e. by all, or by the majority, or by the most notable and reputable of them'. In *N.E.* I 5 we have a similar progression – the many (pleasure), the more refined (honour) and then contemplation, which is presumably the choice of the most notable of the wise (cf. X 8, 1179a16–7).

[17] This also accords well with *Met.* V 1's account of principles, where he says that sometimes we should start from what is easily learnt (1013a1–4).

external prosperity. Now some of these views have been held by many men and men of old, others by a few eminent persons; and it is not probable that either of these should be entirely mistaken, but rather that they should be right in at least one respect, or even in most respects (1098b22–9).

Clearly Aristotle is attempting to put the recommendations of *E.E.* I 6 into practice. Notice also the similarity between *N.E.* I 8 and the second part of the passage that we quoted from *E.E.* I 6:

and this if converted they will do, for everyone has some contribution to make to the truth, and with this as a starting-point we must give some proof of these matters. For by advancing from true but unclear judgements one will arrive at clear ones . . . (1216b30–5)

The reference in *N.E.* I 8 to the need to include pleasure in the final account, together with the reference to what many people have said (1098b27), shows that the first option of I 5 is being in some way accommodated. A few lines later, at 1099a7ff., Aristotle explains at some length how the life of happiness is pleasant. Virtuous actions are by nature pleasant and it is a mark of the virtuous person to find them so. Indeed at 1099a15–20 he appeals to more appearances to show that someone who does not enjoy doing virtuous acts is not genuinely virtuous after all. The connection between happiness and pleasure can be used to determine who is genuinely virtuous and who merely seems so.

Similarly, when he comes to give his final answer to the question of what happiness is in *N.E.* X, and introduces contemplation into the argument, he immediately tries to show how this answer fits with some of the criteria set out in *N.E.* I. In the previous chapter, he rejected amusement as a candidate for happiness and this might make us suspect that the pleasure appearance has been left far behind. But this is not so. In X 7, after announcing that contemplation is the best activity and the most worthy to be called happiness he adds that it is, among other things, the most pleasant of activities:

And we think happiness has pleasure mingled with it, but the activity of wisdom is admittedly the most pleasant of virtuous activities . . . (1177a22–5)

Aristotle has not dismissed the pleasure appearance out of hand, but is at least attempting to give it some role in the argument of X 7.

Given that Aristotle is attempting to follow up on the promises of *E.E.* I 6 at least for the pleasure appearance, we need to see in more detail what role it plays in his account of happiness and hence find an answer to the question about the success of this attempt. The first thing to concede straight off is that the appearance as it stands is false and that for Aristotle happiness is not to be equated with pleasure. But what is significant is the way in which the appearance is false. *Eudaimonia* is distinct from pleasure; the appearance compounds or 'pours together' two distinct things. It therefore recalls the blurred concepts of *Phys.* I 1.

Nevertheless, although it mistakenly identifies things that should be kept apart, there is an association to be made. For Aristotle, true happiness is accompanied by pleasure. Happiness is eventually defined as activity of the rational soul in accordance with virtue. Thus it is not identical to pleasure; yet pleasure is still closely connected to it. Every activity has its own peculiar pleasure which comes about when the activity is unimpeded. Thus virtuous activity will have its own peculiar pleasure. Now any virtuous activity, including intellectual virtue, is valuable in itself and so should not be pursued for the sake of the pleasure that 'supervenes' on it; pleasure is not *the* goal. Yet because it supervenes on what is most valuable in itself, it is called a 'supervenient goal'.[18]

Aristotle does not therefore treat the popular identification of pleasure with happiness as a straightforward mistake. He treats it rather as a case where two elements have been poured together into a compounded concept. Pleasure and happiness are indeed intimately associated, but the relationship is not as simple as the many think. For them, the relationship is a straightforward one of identity; for Aristotle, it is more subtle, pleasure being not *the* goal but a supervenient one. His strategy in dealing with the popular candidate is very much one of separating out two things that have been wrongly, but not unreasonably, fused together.[19] Aristotle's treatment of the majority vote does, then, fit well with the account of *Phys.* I 1.

Furthermore, the connection is an important one. That pleasure is involved in happiness, i.e. in the exercise of virtue, is not some rhetorical gesture to retain something of the majority opinion on

---

[18] *N.E.* X 4, 1174b33 (ἐπιγιγνόμενόν τι τέλος).
[19] Further evidence of this approach comes from an earlier discussion of pleasure at VII 13, 1153b14–15.

Aristotle's part, but a crucial part of his theory. The person who practises virtue does so with pleasure. Someone who, after a titanic struggle within themselves, manages to perform the right act or control their feelings will do so without pleasure, and although later moralists may have seen this as the true case of virtue, Aristotle sees it as inferior to virtue.[20] That pleasure is involved in happiness is a hall-mark of Aristotle's ethics.

All this shows that Aristotle has succeeded to some extent in salvaging an element of the pleasure appearance. Admittedly, there is still a gap between Aristotle's conception of happiness and the vulgar equation of pleasure with happiness. In addition to making pleasure only a supervenient goal Aristotle has to make a further modification. It is not bodily pleasure that is the supervenient goal but the pleasure that accompanies virtuous activities. Nevertheless, I do not think that this renders contentless his claim to have preserved something of their answer. He can point out that pleasures, bodily and non-bodily alike, all belong to the same genus.[21] The best verdict is that Aristotle's treatment of the pleasure appearance is a case of preserving the nugget of truth in an appearance, but a case where his account of discovery is pushed towards its limit.

So much for pleasure and happiness. As for the second of the two appearances listed in *N.E.* I 5, the identification of happiness with honour, there can be no doubting the role that it plays in Aristotle's inquiry. In fact it begins to play this role out in I 5 itself (1095b23–31). Having stated that the option of the more refined is honour, he starts to articulate it. First, he objects that mere reputation cannot be what is at issue, because (we think) that is only an external good and happiness must be something internal. Furthermore, the people who pursue honour do so to assure themselves of their own goodness. In other words, they

---

[20] It might be said that if Aristotle had conceived of virtue as the triumph over temptation he could still have claimed to have accommodated the pleasure appearance; at least the virtue of temperance on this view would be concerned with pleasures. But on this conception pleasure plays a much smaller role than it does in Aristotle's conception of virtue. Pleasure pervades almost all of Aristotle's virtues; 'encratic virtue' involves pleasure only for the case of temperance, and there pleasure is no more salient than pain.

[21] We shall see below how, in the discussion of friendship, he clearly regards the presence of pleasure in virtue friendship as important enough to create a similarity with pleasure friendship (which includes sexual pleasures), thereby ensuring that the latter is a case of genuine, if secondary, friendship.

*themselves* agree that the goal is really moral virtue. At any rate, to the extent that they do seek honour they seek it from those of practical wisdom and on the grounds of virtue. This also shows that what they really pursue is something less superficial than honour, the answer first extracted from them.

If we compare this with the treatment of the pleasure appearance we can see that there is less distance between this appearance and Aristotle's own answer. In I 5 he is not so much making amendments to the view initially set out, but making explicit what is already implicit – the identification of moral virtue with the good. In this sense, he has little problem in showing how his theory fits with one of the appearances, because his answer is already implicitly believed. This appearance continues to guide the inquiry in I 8 where virtue is, along with pleasure, one of the opinions against which the theory of I 7 is tested (1098b24 and 30–1).

It should be noted that even at its more superficial level, where it simply equates happiness with honour, the second appearance of I 5 is not to be rejected out of hand. Honour, according to Aristotle, is an external good (IV 3, 1123b17–21) which is one reason why it could never be identified with happiness. Again we have a 'confusion' on our hands. Nevertheless, as he explains in these lines, it is the greatest of external goods and so is the appropriate prize for someone who has attained the greatest state of virtue. Honour is, or at least should be, a concomitant to virtue and hence happiness. Pleasure is the adornment of happiness, like the bloom of youth; honour is the prize of happiness. Neither is identical to it but both are closely connected with it. Moreover, the connection between honour and happiness is important for Aristotle. He spends a long chapter on the virtue concerned with honour (IV 3) and indeed, in the next chapter, distinguishes this from another virtue concerned with smaller honours. If Aristotle attached such importance to the recognition and management of honour he must have thought the connection between virtue, happiness and honour itself of considerable significance.

Comparing Aristotle's treatment of the first two appearances of I 5 we can see that neither of them are simple falsehoods mentioned only to be dismissed. They are 'confusions' but what they mix together are things that are connected, albeit in a more subtle way, and because these connections are so important they are used to provide valuable clues in the process of articulating ethical theory, i.e. in the process of moving towards the more knowable in nature. It is not merely that these appearances contain an element of truth, but that this element of truth allows them to play a significant role in the inquiry.

Notice also that it is not just the method of *Phys.* I 1 that is at issue in all this. Above I suggested that *An. Po.* II 8 went beyond *Phys.* I 1. What we start off with is a grasp of a part of the thing – in most of the examples there that meant a grasp of one element in the definition. Now this seems to run against what we have in *N.E.* I. However closely happiness is connected with pleasure or honour, neither of them is included in its definition. But here we should remember that the point of *An. Po.* II 8 was not so restricted. The element that is grasped at the early stage need not be a part of the definition; it could equally well be something connected in an important way with the essence, like a 'necessary accident'. Pleasure as being analogous to the bloom of youth, and honour as the prize of virtue seem to fit in an analogous way. Their relationship to happiness is neither that of being part of the essence nor that of being purely coincidental.

So, given that the final answer in book X gives weight to both contemplation and political virtue – whatever the details of their combination – we can see the extent to which the truth in the appearances of I 5 is being preserved. So far, however, I have remained vague about the details of Aristotle's final answer in book X, and so skated over an important problem that must now be addressed. The problem concerns the second and third appearances of I 5, the political and contemplative ideals. The first appearance has been seen to fit in some way with both, but there remains a potential conflict between the political and the contemplative lives which must somehow be resolved in his final account of happiness. We saw that there are, broadly speaking, two ways of interpreting book X: the 'inclusivist' interpretation, according to which the life of happiness consists in both contemplation and virtuous activities pursued for their own sakes, and the 'monolithic' interpretation, where only one activity, that of contemplation, is pursued for its own sake. At first sight it may look as if these two interpretations will yield very different answers to the question of how Aristotle accommodates the appearances of I 5. One might at first say that on the inclusivist interpretation Aristotle does manage a skillful accommodation of both appearances because he weaves both elements into the best kind of life: political activity crowned in some way by philosophic reflection. Let us concede provisionally that the inclusivist approach does succeed in accommodating all the appearances and see what happens on the monolithic one.

If, as this interpretation assumes, Aristotle eventually makes contemplation the sole end of life, how will he accommodate the second appearance of I 5, the opinion of the practically minded? Presumably the answer to this question must come at the beginning of X 8 where he says that the political life is happiest in a secondary way (1178a9). This could be seen as Aristotle's attempt at precisely accommodating the political appearance. Virtue and practical wisdom, as some think, is happiness – but, on Aristotle's final view, only in a qualified, i.e. secondary, way.

But saving the appearances is not as simple as this suggests. In the second part of X 8 (1178b7–32) Aristotle gives a new argument for identifying happiness with contemplation. *Eudaimonia*, we think, is especially a characteristic of the gods. The gods do not engage in acts of moral virtue, but in contemplation. Following this line of reasoning further he ends up saying:

Therefore the activity of God, which surpasses all others in blessedness, must be contemplative; and of human activities, therefore, that which is most akin to this must be most the nature of happiness.

This is indicated, too, by the fact that the other animals have no share in happiness, being completely deprived of such activity. For while the whole life of the gods is blessed, and that of men too in so far as some likeness of such activity belongs to them, none of the other animals is happy, *since they in no way share in contemplation. Happiness extends, then, just so far as contemplation does*, and those to whom contemplation more fully belongs are more truly happy, not accidentally *but in virtue of the contemplation*; for this is in itself precious. *Happiness must therefore be some form of contemplation.* (X 8, 1178b21–32)

As the lines that I have italicised show, it looks as if there can only be happiness where there is contemplation. But if so, what about the second life, a life precisely lacking in contemplation? Given the passage just quoted how can it be happiness in any way, secondarily or otherwise? To call it happiness would just be homonymy.

The monolithic interpretation undoubtedly has a problem in accounting for the fact that the political life is in some way happy.

But this same problem also besets the inclusive interpretation. This, of course, differs from the monolithic in its account of *primary* happiness which now includes activity in accordance with all the virtues, moral as well as intellectual. But most inclusivist interpreters agree with those who advocate the monolithic view in excluding contemplation from the life of secondary happiness. So, in the light of the divinity argument, the same problem applies. What makes the purely political life a life of happiness? In sum, there is a problem about how the *secondary* life can be happy if it involves no contemplation; both interpretations broadly agree on the nature of the second life, and so both are vulnerable to the problem.

What we need to resolve this problem is a clearer understanding of the way in which Aristotle qualifies the happiness of the political life. What does 'secondarily' mean? To answer this question I shall turn back to *N.E.* VIII where in the discussion of friendship Aristotle also makes some use of the primary–secondary relation.

Fundamental to the discussion of friendship is the distinction between three types of friendship: virtue, pleasure and utility friendships. Virtue friendship is primarily and especially friendship because the parties love one another for their true selves. The others are inferior forms of friendship because the parties only associate with one another because of some incidental feature, be it pleasure or utility. Nevertheless, for all their limitations, these types still qualify as types of friendship. There is nothing bogus or counterfeit about them. At one point Aristotle actually attempts to protect these inferior forms of friendship from the temptation to demote them to the status of fakes:

For men apply the name of friends even to those whose motive is utility, in which sense states are said to be friendly (for the alliances of states seem to aim at advantage), and to those who love each other for the sake of pleasure, in which sense children are called friends. Therefore we too ought perhaps to call such people friends, and say that there are several kinds of friendship – firstly and in the proper sense that of good men *qua* good, and by similarity the other kinds; for it is in virtue of something good and something similar that they are friends, since even the pleasant is a good for lovers of pleasure. (*N.E.* VIII 4, 1157a25–33)

Here Aristotle is quite self-consciously saving the appearance that the two inferior kinds are still kinds of friendship. He does this by appealing to some kind of similarity between the primary and the secondary. The point seems to be that in virtue friendship the parties love each other because of the good; in the other types it is because of pleasure or utility, which can still be described as good, though only in a qualified way. It is this similarity that holds them together with virtue friendship. He also has another way of binding the types of friendship together. In VIII 4, he says that pleasure friendship is similar to primary friendship because virtue friends derive pleasure from each other's company; furthermore, since they also derive utility out of their company, utility friendship has something in common with them.[22]

Aristotle uses the primary–secondary relation both to explain the superiority of one type of friendship to the others but also to explain why the inferior types are still entitled to be called types of friendship without homonymy. He may relegate friendships of pleasure and utility to an inferior status but he still keeps them from sliding off the scale of friendship altogether. In general, the primary–secondary relation enables Aristotle both to downgrade one thing in favour of another while also allowing the inferior to count as the type of thing that it is.[23] Let us now turn back from friendship to happiness to see whether these aspects of the primary–secondary relation can be used to solve our problem about the two types of happiness in book X.[24]

The conclusion of the divinity argument is that human lives can be happy only to the extent that their activity has 'some similarity' to contemplation (1178b25–7). The next sentence, with its reference to participating in contemplation, leads us to think that the similarity in question is that humans can engage in contemplation intermittently. This explains why a human life of contemplation is called primarily happy. Nevertheless, even a life of purely political or moral action can be called happy by virtue of

[22] 1156b35–1157a3. See also 1157b4–5 and 1158b1–11.

[23] Another feature about the relation is the role of epistemological priority. In order to understand why secondary friendship is still friendship we must grasp what primary friendship is and how the secondary is connected to it. This is not of course to say that two people who have a friendship of pleasure or utility cannot know that they are friends unless they understand the theory of *N.E.* VIII–IX on primary friendship. But what they lack is the further appreciation of why they can only be called friends in a derivative sense.

[24] My concern has been to determine the nature of the primary–secondary relation in *N.E.* VIII. I do not wish to become embroiled in the question of exactly what the relevant similarities are between the different types of friendship and whether they are close enough to do the work Aristotle requires of them. These issues are tackled in Fortenbaugh (1975) 51–7; Walker (1979); Price (1989) 137–48.

a similarity with the primary life. It is still a life of reason, though not of *nous*, but of practical reason.[25] Earlier in X 8, Aristotle has stressed the way in which the political life depends upon practical reason; in fact, it is rational not only because of its use of practical reason but also because the emotions that play so great a role in it can be called rational by virtue of their ability to respond to and obey reason.[26] The secondary life is thus held together with the contemplative life by virtue of similarity.

Now it could be objected that the similarity to which Aristotle needs to appeal in X 7–8 is too superficial to do the work required of it; for Aristotle (unlike Plato) has stressed in the strongest terms the differences between practical and theoretical reason in book VI, and so has made it difficult to appeal to the similarities between the two lives in their use of reason. But this is exaggerated. Aristotle does indeed stress the differences between the two kinds of reason, no doubt for dialectical, i.e. anti-Platonic purposes. Ultimately, however, he still sees them as belonging to the same genus. This was made clear at the end of *N.E.* I 13, 1103a4–6, where he groups together *phronēsis* and wisdom (*sophia*) in the class of intellectual virtues. What holds them together is stated clearly enough at the beginning of *N.E.* VI 3, 1139b15–18:

Let it be assumed that the states by virtue of which the soul possesses truth by way of affirmation or denial are five in number, i.e. art, scientific understanding, *phronēsis*, wisdom (*sophia*), and *nous*; for belief and opinion may be mistaken.[27]

The two types of happiness are therefore connected by similarities rather as types of friendship were. In more or less the same way that Aristotle uses the similarity relation to protect pleasure and utility relationships from disintegrating into cases of friendship by homonymy, he is able to rescue the political life from the effects of the divinity argument in X 8. In both cases he is able to preserve the way many people speak about things despite his own more austere theories.[28] Aristotle does therefore manage to accommodate the appearances set out in book I in his final answer in book X – and this is true on both the monolithic or

[25] My solution here has something in common with Kraut (1989) 58 and Cooper (1987) 211.
[26] *N.E.* I 13, 1102b13–33.
[27] See also *N.E.* VI 2, 1139a26–9.

inclusive interpretations, although the inclusive interpretation is more generous to the political appearance by placing it within the primary form of happiness.

Finally, we should note how Aristotle not only harmonises the appearances, he also attempts to explain them. His aim is not only to preserve the 'that' but to give the 'why' as well.[29] His theory of pleasure as a supervenient end explains why the activities of politics or contemplation are pleasant (they are unimpeded activities); and the epistemological priority involved in the primary–secondary relation can be used to explain why the political life is a life of happiness.

We have seen in the last four chapters how Aristotle follows Plato in limiting his interests to questions about higher learning, but thereafter gives radically different answers. This is clear both from his curt rejection of recollection as well as from the optimistic approach he takes towards the more familiar to us. I have dwelt on this last point at greatest length, bringing out the detailed nature of Aristotle's gradualist theory and the overlap between his views on the methods of science and the methods of ethics. As we now leave the fourth century BC and turn to the third we can see that although many of the traditional claims about the opposition between Plato and Aristotle may be exaggerated, on this score, at least, the boundary between the two is clearly marked.

---

[28] We should not – and need not – exaggerate the similarities between Aristotle's application of the primary–secondary relation in the cases of friendship and happiness. In both cases, he sees the secondary form as inferior to the primary. But where friendship is concerned, there is a greater distance between the primary and the secondary forms. As a result, he is pejorative about the secondary forms of friendship in a way that he is not about political happiness.

[29] See *E.E.* I 6, 1216b36–9 and *N.E.* I 7, 1098a33–4, though in both passages Aristotle seems keen not to overplay the importance of explanation.

# Perception of the universal

In a Delphic parenthesis at *An. Po.* II 19 100a16–b1, Aristotle says that perception is of the universal:

for although you perceive particulars, perception is of universals – e.g. of man, not of Callias the man.[1]

The same point seems to be made at *An. Po.* I 31, 87b28–30:

Even if perception is of what is such-and-such, and not of individuals, nevertheless what you perceive must be a this so-and-so at a place and at a time.[2]

My interest in these lines should be obvious. In my account of *Physics* I 1 and *An. Po.* II 8 in chapter 5, I have argued that, for Aristotle, perception involves some hazy grasp of the universal and to perceive something involves seeing it as a belonging to a certain kind. Now the idea that perception grasps the essence dimly has been proposed as an interpretation of the above lines,[3] and so perhaps I ought to be leaping at them in support of my overall argument; in fact, things are not quite so straightforward.

If the point of these lines is that even the earliest perception instils in us a dim understanding of the universal, the negative part of the parenthesis becomes very difficult to understand. If 'perception is of the universal' means that perception is aware of the universal, then presumably 'perception is not of the particular' means that in perception we are not aware of particulars. But that

---

[1] καὶ γὰρ αἰσθάνεται μὲν τὸ καθ' ἕκαστον, ἡ δ' αἴσθησις τοῦ καθόλου ἐστίν, οἷον ἀνθρώπου, ἀλλ' οὐ Καλλίου ἀνθρώπου.

[2] εἰ γὰρ καὶ ἔστιν ἡ αἴσθησις τοῦ τοιοῦδε καὶ μὴ τοῦδέ τινος, ἀλλ' αἰσθάνεσθαί γε ἀναγχαῖον τόδε τι καὶ ποὺ καὶ νῦν. The connection between the opening of *An. Po.* I 31 and the perception of the universal in II 19 is commonly made. See Barnes (1993) 266, Kahn (1981) 401 and Mansion (1981) 341, note 24.

[3] See Barnes (1993) 266 and Kahn (1981) 405 with note 21.

is very strange. Just because perception may grasp 'man' indeterminately, why should this preclude it from grasping 'Callias' in his particularity? The same problem bedevils an attempt to make sense of the parenthesis by invoking the distinction between 'seeing' and 'seeing as'. On this interpretation Aristotle is saying that although what we perceive is a particular substance, we see it as a such-and-such; we see Callias, but we see him as a man. The objection to this is that although we may indeed perceive the object as a man, sometimes we do perceive it as Callias, yet the parenthesis says quite simply that perception is not of Callias.[4] This is why, much as I would like to, I cannot connect this parenthesis with my account of *Phys.* I 1 and *An. Po.* II 8.[5]

What then is the point of the parenthesis? One thing that is overlooked in the interpretations just mentioned is that the contrast is not simply between particular and universal, but also between the faculty of perception (for which Aristotle uses the abstract noun, *aisthēsis*) and an act of perceiving (now the verb, *aisthanetai*).[6] The same is true of *An. Po.* I 31, 87b29–30 where the contrast is between the faculty of perception, whose object is a 'such-and-such' (i.e. a species-universal), and perceiving, whose object is an individual at a particular time and place.[7] So the contrast is not only between (two ways of characterising) the *objects* of perception, but also between two ways of characterising perception itself. The interpretations so far mentioned fail to do justice to this, yet surely an accurate account of what is

---

[4] Here I am taking issue with Hamlyn (1976) 179 who paraphrases the parenthesis as 'we perceive Callias as a man, not *merely* as Callias' [my italics]. The insertion of 'merely' is quite unwarranted by the text.

[5] In another attempt to make sense of the perception of the universal or the 'such-and-such' some scholars have taken it as indicating what the *De Anima* calls perception of special objects. At *An.* II 12, 424a22–4 we are told 'perception is affected by colour, flavour or sound, but not as each of them is said, but as such-and-such'. Properly speaking, we perceive that there is white, not that the white thing is the son of Diares; that would be 'incidental' perception. But if the parenthesis of *An. Po.* II 19, 100a16–b1 is a reference to this doctrine Aristotle has chosen a most unfortunate example, because 'man' could not rank as a special object of perception; in fact at *An* II 6, 430b29–30 the perception that the white thing is a man is opposed to the perception that there is white, presumably because the former is a case of incidental perception. Of course, the example of 'man' is crucial to the point in II 19 because it is a case of an *infima species*.

[6] The contrast is very clearly marked in the Greek: αἰσθάνεται μὲν ... ἡ δ' αἴσθησις ... (100a17).

[7] Again, this is emphasised by the Greek: the particle γε at 87b30 emphasises the use of αἰσθάνεσθαι rather than ἡ αἴσθησις.

going on these lines must give an important place to both contrasts.

What is the significance of the distinction between perception and an individual act of perception? Perception (*aisthēsis*) denotes the potentiality, in the more precise terms of the *De Anima*, a second potentiality,[8] while the use of the verb 'perceive' (*aisthanetai*) denotes an actualising of that potentiality on a particular occasion with reference to a particular object. The point, then, is that, whereas the object of the exercise of the faculty is a particular, the object of the faculty itself is general. Presumably, he is saying that when trying to characterise the objects of the *faculty* of perception one should not pick out an individual man, but men in general. An individual exercise of the potentiality has as its object an individual, but the potentiality itself is not so focused; it is not a potentiality only for seeing Callias at one particular time and place.[9]

A similar distinction is made in *Met.* XIII 10, 1087a15–25, where Aristotle talks of potential knowledge being of the universal, actual knowledge of the particular. In the case of grammatical knowledge, for instance, there is one type of knowledge that is of As in general, that is general and potential knowledge, and another – particular and actual knowledge – that is of this particular A.[10] He

---

[8] Alternatively, the first actuality. See *An.* II 5, 417a21ff., esp. b16ff.

[9] I am not claiming that *whenever* Aristotle uses the noun 'perception', *aisthēsis*, he must be talking about the capacity to perceive rather than its exercise on a particular occasion; my point is only that he must be doing so in a context such as I 31 or II 19 where he explicitly contrasts the abstract noun 'perception' with the verb 'perceive'. Outside of these contexts he does use 'perception' to refer to the act of perception: see *De Anima* II 5, 417b22.

[10] I am assuming that by the contrast between a 'this such-and-such' (*tode ti*) and a universal (*katholou*) in this passage Aristotle means us to understand the contrast between the individual and the species rather than the species and the genus, as Lear (1987) 169–71 suggests. My reason for disagreeing with Lear is that the distinction made at 1087a15ff. is proposed as the solution to a problem in 1086b16ff. in which the examples of knowing a 'this such-and-such' are knowing that this individual man is an animal (as opposed to knowing that every man is an animal). Lear admits that in the problem 'this such-and-such' means 'particular', but thinks that when Aristotle comes to solve the puzzle at 1087a14ff. substantial form emerges as the 'this such-and-such', and that this is crucial to the solution. But if Aristotle's solution to the problem depends so crucially on a shift in the sense of the expression 'this such-and-such', I find it extremely unlikely that Aristotle would not have differentiated the two senses explicitly at 1087a18. After all, at least part of Aristotle's solution consists in making a distinction between types of knowledge, potential and actual, and here he is quite explicit about making the distinction. If we are to believe that the solution involves a further distinction, one between different understandings of the phrase 'this such-and-such', we should expect him to be similarly explicit.

also gives an example from perception: 'sight sees the universal colour incidentally because this colour is a colour' (1087a19–20). Thus, when at any time we are actually perceiving, what we have perceptual contact with is a particular colour, but perception in general is of the general – what we have perceptual contact with is not, for instance, this patch of colour but of colours in general.[11] Transferred to the example of *An. Po.* II 19, the point is this. When at any time we are actually perceiving, what we have perceptual contact with is a particular substance, e.g. Callias the man, but perception in general is of the general – what we have perceptual contact with is not, for instance, Callias, but men in general.

This reading of the parenthesis does justice to the dual contrast between the two ways of characterising perception and between the two objects. The question now is what relevance it has to the context. The word 'for' that opens the sentence in translation shows that it is meant to explain something in the previous sentence – presumably, how the universal can come to be in the soul (100a16). Perhaps the line of argument is this. In saying that perception is of the universal or of the such and such, Aristotle is reminding us that particulars exist as such and suches. For Aristotle this is true because the universal does not exist in separation from its particulars.[12] The universal is said of the particulars, and the intelligible form is in the perceptible form. It is because of this that perception is able to instil the universal.

If we assume that Aristotle was arguing against Platonic theory,[13] we can see the significance of making this point. Aristotle wants to claim that perception of individuals can give us the universal. But now he needs to answer a distinctively Platonic challenge. For Plato the form is never encountered in sense perception. Hence the need to posit a type of innate knowledge. But on hearing Aristotle dismiss innate knowledge and assert the ability of perception to instil the universal, the Platonist asks how this can be. Aristotle answers that in a sense we do encounter the universal in perception, because the universal is not separate from the individual substances that we actually perceive. So if the objection that Aristotle is fighting off at

[11] Another passage that may support this interpretation is *An.* II 5, 417b22. Here Aristotle says that actual perception is of the particular. The qualification 'actual' perhaps implies that potential perception is of the universal.

[12] A similar point seems to be made at *An. Po.* I 18, 81b4–5.

[13] That Aristotle's target here is Platonic should not surprise us given that the genetic account began as a reaction against Platonic recollection (99b25–7).

*An. Po.* II 19, 100a16 is a Platonically inspired one, we can see how his answer makes sense.

Such a line of argument can also be extracted from a passage in *Met.* I 9. In the course of a whole barrage of arguments against the forms of the Platonists Aristotle objects that the forms can in no way contribute towards knowing the particulars because the forms 'are not even the substance of these; else they would have been in them' (991a12–13). Although Aristotle does not say as much explicitly the reverse will presumably also hold, separation being a symmetrical relation. If we never encounter the form in perceptible objects it does indeed become unclear as to how the senses can be of use in attaining knowledge of it. In Aristotle's view, Plato's metaphysical gulf between forms and particulars opens up an epistemological one as well.

A similar approach can be found in *An.* III 8, 432a3–8:[14]

Since it seems that there is nothing outside and separate in existence from sensible spatial magnitudes, the objects of thought are in the sensible forms, viz. both the abstract objects and all the states and affections of sensible things. Hence no one can learn or understand anything in the absence of sense ...

Here the argument is that since forms must be in perceptible forms there can be no learning without perception. The point contained in the parenthesis of *An. Po.* II 19 is not quite the same but similar. Since particulars exist as such and suches, i.e. since the form does not exist separately, perception can instil the universal in us. *An.* III 8, 432a3–8 says at this point not that perception can instil the universal but that we need perception if we are to learn the universal.

So the background to the parenthesis of *An. Po.* II 19 is that of an argument between Plato and Aristotle over the separation or inherence of forms and of the epistemological consequences. As long as forms are not seen as separated, the idea of perception instilling the universal becomes much less problematic.

[14] See Kahn (1981) 406 for a connection between the perception of the universal in *An. Po.* II 19 and *An.* III 8.

# SECTION THREE

## *Hellenistic Concepts*

# Introduction

From our perspective, there are two especially important developments in the Hellenistic era. The first concerns the issue of ordinary concept formation. As we have seen, this subject had held little interest for either Plato or Aristotle, but with Epicurus and the Stoics things are very different. Epicurus showed a strong interest in explaining the formation of primary concepts – 'prolepses', as he called them – especially the prolepsis of the gods. As for the Stoics, we have already anticipated their interest in ordinary learning when we saw how they developed a stage-by-stage account of how we form concepts in the first seven years of life.[1] That the Hellenistic philosophers were interested in ordinary learning is uncontroversial and not something that needs to be laboured; it can instead be allowed it to speak for itself over the next two chapters. But when set against the Platonic and Aristotelian indifference to the subject, it gives rise to a new question: why was it the Hellenistic period in which the issue was placed on the agenda for the first time? We shall turn to this question on pp. 217–18 below after we have examined the Hellenistic theories in more detail.

The other thing that happened in the Hellenistic era was the emergence of a new theory of innateness. The burden of section I was that Plato's theory of recollection is not be be seen as a theory of 'innate ideas' in the seventeenth-century sense, a theory in which nature, or God, has endowed us at birth with concepts that help to form 'the inner core and mortar of our thoughts', as Leibniz was to put it.[2] This kind of theory attempts to explain ordinary concept formation and so is in a sense far more optimistic than Plato's about the extent to which such innate resources are actually used by most people. Having bestowed such generous

---

[1] See p. 110 above.  [2] *New Essays* I i = Remnant and Bennett (1982) 84.

endowments upon us at birth, Nature does not seal them away under a layer of wax; it ensures that they come to the surface and play a role in our everyday thought. But if we now have a gulf between the seventeenth-century innatists and Plato, we have not cut them off from antiquity altogether, because such a theory of innate ideas, even if it had little to do with Plato, was the invention of some philosopher or philosophers in the Hellenistic era. In this section we shall discover who is to take the credit for this achievement.

The kind of optimistic innatism that I have just outlined appears in the first century BC, in Cicero, *Ends* V 59–60, often considered to be strongly influenced by the syncretist philosopher, Antiochus of Ascalon:

In generating and developing the human body, nature's procedure was to make some parts perfect at birth, and to fashion other parts as it grew up, without making much use of external and artificial aids. The mind on the other hand she endowed with its remaining faculties in the same perfection as the body, equipping it with senses already adapted to their function of perception and requiring little or no assistance of any kind to complete their development; but the highest and noblest part of man's nature she neglected. It is true she bestowed an intellect capable of receiving every virtue, *and implanted in it at birth and without instruction embryonic notions of the loftiest ideas, laying the foundation of its education,* and introducing among its endowments the elementary constituents of virtue. But of virtue itself she merely gave the germ and no more. Therefore it rests with us ... in addition to the elementary principles bestowed on us, to seek out their logical developments, until our full purpose is realized.[3]

Earlier in this book (43) we have been told that children have within them the 'seeds' of virtue which are capable of being developed and perfected with the use of philosophical reason. But the claim in 59 that there are innate notions goes beyond this. The chapter opens with a parallel between the body and the mind. In the case of the body, a distinction is made between the organs that are perfected at birth and those that nature will develop later on. A similar point is made about the mind: the senses have been provided for at birth so that they need little or no help later on, but the highest part of the soul has been disregarded. However, Cicero

---

[3] Trans. Rackham (1931). The Latin for the words I have put in italics is 'ingenuitque sine doctrina notitias parvas maximarum et quasi instituit docere'.

adds a qualification to this last claim saying that the capability for virtue and the notions themselves have been provided (though not their development). Given the parallel that is at work in the chapter this means that the notions, like the senses and the first category of bodily organs are there at birth.[4]

Not only does Cicero think we all have such innate notions, he also shows considerable optimism that they will start to manifest themselves in everyone. In 61 he talks of this happening in young children, pointing to their love of praise and hatred of blame, their memory of favours done and their desire to reciprocate. But these are only nature's first sketches. The picture is filled in at adulthood where the notions are responsible for producing universal consent over a number of general moral principles (62): we all reject baseness and approve of goodness; we all condemn those who spend their youths in debauchery; we all esteem modesty and orderliness in the young. He stresses in 63 that the 'we' here is not the educated and well-brought up but also the uneducated.[5]

We find a similarly optimistic brand of innateness later on, in the writings of the Stoic, Epictetus. First, here he is committing himself to innatism:

We do not come into being with a natural concept of a right-angled triangle, or a half-tone musical interval, but are taught each of these by some technical or systematic instruction, and so those who do not know them do not even think that they know them. Who, on the other hand, has not come into being with an inborn concept of good and evil, fine and base, appropriate and inappropriate, of happiness, of what is proper and what is one's fate, and of what one ought and ought not to do?[6]

Unlike Plato, Epictetus limits his innatism to moral notions and his exclusion of geometrical notions seems like a criticism of the *Meno*.

[4] Crucial is the use of the expression 'implanted in it at birth' (*ingenuit*). In II 124 Cicero's Stoic spokesmen use this same verb when claiming that nature has implanted an instinct to self-preservation in all animals. On the Stoic doctrine being referred to here, the instinct to self-preservation is innate in the strong sense of being prior to any sense impressions. The verb implies something built into a creature as part of its birthright. See also *Ends* V 33.

Cicero seems to adopting a similar approach to *Ends* V 59 in *Laws* I 27 and 59; in I 28, 43 and 62 he claims that we are in some way innately disposed towards justice and society.

[5] For other appeals to general consent in Cicero see *Laws* I 24–5. Cicero is not always so optimistic about the propensity of our innate notions to operate in our lives: in *Tusculan Disputations* III 2 he talks about the way in which these natural sparks can be extinguished.

[6] *Discourses* II 11.2–3: ὀρθογωνίου μὲν γὰρ τριγώνου ἢ διέσεως ἡμιτονίου οὐδεμίαν φύσει

But also unlike Plato, he is considerably more confident about the ability of these innate ideas to come to the surface:

> Prolepses are common to all men, and one prolepsis does not conflict with another. For which of us does not assume that the good is expedient and choiceworthy and that in every circumstance we should go after it and pursue it? . . . So whence does the conflict arise? In fitting prolepses to particular entities . . .[7]

The term 'prolepsis' was a technical term originally introduced by Epicurus and then taken over by the Stoics, but it is doing more or less the same work as the term 'concept' (*ennoia*) in the previous passage. So the innate ideas mentioned in that passage make their way into people's consciousness to such a degree that there is quite widespread consent about them.

By the early centuries AD, then, we find a clear commitment to a very un-Platonic kind of innateness. But was this theory an invention of Antiochus' own, or had it already appeared on the scene? If so, when – in the earlier Stoa, or perhaps even before that? Look at this passage, from *N.D.* I 43–4, where Cicero is reporting Epicurus' account of our concept or 'prolepsis' of the gods:

> For he alone saw, first, that the gods existed, because nature herself had imprinted the conception of them in all men's minds. For what human nation or race does not have, without instruction, some prolepsis of the gods? . . . For since the belief has not been established by any convention, custom or law, and retains unanimous consent, it must necessarily be understood that there are gods, given that we have ingrained, or rather *natural*, knowledge of them. But that on which all men's nature agrees must necessarily be true. Therefore it must be conceded that there are gods.[8]

Where I have used the word 'natural', in the original Latin Cicero uses the word *innatus*, and although this can merely mean 'natural', it can also have the stronger sense of 'innate'. Accordingly, some scholars have taken him to be talking about an innate idea of the gods. Furthermore, the concept is said to give rise to beliefs that

---

ἔννοιαν ἥκομεν ἔχοντες, ἀλλ᾽ ἔκ τινος τεχνικῆς παραλήψεως διδασκόμεθα ἕκαστον αὐτῶν καὶ διὰ τοῦτο οἱ μὴ εἰδότες αὐτὰ οὐδ᾽ οἴονται εἰδέναι. ἀγαθοῦ δὲ καὶ κακοῦ καὶ καλοῦ καὶ αἰσχροῦ καὶ πρέποντος καὶ ἀπρεποῦς καὶ εὐδαιμονίας καὶ προσήκοντος καὶ ἐπιβάλλοντος καὶ ὅ τι οὐ δεῖ ποιῆσαι καὶ ὅ τι δεῖ ποιῆσαι τίς οὐκ ἔχων ἔμφυτον ἔννοιαν ἐλήλυθεν.

[7] *Discourses* I 22.1–3, trans. Long and Sedley (1987) I 248, modified.
[8] Trans. Long and Sedley (1987) I 141, modified.

command universal consent; if so, the concept has not remained buried in people's minds, but plays an active role in their conscious thought. So perhaps it was Epicurus who reinstated innatism after Aristotle, at least for one concept, but gave his innatism the more optimistic turn we found lacking in Platonic recollection. Many scholars, however, have been puzzled by all this. Firstly, most of our other evidence suggests that for Epicurus concepts were empirically derived.[9] Secondly, whether or not he was an innatist, Epicurus was not the sort of philosopher to celebrate the achievements of common sense:

I would rather speak with the frankness of a natural philosopher, and reveal things which are expedient to all mankind, even if no one is going to understand me, than assent to the received opinions and reap the adulation lavishly bestowed by the multitude.[10]

This passage is an accurate reflection of the counter-intuitiveness of Epicurean philosophy. On all the topics that matter most to him – pleasure, death and the nature of the gods – majority opinion is subjected to a sustained barrage of criticism. In the third instance, Epicurus readily admits that people are correct to acknowledge the existence of gods, but is relentless in condemning their belief that the gods interfere in human affairs.

Perhaps, then, Cicero had misunderstood Epicurus on both counts; he was neither an optimist nor an innatist. Another possibility, however, is that the non-Platonic type of innateness first apppeared in the early Stoa, in the philosophy of Zeno, Cleanthes and Chrysippus. Plutarch seems to attribute to the earlier Stoics the view that certain moral notions 'are generated connaturally from principles within us'.[11] If we take this at face value we should see Epictetus' moral innatism simply as Stoic orthodoxy. Moreover, the same might be said of his belief that the innate ideas make their way to most people's consciousness. As well as using Epicurus' term, prolepsis, to refer to basic concepts the Stoics

---

[9] See, for example, Diogenes Laërtius, X 33: 'a prolepsis, they say, is as it were a perception, or correct opinion, or conception, or universal "stored notion" (i.e. memory), of that which has frequently become evident from outside.' (I am following the punctuation adopted by Long and Sedley (1987) I 87–8, because, if the words 'of that which has frequently become evident from outside' (τοῦ πολλάκις ἔξωθεν φανέντος) apply only to the memory, it means that Diogenes is earlier describing a prolepsis merely as a correct opinion, or a perception which is improbable.)

[10] *Vatican Saying* 29, trans. Long and Sedley (1987) I 155.

[11] *Common Conceptions (De Communibus Notitiis)* 1070c-d.

also used the expression 'common notion', presumably to point out the widespread agreement that these notions commanded.

But again, this account of the early Stoa is widely regarded as misleading, if not simply false. On the question of innateness, it seems difficult to deny the empiricism of the Stoics in the light of the fragment to which we referred in chapter 4:

When a man is born, the Stoics say, he has the commanding part of his soul like a piece of paper ready for writing upon. On this he inscribes each one of his conceptions. The first method of inscription is through the senses. For by perceiving something, e.g. white, they have a memory of it when it has departed. And when many memories of a similar kind have occurred we then say we have experience. For the plurality of similar impressions is experience. Some conceptions arise naturally in the aforesaid ways and undesignedly, others through our own instruction and attention. The latter are called 'conceptions' only, the former are called 'prolepses' as well. Reason, for which we are called rational, is said to be completed from our prolepses during our first seven years.[12]

Furthermore, its seems misleading to say that the Stoics had a great respect for common sense. Take the famous Stoic claim that presence or absence of pleasure, health and wealth makes no difference to happiness: the happiness of the sage remains intact even while being tortured on the rack.[13] This is hardly a view to command widespread consent. Furthermore Plutarch, in *Stoic Self-contradictions* 1041f, tells us that Chrysippus almost relished the counter-intuitiveness of some his own views on justice:

For this reason then, owing to the extreme magnitude and beauty of justice we seem to be talking fiction and not on the level of man and human nature.[14]

If the Stoics thought that not only do we have a stock of innate moral ideas but also that, on the whole, they come to the surface,

---

[12] See p. 109 above. Aëtius, IV 11 = *SVF* II 83, lines 13–23, trans. Long and Sedley (1987) I 238, modified: οἱ Στωικοί φασιν· ὅταν γεννηθῇ ὁ ἄνθρωπος, ἔχει τὸ ἡγεμονικὸν μέρος τῆς ψυχῆς ὥσπερ χάρτην εὔεργον εἰς ἀπογραφήν· εἰς τοῦτο μίαν ἑκάστην τῶν ἐννοιῶν ἐναπογράφεται. πρῶτος δὲ ὁ τῆς ἀναγραφῆς τρόπος ὁ διὰ τῶν αἰσθήσεων. αἰσθόμενοι γάρ τινος οἷον λευκοῦ ἀπελθόντος αὐτοῦ μνήμην ἔχουσιν. ὅταν δὲ ὁμοειδεῖς πολλαὶ μνῆμαι γένωνται, τότε φαμὲν ἔχειν ἐμπειρίαν· ἐμπειρία γάρ ἐστι τὸ τῶν ὁμοειδῶν φαντασιῶν πλῆθος. τῶν δὲ ἐννοιῶν αἱ μὲν φυσικῶς γίνονται κατὰ τοὺς εἰρημένους τρόπους καὶ ἀνεπιτεχνήτως, αἱ δὲ ἤδη δι᾽ ἡμετέρας διδασκαλίας καὶ ἐπιμελείας. αὗται μὲν οὖν ἔννοιαι καλοῦνται μόνον, ἐκεῖναι δὲ καὶ προλήψεις. ὁ δὲ λόγος καθ᾽ ὃν προσαγορευόμεθα λογικοὶ ἐκ τῶν προλήψεων συμπληροῦσθαι λέγεται κατὰ τὴν πρώτην ἑβδομάδα.

[13] See Cicero, *Tusculan Disputations* V 73–83 and *Ends* III 42.

[14] Trans. Long and Sedley (1987) I 423.

how is it that the results of their philosophy should clash with common moral sense in this way?

The purpose of the next two chapters is to determine whether the invention of the theory of innate ideas, a theory that was to play so important a role in post-Renaissance philosophy, can be dated back as far as Epicurus, or the early Stoa, or whether it was a later phenomenon. This involves answering two pairs of questions: were either Epicurus or the Stoics innatists, and did either of them manifest a respect for common sense?

Before we move on to these questions we need some background, specifically about the nature of this new item, the prolepsis,[15] that was first introduced into philosophy by Epicurus and then appropriated by the Stoics. Epicurus introduced it to perform essentially two roles – one, as we have seen, as a criterion of truth, the other to account for conceptual thought and our ability to use and understand language.[16] The criterial role is mentioned by Diogenes Laërtius in X 31 (alongside that of perception and feeling), and reinforced in 33. In order to be able to know whether the approaching object is a cow, we need the notion of a cow already in our minds to check the truth of our conjecture. In any dispute, in fact, we should refer the matter to our prolepses for arbitration. This is also the procedure recommended in Cicero,

---

[15] There have been some problems about how to translate the Greek word *prolēpsis*. A common translation is 'preconception' but this has unfortunate connotations of subjectivity or prejudice which are inappropriate given Epicurus' use of *prolēpses* as criteria of truth.

What tends to be overlooked in all this is that 'prolepsis' is an English word in its own right. Its commonest use is to denote a figure of speech, an anticipation, as when someone anachronistically refers to something by a name or description that it did not have at that time. But prolepsis has also been used in the same way as in Hellenistic times: the *OED* quotes two interesting cases, one of which is from Bishop Stillingfleet (an opponent of Locke's over the innateness of ideas, among other issues). He talks of prolepses of the existence of God and of the immortality of the soul. The other case quoted in the *OED* comes from a writer claiming that the idea that nature could create hard shells for no purpose at all is contrary to our prolepsis of the prudence of nature. The first example is of prolepsis as a moral criterion, the second as a natural one. On the use of the word 'prolepsis' in seventeenth-century philosophy, see pp. 238–9 below.

The subject of Epicurean prolepsis has generated a substantial literature. The cast includes Long (1971a), Manuwald (1972), Striker (1990) 147–151, Goldschmidt (1978), Schofield (1980), Asmis (1984), Glidden (1983) and (1985) and Long and Sedley (1987) I 87–101.

[16] According to Cicero, *N.D.* I 43, an Epicurean prolepsis was a preconceived mental picture of a thing without which nothing can be understood, investigated or discussed. On this see Long (1971a) 120.

*N.D.* I 43, and in D. L., X 123–4: our prolepsis of the gods is epistemologically basic in the sense that any belief we have about the gods must be in agreement with it. The prolepsis itself has no further standard upon which to rest.

Most scholars have also assumed that in the *Letter to Herodotus* 37–8 the same point is being made, although Epicurus does not actually use the word *prolepsis*:[17]

First, then, Herodotus, we must grasp the things that underlie words, so that we may have them as a reference point against which to judge matters of opinion, inquiry and puzzlement, and not have everything undiscriminated for ourselves as we attempt infinite chains of proofs, or have words which are empty. For the primary concept corresponding to each word must be seen and need no additional proof, if we are going to have a reference point for matters of inquiry, puzzlement and opinion.[18]

In this passage the prolepsis is to be used to stem a regress of explanations; it itself is in no need of further judgement but is self-evident. The problem that prolepses are being used to solve here is one that Aristotle raises in *An. Po.* I 3: if the explanans is itself always in need of a further explanans then we set up an infinite regress of proofs, which can satisfy only the sceptic. As we saw, Aristotle solves the problem with *nous*, the unmediated grasp of first principles; Epicurean prolepsis may be seen as the alternative solution.[19]

The second role prolepses performed was that of acting as

---

[17] See, for instance, Schofield (1980) 291, 297; Striker (1990) 147; Long and Sedley (1987) I 89.

[18] Trans. Long and Sedley (1987) I 87: πρῶτον μὲν οὖν τὰ ὑποτεταγμένα τοῖς φθόγγοις, ὦ Ἡρόδοτε, δεῖ εἰληφέναι, ὅπως ἂν τὰ δοξαζόμενα ἢ ζητούμενα ἢ ἀπορούμενα ἔχωμεν εἰς ταῦτα ἀναγαγόντες ἐπικρίνειν, καὶ μὴ ἄκριτα πάντα ἡμῖν εἰς ἄπειρον ἀποδεικνύουσιν ἢ κενοὺς φθόγγους ἔχωμεν. ἀνάγκη γὰρ τὸ πρῶτον ἐννόημα καθ᾽ ἕκαστον φθόγγον βλέπεσθαι καὶ μηθὲν ἀποδείξεως προσδεῖσθαι, εἴπερ ἕξομεν τὸ ζητούμενον ἢ ἀπορούμενον καὶ δοξαζόμενον ἐφ᾽ ὃ ἀνάξομεν.

[19] Although this interpretation of X 37 is widely held, there is one voice of dissent. Glidden (1983) 187ff. has argued that we should not be so eager to read the theory of prolepsis into this passage. However, the linguistic parallels between 33 and 37 are quite striking: both the prolepses of 33 and the concepts of 37 'underlie' language (ὑποτεταγμένα τῷ ὀνόματι/τοῖς φθόγγοις) the concepts of 37 are called 'primary', the prolepses of 33 are what 'primarily' underlie language; in both passages we are to 'refer' (ἀνάγειν) our judgements and inquiries (δοξαστόν, δοξαζόμενα and ζητούμενα) to the prolepsis (33) or primary concept (37). A further reason for assuming that 37 is talking of prolepses is that in 37 we are told to 'attend' (βλέπεσθαι) to our primary concept, and the same verb is used later on in the letter to Herodotus in a very similar sense but with prolepsis as its object (72). In the face of such parallels it is difficult to resist the temptation to read the theory of prolepsis into 37.

necessary conditions of forming opinions. We have already seen that in D. L., X 33 a prolepsis is the tribunal to which we refer matters of inquiry and dispute, but the same chapter also makes them necessary for the very framing of the question to be settled:

And what we inquire into would not have been a matter for inquiry had we not had prior knowledge of it. For example, 'Is the thing standing over there a horse or a cow?' For one must already have known the form of a horse and that of a cow by means of a prolepsis.[20]

Furthermore, it is not difficult to infer from this that prolepses are necessary for forming judgements as well as asking oneself questions. They would even be necessary for making mistakes. If, instead of asking Diogenes' question, someone immediately called the object a cow (when in fact it was a horse) they would have needed a prolepsis to fit to their perception. I take it that recognition for Epicurus involves interpreting a sensation by means of this proleptic knowledge.[21]

Associated with this second role is an intimate connection between prolepsis and language. Prolepses are pre-verbal. We are told in D. L., X 33 that it is in virtue of our prolepsis of man that when someone says the word 'man' the form of man appears to us. Later on in the same paragraph Diogenes says that we could never have given something a name unless we had previously known it by way of a prolepsis. This connection between prolepsis and language is reinforced by Epicurus' own words in the letter to Herodotus (D. L., X 37). He tells Herodotus that we must first grasp the things that underlie the words – the primary notion, as he calls it in the next sentence – if, among other things, our words are not to be empty. For example, the word 'man' would be no more than a noise to us if we heard it without already possessing the concept. This is a negative way of making the same point as Diogenes when he says that, on hearing the word, the shape or delineation of the thing appears in our minds.

The two roles that Epicurus made his prolepses perform were maintained when the theory of prolepsis was appropriated by the Stoics. When Diogenes tells us that Chrysippus introduced

---

[20] Trans. Long and Sedley (1987) I 87–8, modified. This passage suggests that Epicurus saw his theory of prolepsis as a response to Meno's paradox. On this see, for instance, Goldschmidt (1978) 156, and Asmis (1984) 49.

[21] Lucretius, IV 379–85.

prolepses into Stoic theory, he says that Chrysippus was adding
them to the list of criteria;[22] that they were also to act as elements
in cognitive psychology is clear from the Aëtius passage that we
have already quoted, *SVF* II 83. We are told how prolepses are
constitutive of human reason. Prolepses are thus the preconditions
or materials for the faculty in virtue of which language and discur-
sive thought are possible, a faculty formed early on in our lives,
before the age of seven (or fourteen). So much is uncontroversial.
Problems begin to arise with the introduction of the expression
'common notion' (*koinē ennoia*). Often this seems to be used syn-
onymously with *prolēpsis*. But it may not be true that all prolepses
were common notions, because there is a suggestion in Plutarch
that Stoics distinguished 'common' from 'special' prolepses, the
latter being technical notions employed within the Stoa itself. If
so, a common notion corresponds only to a common prolepsis.[23]
Throughout the following chapters I shall use the term prolepsis
in the sense of 'common prolepsis' and treat it as equivalent to
'common notion'.

[22] D. L., VII 54.
[23] This point was made by Sandbach (1971) 23–4. See Plutarch, *Common Conceptions* 1084d;
cf. also 1062a.
    Todd (1973) 51–4 has disputed even the equivalence between common notions and
common prolepses. He bases this on his claim that one of our texts, the account of
Stoic physics in Alexander's *De Mixtione* 216.14–218.6 (*SVF* II 473), only makes sense if
we see prolepsis as one kind of general concept and common conceptions as the results
of a further stage of generalisation and abstraction. I am unconvinced by his claims
about this passage and would also point out that most of the ethical texts, which he
does not discuss, treat prolepses and common notions in tandem. I find it unlikely
that there is any significant difference between prolepses and common notions and
shall instead stay with Sandbach's position on this issue.

# CHAPTER 7

# Hellenistic philosophy and common sense

Both Epicurus and the Stoics thought we have natural concepts – prolepses or common notions – whose reliability and clarity acts as the touchstone of all inquiries. In the next chapter we shall ask whether either Epicurus or the Stoics thought that these concepts were, in any sense of the word, innate, or whether they were natural only in the sense of being derived from experience rather than teaching or tradition. In this chapter we shall focus on their attitude to common sense. Plato would have agreed that all of us possess such foundational knowledge; the problem is that it is buried deep in the soul, hidden beneath a layer of wax. Most people are thus quite unaware of the knowledge they possess. The Hellenistics, on the other hand, seem to hold that our criteria are manifest to everyone: how else could they appeal to universal consent as they seem to? So far, then, we seem to have an optimistic theory about nature giving us reliable concepts that are put to work throughout our lives. The problem is that both these philosophers can also be extremely critical of common sense. In other words, they start by showing an Aristotelian respect for our ordinary cognitive resources, and then offer an almost Platonic view about human propensity to error. The point of this chapter is to determine where these philosophers really stood on this issue.

## [1] EPICURUS

There are two reasons for thinking that Epicurus was a philosopher who felt obliged to tailor his theories to common sense. The first, as we have seen on pp. 162–3, comes from Cicero, *N.D.* I 44–5 where Epicurus seems to be using an argument from common assent; anyone who employs such arguments must be impressed by the reliability of common sense. The second arises

from the fact that a prolepsis had to play two separate roles
in Epicurean epistemology: one as a criterion of truth, analogous to Aristotelian knowledge of first principles, the other as
a constituent of ordinary thought. If prolepses are constitutive
of ordinary thought, they must be the property of anyone who
can think, rather than the hard-earned results of philosophical
labour. If they are also criteria of truth, almost everyone has
in their hands, readily available, the foundations of knowledge.
Epicurus must therefore be extremely optimistic about the cognitive achievements of the ordinary person. On the other hand,
we saw how surprising it would be for Epicurus to be described
as a common sense philosopher given his frequent criticisms of
popular belief in matters moral and religious. Epicurus cannot
have it both ways.

In discussing this problem I shall focus predominantly on his
discussion of the prolepsis of the gods. This is partly because our
sources serve us well in this area, but also because theology is an
issue where the problem arises so acutely. Both Epicurus' own
critique of majority opinion in the *Letter to Menoeceus* 124 and the
association between prolepsis and universal assent in *N.D.* I 44–5
are set in a theological context.

One answer to the question of how Epicurus could respect
common intuition while still remaining critical of majority opinion
might be to take a leaf out of Aristotle's book. He allowed the more
familiar to us – the appearances – to act as some sort of check
on the results of an inquiry, but still remained able to criticise
them. This was because although the appearances are roughly
or partially correct they might still be in need of refinement and
definition. It was in this way that Aristotle could be optimistic
about the reliability of the appearances whilst also stressing the
need for philosophical or scientific inquiry and even, on occasion,
impugning common sense.

Unfortunately, Epicurus seems to compound his problems by
ruling out any need for the refinement or articulation of prolepses.
Here are some passages to illustrate his views on the philosophical
significance of definitions:

In the other branch of philosophy, logic, which concerns inquiry and
argument, your master [Epicurus] seems to me unarmed and naked. He
abolishes definitions. He teaches nothing about division and partition.
(Cicero, *Ends* I 22)

Epicurus says that names are clearer than definitions, and indeed it would be absurd if instead of saying 'Hello Socrates' one were to say 'Hello mortal rational animal'. (Anonymous Commentary on Plato's *Theaetetus* 22.39–47)

Epicurus' reasons for this curt rejection of the value of definitions can be gleaned from the following passage:[1]

For if we were going to explain the words known to everybody, we would explain either all or some. But to explain all is impossible, whereas to explain some is pointless. For we will explain them either through familiar locutions or unfamiliar. But unfamiliar words seem unsuited to the task, the accepted principle being to explain less well known things by means of better known things; and familiar words, by being on a par with them, will be uninformative for illuminating language, as Epicurus says. For the informativeness of language is characteristically ruined when it is bewitched by a defintion, as if by a drug.

As we have already seen, words have their meaning because of the user's proleptic knowledge; we have also been told that prolepses are 'clear' (*enargeis*, D. L., X 33). The informativeness of language mentioned at the end of this last passage most likely refers to the fact that when we hear a word a clear prolepsis corresponding to it comes before our minds. The clarity of that concept cannot be improved upon by weaving words together; more words will bring more prolepses before us which are no clearer than the original one. So whatever we think we learn from definitions is purely a verbal affair. They teach us nothing about reality that we do not already know from our proleptic knowledge. In other words, our proleptic understanding of a certain term, '*x*', is sufficient,[2] and nothing is gained by asking the question, 'what is *x*?', because to understand the question is to answer it. Definitional inquiry is a waste of time; you simply inquire into what you already know. For Epicurus, 'words known to everybody' really means what it says.

So our attempt to solve our problem by finding some deficiency in the prolepsis will not work, and Epicurus is now looking even

---

[1] Erotianus, *Vocum Hippocraticarum Collectio* 34.10–20. As with the previous two quotations, the translation is from Long and Sedley (1987) I 99. It is difficult to say exactly how much of this argument is being attributed to Epicurus, but, as Asmis (1984) 39 note 15 has suggested, it seems safe to assume that Epicurus is being represented from '[and] familiar words . . .' to the end of the quotation.

[2] See Cicero, *Ends* II 6: 'who is there who does not know what pleasure is? Who needs a definition to assist him to understand it?'

The argument reported by Erotianus is, of course, reminiscent of Meno's paradox.

more optimistic than Aristotle about the reliability of the concepts available to everyone. Prolepses are not just more familiar to us but more familiar in nature as well. So our problem is exacerbated; if a prolepsis is not only common to everyone but also perfectly clear, trustworthy, and the standard to which we can refer all other judgements about the gods, what are we to make of Epicurus' castigation of common sense?

There are clearly elements of pessimism and optimism in Epicurus' epistemology and they need to be disentangled from each other. Our best hope of doing this lies in the passage in the *Letter to Menoeceus* 123–4 where Epicurus talks disparagingly about ordinary religious belief:

Firstly, consider God to be an immortal and happy being, as the common notion of God indicates, and do not attribute to him anything that is inconsistent with his immortality or inappropriate to his happiness, but believe everything which can preserve his happiness together with his immortality. For there are indeed gods, and knowledge of them is clear, but they are not as the majority of people conceive them to be: for they do not preserve the gods as they conceive of them. It is not the man who denies the gods of the many who is impious, but he who attributes the opinions of the many to the gods. For the claims of the many about the gods are not prolepses, but false suppositions (*hupolēpseis*).[3]

In the last sentence, Epicurus carefully distinguishes between the prolepsis itself and false suppositions or super-added judgements (*hupolēpseis*) which will include the belief that the gods interfere in human affairs. He never denies that the prolepsis is widely shared, let alone that it is true and reliable; it is the super-added judgements that carry all the blame for widespread errors about divine interference. So the common conception of the gods is not simply the prolepsis, but a compound of the prolepsis and false suppositions. This begins to explain how Epicurus is able to castigate some common sense views while at the same time maintaining that the prolepsis is widely shared and reliable: when he impugns common sense he attacks only a part of it, the super-added judgement.

This passage demonstrates that, for Epicurus, pessimism and optimism are held in balance, and are not, as it first seemed, so grotesquely at odds with each other. Epicurean prolepses are natural concepts, formed quite independently of any educational or cultural

---

[3] Trans. Long and Sedley (1987) I 140, modified.

process. This is the source of their reliability and clarity. Epicurus' limited optimism stems from the fact that not only does everyone possess such concepts, the concepts are at work in their ordinary thought. On the other hand, he also thought that we have a dangerous propensity to superimpose a large number of other beliefs on these prolepses and to be unable (without the help of Epicurean philosophy) to distinguish the two elements. These superimposed conceptions are unnatural, cultural accretions and it is their widespread acceptance that explains Epicurus' pessimistic diagnosis of human cognition.

This also tells us more about the Epicurean conception of the nature and role of philosophy. Despite the fact that philosophy does rely upon universally held prolepses, it is still a revisionary enterprise fired by a crusading, almost evangelical spirit. The philosopher's task is not one of definition or clarification of concepts, but one of paring away the false accretions that most people have added to their prolepses, like someone restoring a grossly over-decorated building to its original simplicity. And this is just what Epicurus is trying to do in the *Letter to Menoeceus* 123–4.

But if we wish to maintain that Epicurus can coherently criticise the views of the many, what are we to say of the two reasons for supposing him to be a common-sense philosopher, i.e. someone who feels bound to respect all opinions that command widespread assent? The first was that prolepses were both criteria of truth and common to everyone. On the view we are now developing we can see that neither of these claims, though true, need make him a common-sense philosopher. Everyone may be in possession of the prolepsis of the gods, but there are any number of false beliefs which they can add to their prolepsis. Hence the majority of common-sense views could quite well be false.

However it could be said that Epicurus has by such devices merely landed himself in a worse set of problems. How do we separate prolepses from super-added judgements? The implication of the *Letter to Menoeceus* 123–4 is that what the prolepsis itself is need not be evident to the person who has it. It is evident in an objective sense, i.e. in that it is an entirely accurate picture of the common property of godhood and requires no further clarification. But this does not imply subjective clarity; a prolepsis does not have 'prolepsis' written all over its face. Our prolepses are by no means easy to distinguish from the other, more dubious notions we may have about divine interference in human affairs. In fact, Epicurus' opponents think that these beliefs are as basic as the proleptic beliefs. In Epicurean terms they can think that their super-added judgements are prolepses. But how does he decide which beliefs are part of the prolepsis and which are not?

It looks as if the Epicurean solution to this problem was to embark upon a history of the concepts of primitive man, as Lucretius does in *De Rerum Natura* V. Such anthropological accounts are part of the philosophical programme of separation and are meant to enable us to strip off the layers of sophistication and to reach back to the natural and original primary concept which preceded even language.

But what of the other reason for supposing Epicurus to be a 'common sense' philosopher, Cicero's reference to consensus arguments in *N.D.* I 44–5? Before we tackle the text in detail, we need to establish what Epicurus would have to say about common consent in the light of the theory set out so far. Among beliefs that command common consent there will be true ones – the proleptic beliefs – but also false ones. Where the consent is based on the prolepsis it is a 'natural' consent; otherwise it is merely 'cultural' consent. There is no point therefore in simply appealing to any belief that happens to command common consent until you know which kind it is.

With this distinction in mind let us turn to Cicero, *N.D.* I 44–5. There are actually three sentences in this passage that talk of common consent:

(1) For since the belief [sc. in the existence of gods] has not been established by any convention, custom or law, and retains unanimous consent, it must necessarily be understood that there are gods, given that we have an ingrained or rather natural knowledge of them. (2) But that on which all men's nature agrees must necessarily be true. Therefore it must be conceded that there are gods. (3) Since this is agreed among virtually all – the uneducated, as well as the philosophers – let us allow the following to be agreed: that what I call our preconception, or prenotion [sc. prolepsis], of the gods – is such that we think the gods blessed and immortal.[4]

Sentence (2) does not present any problems for our interpretation because Cicero does not have Epicurus appeal to what

---

[4] Trans. Long and Sedley (1987) I 141, modified: (1) cum enim non instituto aliquo aut more aut lege sit opinio constituta maneatque ad unum omnium firma consensio, intellegi necesse est esse deos, quoniam insitas eorum vel potius innatas cognitiones

people actually say, but what *their nature* agrees to. We have seen how underlying the distinction between prolepsis and super-added judgements (*hupolēpseis*) is a distinction between what is formed naturally and what is the result of cultural accretion. In this passage Cicero is merely inferring the truth of a universally accepted belief in cases where the agreement happens at the level of nature, i.e. derives from a naturally formed prolepsis. That fits in perfectly well with the account we have given of Epicurean prolepsis and in no way commits Epicurus to the argument from every case of universal consent but only 'natural' consent.

We can also interpret sentence (3) as an appeal to a specifically natural consensus. Here he focuses upon the agreement of 'virtually all – the uneducated (*indocti*), as well as the philosophers'. The appeal to the uneducated picks up the reference in the previous sentence to the fact that the belief in the gods is the result not of convention but of nature. It is especially important for Epicurus to focus on those innocent of cultural and educational influence, the *indocti*. This is his best way of getting back to the prolepsis itself. (3) should not therefore be read as trying to get back to a belief that everyone happens to have, regardless of whether that belief is natural or not.

Sentence (1) is more involved. The best way to make sense of it is to see it as the following argument:

[a] the belief in the gods has not been established by any convention, and retains unanimous consent. Hence,
[b] we have a natural knowledge of them. Hence,
[c] it must necessarily be understood that there are gods

Cicero's Epicurean spokesman, Velleius, starts from the claim that belief in the gods does not derive from any kind of cultural origin; from this he infers that these beliefs must be natural; finally he infers from the naturalness of the beliefs that they must be true. The point of the passage is to argue that, as long as the belief in question has a natural rather than a cultural origin, it can be trusted. Now the apparent appeal to universal consent comes in [a]

habemus; (2) de quo autem omnium natura consentit, id verum esse necesse est; esse igitur deos confitendum est. (3) quod quoniam fere constat inter omnis non philosophos solum sed etiam indoctos, fatemur constare illud etiam, hanc nos habere sive anticipationem, ut ante dixi, sive praenotionem deorum ... hanc igitur habemus, ut deos beatos et inmortales putemus.

and it was this that aroused our interest in the sentence. But if my interpretation of the pattern of the argument is correct, the consensus being talked about in [a] is being specifically opposed to the kind of consensus that might arise from convention. It is therefore best understood as a natural rather than a cultural consensus.

So this passage should not be taken as evidence that Epicurus appealed to *any* kind of consensus.[5] Instead it conforms well to the theory that we have attributed to Epicurus, and its appeal to the untutored state of natural beliefs shows remarkable affinities with Lucretius' account of the development of religious belief in V 1169ff. In fact, Cicero has given us a phrase that very neatly encapsulates Epicurus' position: we should follow not what everyone happens to say, but what *their nature* agrees upon. In other words, philosophers can rely upon the naturally formed prolepsis while being able to impugn the super-added judgements as much as need be.

To lend further support to this interpretation let me point out a parallel to these features of the prolepsis theory. Another criterion of truth alongside prolepsis is sense perception, and here too Epicurus wanted both to maintain the absolute reliability of the criterion – 'all perceptions are true' – and to allow for the occurrence of error, in this case, optical illusion. The way in which he tried to keep these two features of his theory in balance is remarkably similar to the way he did so in the case of prolepses.

Take a standard Hellenistic example of an optical illusion: a large and square tower appears round and small at a distance.[6] On Epicurus' theory, a series of films of atoms or 'images' flow from the tower and, coming into contact with a viewer's eyes, produce an impression that corresponds precisely to the actual state of the images upon contact. However, between leaving the original tower and meeting the distant viewer the images collide with many other atoms so that eventually their edges get rubbed away leaving them rounded and smaller. So when a large square tower looks round and small to us at a distance it is not that our eyes are guilty of deception. They are reporting with perfect accuracy on an impression produced in exact accordance with the images. In this sense, all perceptions are true.

[5] For a different approach to this issue see Obbink (1992) 200–2. He rightly sees the problem in attributing to Epicurus any appeal to the argument from universal consent, but mistakenly assumes Cicero is attributing it to him.

[6] See Sextus, *M.* VII 203ff., esp. 208–9.

To make a statement about the tower itself we have to go beyond our perception and make a judgement about the state of the tower itself. We could wait until we have a nearer view and only make the provisional judgement that we have had a view of something small and round. Here we have stopped short at a description of what we have perceived. But if we form the opinion that the object itself is like the well-travelled images we have fallen victim to an illusion, the error being to think that the tower itself is round. This supposition, however, is in no way the work of perception but an act of interpretation on the part of the mind which, on this occasion, happened to be false.

Here we already have a clear parallel to the conceptual illusion about the gods; everyone is in possession of the criterion which is clear and reliable, but they have superimposed a false judgement upon it. There is a further point of analogy; in both types of illusion Epicurus thinks it necessary to labour the distinction between criterion and supposition, and does so because we are apt to confuse the two. In the case of optical illusions this must in turn be explained by the fact that a raw perception and one interpreted by judgement are so alike as to be easily confused. A reason for this might be that in the case of many optical illusions our interpretation of the image is made immediately and unconsciously, an implication of which is that we may never have been aware of the image as it actually is. This in turn can make it very difficult not to confuse the interpretation with the perception itself.[7]

Just this point emerges from Lucretius' diagnosis of optical illusions in IV 379–468. Having just mentioned the illusion where our shadow seems to follow in our footsteps and to imitate our gestures (364–78), he in effect defends the claim that all perceptions are true: 'nor in this [the shadow illusion] do we admit that the eyes are in any way deceived' (379). Our senses tell us whether there is light or dark in a particular place (380–1); the claim that the shadow actually walks behind us is the work of the mind superimposing judgements onto the information provided by the senses.

Although Lucretius stresses the distinction between the criterial

[7] Epicurus commonly called his criteria, including perception, 'clear' (see, for instance, *Letter to Herodotus* 48, 52 and 82). This does not mean, however, that the criterion is clear to us as a criterion (as opposed to a mere opinion); it only means that perception gives a perfectly clear or accurate picture of the images.

information and the super-added judgements only in relation to the example of the shadow, there can be no doubt that a similar point should apply to all the other examples he goes on to list in lines 387–461. After going through all these cases, he concludes (462–8):

We see many other wonderful things of this kind which all try, as it were, to break the good faith of our senses – in vain, since the majority of them deceives because of opinions of the mind which we add ourselves, with the result that things which have not been seen with our senses are thought to have been seen. For nothing is more difficult than to separate out clear evidence from the doubtful things that the mind adds immediately of its own accord.

In optical illusions there is a hidden interpretative component in addition to the reception of sense images. The fact that 'nothing is more difficult' than the separation of these two can only imply a strong similarity between criterion and judgement as far as the subject is concerned. The former is clear (*aperta*) in an objective sense, but, obviously in this context, not in a subjective one. As Lucretius goes on to show in his use of the word 'immediately' (*protinus*, 468), such interpretations are immediate and, presumably, unconscious, hence there was never a moment when we were aware of the raw criterion alone. This would explain why we are tempted to take the interpreted perception as the perception itself. It also shows just how well the diagnosis of optical illusions carries over to conceptual illusions. In both cases the person has the relevant criterion but adds false judgements beyond this and confuses the compound of criterion and judgement with the criterion itself.[8]

This analogy, as well as helping to clarify and perhaps confirm our account of conceptual illusions, recalls the problem for Epicurean epistemology that we discussed above, namely, that of distinguishing in any individual case between criterion and added supposition given that they are so easily conflated. In the perceptual case our best strategy is to take a closer look at the object in question. The analogue of this approach in the conceptual case is the anthropological approach mentioned above. By turning back to the age before culture had developed very far, we are taking, as it were, a closer look at the natural state of human beings.

---

[8] Another parallel can be found in Epicurus' treatment of the third criterion of truth, the feelings. For a discussion of this see Scott (1989).

## [2] THE STOICS

If we were initially puzzled by the Epicurean attitude to universal consent, the Stoic texts present at least as many problems. In some places there seem to be unequivocal appeals to universal consent, in others they seem almost to delight in the counter-intuitive nature of their doctrines. Examples of the appeal to universal consent, concerned with theology, are cited by Sextus in *M.* IX 132–8. The argument of one of them, for instance, is that if there were no gods there would be no science of divination; but it would be absurd to deny something everyone believes in, so the gods exist. And here is Seneca on the use of universal consent in *Letter* 117.6:

We are accustomed to concede much to a prolepsis that all men share; and for us the fact that everyone agrees about something is an indication of its truth. For example, we infer that the gods exist, for this reason, among others – that everyone has implanted in them a notion about the gods, and there is no race so far beyond the reach of laws and customs that it does not acknowledge the existence of at least some kind of gods.9

On the other hand, there is no doubt that they did often attack popular belief and we saw in the introduction to this section how in *Stoic Self-contradictions* 1041f Plutarch gleefully quotes Chrysippus acknowledging the counter-intuitiveness of some Stoic theories. But we do not even have to rely on Plutarch's evidence alone but can turn to the Stoics themselves. For example, in *Letter* 94.52–4, Seneca laments the way in which false opinions and values can affect whole societies and individuals within them. The love of wealth is an example. He describes the way in which each person imbibes the opinion and passes it on. Whole nations are affected and we need a teacher to counteract the influence of common opinion.10 In *Letter* 115.11, Seneca again laments the love of gold and silver and yet says that it is something on which the *whole* people, though at odds on many other things, agree.11

---

9 'Multum dare solemus praesumptioni omnium hominum, et apud nos veritatis argumentum est aliquid omnibus videri. Tamquam deos esse inter alia hoc colligimus, quod omnibus insita de dis opinio est nec ulla gens usquam est adeo extra leges moresque proiecta, ut non aliquos deos credat.'
10 *Letter* 94.52; cf. also 55.
11 For another example in Seneca see *Letter* 82.23 berating the popular fear of death.

This apparent ambivalence to universal consent was made notorious by Plutarch whose work, *On the Stoic Common Conceptions* is entirely devoted to exposing the Stoics' allegedly double standards on this issue. The Stoics, he claims, are committed to salvaging the truth of the common conceptions; yet, time and time again, they produce theories that are totally at odds with common sense. The Stoics then compound their hypocrisy by actually accusing the Academics of overturning the common conceptions.[12]

Now I think that there is ultimately a problem for the Stoics here. The issue is how severe a problem it is. If Plutarch is correct, the Stoics are guilty of a particularly gross contradiction; they infer the truth of a claim from its widespread assent, but deny the truth of several claims which command widespread assent. I shall argue that this is not a fair interpretation of their theory. Instead they had a more cautious Aristotelian approach which allowed them to endorse many aspects of common sense while criticising it in others. Nevertheless their revisions were occasionally such that they went beyond the point where they could be said to be using common sense at all.

There are two questions we need to answer: first, to what extent, if any, were the Stoics really committed to respecting widespread agreement, and second, if they did respect it, how is this connected to the doctrine of common notions? Plutarch's answer to these questions seems to have been that the Stoics did indeed claim to take common consent seriously, so much so that they made it a criterion of truth. This was precisely the doctrine of the common conceptions; these derive their right to be criteria of truth from the fact that they are commonly held. On this view then the Stoics promised to follow the principle 'if most people say $p$, then $p$', but then as often as not said 'most people say $p$, but not-$p$'.

If this is true, so much the worse for the Stoics. But there is a more charitable, and indeed plausible, approach, the crucial point of which is to keep the doctrine of common notions quite distinct from an appeal to universal or common consent. Remember how for Epicurus a prolepsis is formed by some kind of natural process rather than by opinion, culture or convention. Now the Stoics accepted this feature of the theory of prolepsis; what distinguishes our prolepses is the fact that they are formed naturally, without

---

[12] For some references to relevant texts on this issue see Cherniss (1976) 625–30.

attention or teaching. It is from their naturalness that they derive their criterial status. The point of the doctrine of common notions is that there are certain concepts which, because of their origin, can be used as the basis of other inquiries. So far the theory is much the same as in Epicurus.[13]

But why are these notions called 'common'? Simply because, as a matter of fact, they are common; most people, though not necessarily all, would subscribe to them. Their commonness derives from their naturalness. Since they are the result of a natural process, they are likely to belong to the vast majority of people, whereas if they had been the results of a particular culture or of a laborious process of education, they would not be so prevalent. But what is crucial here is that the prevalence of the opinions is not the source of their criterial status. Rather, their naturalness is the joint source of this status and of their prevalence. So the doctrine of common notions amounts to this: some notions derive from nature and so are criteria; also, as a matter of fact, and because of the natural origin, these notions are common. That is all. The doctrine of common notions is kept distinct from an appeal to universal or common consent.[14]

So far there is no substantive difference with Epicurus, for whom prolepses were also both natural and widely held. Where they did differ from Epicurus is in the fact that they did – independently of their doctrine of common notions – make a rather qualified appeal to common consent and they did so in a way very similar to Aristotle. We saw in chapter 6 how Aristotle was not committed to preserving the exact truth of anything that commanded widespread assent. Such opinions might, strictly speaking, be false and confused; yet they might still contain some important element of truth. That is why we should keep our eye on the appearances and try to show how our results in some sense conform to them. A closer

---

[13] On the closeness of Epicurean and Stoic prolepses in this respect see Schofield (1980) 298.

[14] It may now seem mysterious as to why the Stoics should have singled out the epithet 'common' for these notions if their commonness is only indirectly connected to their role as criteria. To give the word 'common' more work to do we could instead take it in the same sense we find it in common reason or *logos*. By this expression the Stoics meant to describe the way in which reason, nature or the *logos* is all-pervasive. Now, if we derive the notions directly from nature or the *logos* itself they can be called common notions. The point of calling them common is to signal their connection with nature and hence their reliability.

look at the texts where the Stoics seem to be appealing to universal
consent will show that they took a similarly moderate approach.

There are three arguments in Sextus, *M.* IX 124–38, usually
attributed to the Stoics, that seem to appeal to universal consent.
The first comes in 124:

if gods do not exist, holiness is non-existent, it being a 'kind of god-ward
justice'; but according to the common notions and prolepses of all men
holiness exists, and because of this a holy thing also exists; and therefore
the divine also exists.[15]

Despite appearances, this argument need not be read as an appeal
to universal consent. The appeal is merely to the common notions
and prolepses which, Sextus adds, are held by everyone. If, as I
have claimed, the doctrine of common notions is distinct from the
appeal to universal consent, this argument is not making such an
appeal either. Sextus is merely reporting that all men have these
notions, not trying to infer something from such universality.

The next passage is 132:

if gods do not exist, neither does prophecy exist, it being 'the science
which observes and interprets the signs given by gods to men'; nor yet
inspiration and astrology, nor divination, nor prediction by means of
dreams. But it is absurd to demolish such a multitude of things which
are already believed in by all men. Therefore gods exist.[16]

This passage which, unlike the previous one, does not mention the
doctrine of common notions, does appeal to widespread consent.
But it can be read as making only a weak appeal. The Stoics are
not saying that whenever there is general agreement about some
opinion, they will accept the opinion as it stands. They are saying
that it would be absurd to demolish so many universally accepted
beliefs. In this case, the accumulation of agreement is so enormous
that it cannot be disregarded. This does not mean either that an
individual case of universal assent could not be treated critically or
that, when it comes to preserving[17] the opinions, they keep them
exactly as they are. 132, then, only offers evidence for a relatively
modest appeal to common consent such as we find in Aristotle.

---

[15] As with the two following passages, the translation is from Bury (1933–49), modified.
[16] The Greek for the penultimate sentence is: ἄτοπον δέ γε τοσοῦτο πλῆθος πραγμάτων
ἀναιρεῖν πεπιστευμένων ἤδη παρὰ πᾶσιν ἀνθρώποις.
[17] This is the opposite, I take it, of 'demolishing' (ἀναιρεῖν). Compare this use of this
word with Aristotle's in *N.E.* X 2, 1173a1.

The third passage comes at 138:

therefore god is a living being; and in support of this argument is adduced also the common conception of mankind, since ordinary people and poets, too, and the majority of the best philosophers bear witness to the fact that god is a living being.[18]

This shows some remarkably Aristotelian affinities. Common opinion is being summoned to come to the aid of an argument that has already been given. This is similar to the way in which Aristotle, in *N. E.* I 8, summoned the opinions of the many and the wise to give support to the more technical argument offered in the previous chapter. Furthermore, in the important passage on method in *Eudemian Ethics*, I 6, 1216b26–35, Aristotle had talked of the appearances as witnesses.[19] We saw how in Aristotle's case none of this implied an unqualified resort to the popular vote, merely the more cautious use of them as supporting an argument already produced. So there is no reason why the same should not be said of the Stoics.[20]

This still leaves Seneca, *Letter* 117.6 which contains the sentence, 'the fact that everyone agrees about something is an indication of its truth'. But again, remember Aristotle's approach to the appearances in *N. E.* X 2, 1172b36–1173a1: 'for we say that that which everyone thinks really is so'. Few scholars use this to undermine the fact that he attempts to extract something of value from the prevalent opinions without endorsing them exactly as they stand. The same can be said for Seneca. We can, moreover, temper the force of his assertion by the following considerations: first, he has just said that his school attaches importance not to to universal consent as such, but to a *prolepsis* that everyone shares.[21] Second, the first example he gives of universal consent is the belief in the gods which is said to be 'implanted in everyone'. The Latin word for 'implanted' is *insita*, and is etymologically related to the

---

[18] ζῷον ἄρα ἐστὶν ὁ θεός, συμπαραλαμβανομένης τούτῳ τῷ λόγῳ καὶ τῆς κοινῆς τῶν ἀνθρώπων ἐννοίας, εἴγε καὶ ὁ βίος καὶ οἱ ποιηταὶ καὶ ἡ τῶν ἀρίστων φιλοσόφων πληθὺς μαρτυρεῖ τῷ ζῷον εἶναι τὸν θεόν.

[19] Elsewhere he uses the laws of certain cities to support his arguments and refers to them as witnesses. See *N.E.* II 1, 1103b2–6 and III 5, 1113b21–6.

[20] For a different interpretation of these passages from Sextus see Obbink (1992) 209–16. He seeks to excise all reference to actual common consent from them. I agree that this can be done in the first case, but find his attempt to do so for the others too forced.

[21] 'praesumptioni omnium hominum'.

word for 'seed', *semen*. This can be connected to another passage in Seneca, *Letter* 120.4, where he refers to naturally instilled concepts as 'seeds given by nature'.[22] Thus a belief that is 'implanted' (*insita*) is not any belief that happens to command universal consent, but one *naturally* instilled. Finally, in the next example, the immortality of the soul, he says 'we are influenced in no small degree by the general opinion of mankind, who either fear or worship the spirits of the lower world'. The first part of this does not imply any rigid commitment to universal consent and the second half cites beliefs that the Stoics did not accept as they stood, but only in a modified way. Thus the context of *Letter* 117.6 gives us good reasons against assuming that the words, 'the fact that everyone agrees about something is an indication of its truth', imply a strong appeal to universal consent.[23]

To recapitulate: the first thing is to keep the doctrine of common notions apart from the appeal to common consent. Common consent is not *per se* one of the criteria of truth. Rather, their doctrine of common notions was very similar to the Epicurean theory of prolepsis in the way in which it derived the status of the notions from their naturalness. Having explicated the doctrine of common notions without any reference to common consent we can then, as an additional point, allow the Stoics a moderate or Aristotelian respect for some opinions commanding widespread assent. But they were not committed to following *all* cases of common consent; and where they did follow it their method did not prevent them from subjecting it to some modification and refinement.[24]

[22] See also *Letter* 73.16 which talks of divine seeds (*semina*) implanted in human bodies. The importance of the etymological connection between *semen* and *insita* has been brought out by Dragona-Monachou (1976) 188.

[23] Although he declares his school's approval of common consent at the beginning of this paragraph, he then indicates that on this occasion he will be using a different approach: 'I shall not appeal to the crowd, as defeated gladiators do; let us engage in close combat with our weapons.' Nevertheless, after engaging in argument for a number of paragraphs, he becomes impatient and wants to return to common notions (18). Compare the way in which Aristotle in *N.E.* I criss-crosses between appearances (chs 4–5 and 8) and argument (ch. 7). See also *E.E.* I. 6, 1216b35–17a10 for a touch of impatience with those who expect arguments when they should be using appearances.

[24] Note that unlike Epicurus, Chrysippus seems to have believed in the value of definitions and to have used the prolepses and common notions as their starting-point. In *Common Conceptions* 1059b-c Plutarch tells us that Chrysippus had articulated each of the prolepses and common notions. The articulation of common notions was also a favourite topic of Epictetus (*Discourses* II 11.18, II 17.7, 10 and 13). On the Stoic articulation of prolepses see Goldschmidt (1979) 161–2.

The reason for their merely cautious approval of common consent rests in their belief that even though nature endows us with prolepses, things can go wrong through culture and education. Reason (which is constituted out of prolepses) can be perverted.[25] The two sources of perversion are contact with other people and the attractiveness of things, i.e. the pleasure they give us.[26] So it may well happen that we originally formed a prolepsis, but then perversion set in and distorted it; or the perversion may have happened while the process of natural formation was going on. When perversion takes place on a grand scale the result will be universal consent of the kind Seneca berates, a sort of 'perverted' consent. Not all notions, however, will be perverted beyond all hope or usefulness:

When someone asked him [Epictetus] what 'general perception' (*koinos nous*) was, he replied, 'Just as a sense of hearing would be called general but that which distinguishes between tones is no longer general but technical, so there are certain things which those men who are not altogether perverted see by virtue of their general faculties.'[27]

This allows for some prolepses to remain unperverted or at least reasonably intact. Here the Stoics would cite the prolepsis of the gods as an example. According to our prolepsis, the gods exist as happy and provident beings; popular belief, to its credit, accords with this.[28] And it will be in these cases that the Stoics will permit themselves an appeal to universal consent. In other words, when Seneca, for instance, speaks approvingly of the use of universal consent, he is not endorsing all appeals to it, only 'natural' consent – those where the process of perversion has not gone too far.

Again we can see parallels with the Epicurean theory of prolepsis. Epicurus thought that although we are all in possession of prolepses we are apt to confuse them with super-added false opinions. On the strength of this I distinguished between natural and cultural consent just as I have distinguished between perverted

---

[25] The texts relating to the perversions that affect reason are collected together in *SVF* III 228–36.

[26] Seneca is presumably discussing the first sort of perversion in *Letters* 94.52–4 and 115.11.

[27] Epictetus *Discourses* III 6.8, trans. Oldfather (1925–8).

[28] Epicurus, they would point out, is mistaken about what the prolepsis is, and therefore excessively harsh in his condemnation of popular belief. See Plutarch, *Stoic Self-contradictions* 1051d-e and *Common Conceptions* 1075e.

and natural consent for the Stoics. The crucial difference between the two philosophies must be that the Stoics thought such cases of perversion less common than Epicurus did. Were this not so it would be very difficult to explain why they made even a qualified appeal to common consent. This then raises the question of why the Stoics took a less pessimistic view about our susceptibility to perversion. The answer most likely lies with their teleology. In a very Aristotelian way they would presumably claim that in most cases nature will ensure that there is something left of the prolepsis and that 'natural' consent is still more common than 'perverted' consent.

Ultimately, then, the Stoics can be acquitted of Plutarch's charge of gross contradiction because they allowed themselves room for the refinement of some common opinions and for the rejection of others. Nevertheless, this still leaves a serious problem for them. It seems that they did depart from the common conceptions more regularly than Aristotle and so exacerbated the problem of how to decide which beliefs are based on nature and which on perversion. We saw above that the Epicureans had the beginnings of a answer in their anthropological approach. But since it is not at all clear what the Stoic analogue was supposed to be, the suspicion will always remain that they did to some extent pick and choose among the common conceptions to suit the doctrines of their own school.

# CHAPTER 8

# *Innateness in the Hellenistic era*

## [1] INNATENESS AND EPISTEMOLOGY

Epicurus and the Stoics appealed to the natural origin of our prolepses to explain their reliability. In doing this they were certainly differentiating prolepses from concepts formed by education or some other cultural process. But if prolepses are formed by a process of nature, that process could be the result either of innateness or merely of sense perception, which was construed by both schools as an essentially natural process. As I have already said, there is considerable controversy among scholars, both in the case of Epicurus and of the Stoics, as to whether any of these natural notions were actually innate notions.

One explanation for the divergence of opinion among scholars is the state of the evidence, especially in the case of Epicurus. But this is not the only one. When we attempted to determine Aristotle's attitude to innatism in chapter 3, we came up against the need to distinguish different varieties of innatism and to clarify the opposition between innatism and empiricism. The same goes for the Hellenistic philosophers. The scholarly controversies that have raged over which, if any, of these philosophers espoused innatism have arisen partly out of a lack of clarity on these philosophical issues. So before turning to the texts, we need to recall some of the points made about the innateness debate in chapter 3.

On pp. 91–3, we drew a distinction between two different ways in which we might talk of innate knowledge, beliefs or concepts: according to one theory these items might be latent in the mind from birth; according to another we have inborn predispositions to acquire them. In this chapter we shall be focusing on the latter variety. As we saw, dispositionalism is not reducible to the thesis that we have mere capacities to acquire knowledge, beliefs or concepts. Instead, the mind is selectively disposed to favour the formation of certain concepts or beliefs, whatever its experience might be. Descartes' analogy of an innate disease helped to clarify this. A child born with an innate propensity to a disease does not suffer from that disease at birth but is preformed to catch that rather than other diseases in the course of its life. Having established dispositionalism as one form of innatism we went on to argue that the difference between empiricism and innatism could be construed as being one of degree. Empiricists need not be committed to denying the existence of any such inborn predispositions, but they keep their number, as well as their role in the explanation of learning, down to a minimum.

There are now two further distinctions we need to mention. Both arise from the way I have just talked indifferently between concepts, beliefs and knowledge being innate. To start with, there is a distinction between a theory of innate concepts and innate beliefs. One might hold that human beings have innate concepts of God or of substance, or one might advocate innate beliefs such as 'God exists'. However, I do not wish to make much of this distinction. We have already encountered it when discussing Aristotle, *An. Po.* II 19 where we argued that the possession of a concept will entail the holding of certain beliefs.[1]

But there is another distinction that is more important, and touches upon the issue of innate *knowledge*. We should distinguish innatism as a psychological thesis from innatism as an epistemological one. What exercised Locke and Leibniz, for instance, was not merely the psychological claim that we are innately disposed to form some beliefs rather than others, but that these ideas or beliefs are epistemologically basic, acting as the foundation of moral, theological, mathematical, or logical knowledge. Leibniz was well aware that mere sense experience could not justify knowledge of necessary truths (as opposed to the particular instances of which experience informs us) and so appealed to an inner source of justification.[2] And Leibniz was not alone in looking beyond the confines of human psychology when he defended innatism. Both Descartes and the Cambridge Platonist Henry More had started out from the idea of God, which is innate, as part of

---

[1] See p. 110 above with n. 5.
[2] *New Essays*, Preface = Remnant and Bennett (1982) 49; see Hacking (1975) 63.

an argument to prove His existence.[3] It was therefore crucial to them that this innate idea was trustworthy. In the realm of practical principles the situation was the same; many of the philosophers and clerics whom Locke had attacked had not been interested merely in claiming innateness for moral principles but, ultimately, in justifying their acceptance.[4]

Now it may seem the issue of innatism is at best only tenuously connected to the justification of knowledge. That we have innate beliefs may be an interesting thesis for the cognitive psychologist, but even if true, is not sufficient to justify those beliefs. Such a psychological thesis has little epistemological power. Even in Locke's time it had been argued that the mere fact of our having an innate belief hardly justifies its acceptance. Our heads could be stuffed with any old rubbish.[5]

How did the proponents of innatism meet such a challenge? Some appealed to the naturalness of innate ideas. Certain principles command universal assent and are prior to experience; hence their ubiquity is not a product of some feature in the world but must proceed from human nature itself, i.e. they are woven into our very fabric as essential and necessary to it. Certain philosophers thought it enough to stop the argument there because for them anything so intrinsic and necessary to human nature should command unquestioning respect. In its reverence for human nature this argument already makes an implicit appeal to providence and so it is not surprising that it sometimes derived explicit support from theology. As these innate principles are part of human nature they must have been put there by the artificer of human nature, God. On such theories, therefore, it is ultimately theology that gives innatism its epistemological clout.[6]

But whatever reasons philosophers gave for their trust in innate principles, the point to stress here is that there is a fundamental choice to be made between psychological and epistemological versions of innatism. The psychological version confines itself to the claim that by the nature of our own minds we are inclined to form certain specific beliefs. The epistemological version goes

---

[3] See Descartes, *Meditation* III and More (1662) 20–1 = Patrides (1969) 226–7.
[4] For a discussion of the strong moral motivation behind the doctrine of innate ideas see Yolton (1956) 28–35.
[5] This objection was made by Parker (1666) 55.
[6] For this approach see, for instance, Herbert of Cherbury in Carré (1937) 126.

beyond this to talk about the justification of certain beliefs, and has often been associated with an unquestioning respect for human nature, if not an outright appeal to theology.

### [2] EPICURUS AND INNATENESS

Now that we have a clearer understanding of the hazards involved in talking about innate ideas and innate knowledge, we can turn back to the conflicting evidence. In Epicurus' case, we found a reason for adopting an innatist interpretation in Cicero's discussion of Epicurean theology in *N.D.* I 44. Here the Epicurean spokesman, Velleius, says quite simply that the prolepsis of the gods is *innata*. This seems to provide strong evidence that at least one prolepsis was innate. On the other hand, Diogenes Laërtius, talking of prolepses quite generally, said that they are memories of what has frequently appeared *from outside* (X 33).

In this section I wish to show that, despite Cicero's use of the word *innata*, we should not interpret Epicurus as being an innatist.[7] I shall start by sketching two interpretations, one that makes Epicurus an empiricist, the other a dispositional innatist about the formation of our concept of the gods.

On the more traditional of these interpretations, the notion of the gods derives from perception. Like all other beings in the Epicurean universe, the gods are entities composed of atoms and are capable of being perceived. All perception depends on thin films of atoms which stream off the object in a continuous series. These films form likenesses of the object and so present a picture of the object to any perceiver with whom they come into contact. When it comes to the perception of the gods, however, the theory is slightly modified because the atoms of which the gods are composed are unusually fine and the normal process of perception is too crude to cope. Instead, the mind perceives the atoms on its

---

[7] There is one reason for attributing innatism to Epicurus that should be rejected at the outset. This is the claim that Epicurus is committed to the theory just for using the word 'prolepsis', whose literal meaning is 'anticipation'. According to de Witt (1954) 145, the only thing a prolepsis could anticipate is experience. Thus every prolepsis has to be prior to experience and for this reason innate. But it is quite clear from Diogenes in what sense prolepses are anticipations: we need them prior to confirming our judgements. This does not exclude the possibility that sense perceptions are themselves prior to prolepses.

own in a process that usually takes place in dreams. As a result of focusing on these dream images the mind forms its first notions of the gods. However, this only brings the mind as far as conceiving of the existence of the gods. When it comes to their other features, such as blessedness and immortality, the mind relies on a process of inference, as I shall set out in more detail below.

A very different interpretation, one which makes Epicurus an innatist about the prolepsis of the gods has recently been proposed by A. A. Long and D. N. Sedley. They argue for an unorthodox view of Epicurean theology in general which uses innatism as an important ingredient.[8] On their view, Epicurean gods do not exist in any substantial or biological way, as is supposed on the previous interpretation, but as thought constructs of human beings. God is really an ethical goal – the paradigm of human happiness. So Long and Sedley deny that we receive films of atoms flowing from actually existent gods. We create the prolepsis starting out from perceptions of happy and long-lived men; we then perform a process of intensification on these images to form a prolepsis of supremely blessed gods. It is in this process, which happens automatically and without any conscious mental effort, that dispositional innatism enters into the story. All human minds have an innate predisposition to process images of human beings in this special way.

To decide between these interpretations we need to focus upon three texts. We have already mentioned Cicero, *N.D.* I 43ff., but there are also detailed accounts of the origin of the prolepsis of the gods in Sextus, *M.* IX 43–7 and Lucretius, V 1161–93. The crucial lines in the Lucretius passage are 1169–82:

already in those days the races of mortal men used to see with waking mind, and even more so in their dreams, figures of gods, of marvellous appearance and prodigious size. They attributed sensation to them, because they seemed to move their limbs and to give utterance with voices of a dignity to match their splendid appearance and great strength. They endowed them with everlasting life, because their appearance was in perpetual supply and the form remained unchanged, and more generally because they supposed that beings with such strength could not be easily overcome by any force. And hence they supposed them to be supremely blessed, because none of them seemed oppressed by fear of death, and also because in their dreams they saw them perform many marvellous acts with no trouble to themselves.[9]

[8] Long and Sedley (1987) I 144–9.  [9] Trans. Long and Sedley (1987) I 139.

In the preamble to this section, Lucretius has promised to explain how human beings came to entertain false notions about the gods (1161–8), but before he does this he provides us, in the passage quoted, with an account of how they came to hold the true beliefs. Just after this passage, at 1183, he launches into an account of how false suppositions about the gods arose. But it is important to note that everything attributed to the gods up to 1183 is correctly attributed, and that two out of the three attributes listed, blessedness and immortality, are explicitly claimed by Epicurus himself to be part of the prolepsis (*Letter to Menoeceus* 123). For the moment, I shall assume that Lucretius is actually talking about how we form the prolepsis, but shall defend this assumption below.

The section quoted can itself be divided into two uneven parts: 1169–71 and 1172–82. In the first, Lucretius merely reports that men saw figures of gods. This is a purely perceptual stage, with no inferential processes involved. In the following lines, however, Lucretius lists all the conclusions men drew from their initial perceptions. There are three inferences: (1) 1172–4, men inferred that the gods had sensation because they moved their limbs and could speak; (2) 1175–8, they inferred that they were immortal from the constant supply of images, from the fact that their forms remained unchanged and from their apparent insuperability; (3) 1179–82, they attributed to the gods supreme blessedness because they had no fear of death and because they performed great deeds without any effort.

There are two things to stress in all this. First – to answer our overall question straight off – the whole process described in 1169–82 is empiricist. Innatism, even of the dispositionalist variety, plays no role in the process. We start out from images of gods given in sensation and then infer, presumably on the basis of our experience of men, the three attributes of the gods. This passage is clearly incompatible with the innatist account proposed by Long and Sedley. Central to their view of the way the prolepsis of the gods is formed is the idea that we start out from images of *human beings* and then intensify these into concepts of gods. But Lucretius is very clear that what first appeared to us were not men but gods (1169–71): 'men used to see with waking mind, and even more so in their dreams, figures of *gods* (*divom*)'. This commits us to an interpretation where the gods actually exist, emitting films of atoms. These are what people receive in the first instance, before they start inferring the attributes of the gods.

The second point concerns the fact that the process through which we attain our prolepsis of the gods involves a string of inferences. This is a point that we might be reluctant to accept, perhaps for two reasons. First, we might ask how an inference can be used to form a prolepsis when prolepses are themselves meant to be the basis of all inferential thinking. Second, Epicurus thought that inferences involve a risk of error, unlike the passive reception of sensations.[10] Yet if a prolepsis is to act as a criterion of truth, how could Epicurus have allowed it to be formed by a process susceptible to error?

Now like it or not, Lucretius makes it clear that inferences are involved in the formation of the prolepsis of the gods. So our response should be not to try and remove all traces of inferential thinking from prolepsis-formation but to disarm the objections. The first objection can be disposed of easily. A single prolepsis is not the basis of *all* reasoning. It is used as a yardstick for the truth of only a certain class of beliefs, in this case those about the gods. There is nothing amiss, then, in forming a higher level prolepsis on the basis of certain sensations and other prolepses (about men) and then using that prolepsis to test the truth of a new set of beliefs.

The second objection, it should be conceded, has considerable force. All we can do is to attempt to weaken the objection somewhat by drawing on the following section, V 1183 ff., where Lucretius talks about the origin of the false beliefs. Here he says that, as a further point, men found themselves unable to explain the regularity of natural phenomena and so 'took refuge' in attributing the explanation to the gods. Once they had done this they inferred that since the gods controlled the movements of the sun and the stars they must live in the place from which such control is possible, the heavens. Now although the second part of this is an inference, the first part, the attribution to the gods of interference in the natural world is presented as a slightly desperate attempt to remedy human ignorance. We are not, as in the previous section, presented with a chain of premises and conclusions, but merely with a causal explanation for a false belief. Lucretius is perhaps deliberately making a distinction between the

---

[10] On the epistemological innocence of perception, see Lucretius, IV 379–86 and Sextus, *M*. VII 209–10.

two kinds of thought process. If he had represented all the acts of reasoning in exactly the same way, he would be extremely vulnerable to the second problem. It cannot be denied that there is still a problem for Epicurus, but at least he has opened up a way of reply and seems to be aware of the need to do so.

Before leaving Lucretius, I need to defend my assumption that he is indeed talking about the formation of the prolepsis of the gods. It could be pointed out that he is not talking about what all humans of all times and places do, but only of what the earliest people did;[11] if he is talking of something peculiar to them, and if prolepses are common to everyone, he cannot be talking about prolepses. Two things need to be said here. First, although it is to early men that he attributes the thought process of 1169ff. there is no reason to say that he thinks *only* early men did this. On the contrary, the words 'already in those days' (*etenim iam tum*, 1169) imply that people have continued to have the same images and that Lucretius is deliberately not limiting the process to early men. Secondly if this is not an account of how the prolepsis is formed, what need would they have of a prolepsis? They could have apprehended all the attributes of the gods without it. Perhaps, it will be replied, they should use the prolepsis to check that they have the right answers. But then why would Lucretius remain completely silent about this especially when it would help his case in distinguishing the process of making correct inferences from the attribution of interference in the world?

Let us now turn to our second text, a passage in Sextus, *M.* IX 43–7 where Epicurean theology is coming under sceptical attack:

The same reply can be made to Epicurus' belief that the idea of the gods arose from dream impressions of anthropomorphic images. For why should these have given rise to the idea of gods rather than outsized men? And in general it will be possible to reply to all the doctrines we have listed that men's idea of god is not based on mere largeness in a human-shaped animal, but includes his being blessed and imperishable and wielding the greatest power in the world. But from what origin, or how, these thoughts occurred among the first men to draw a conception of god, is not explained by those who attribute the cause to dream impressions and to the orderly motion of the heavenly bodies. To this they reply that the idea of god's existence originated from appearances in dreams ... but that the idea of god's being everlasting

11 See Manuwald (1972) 35.

and imperishable and perfect in happiness arose through a process of transition from men. For just as we acquired the idea of a Cyclops ... by enlarging the common man in our impression of him, so too we have started with the idea of a happy man, blessed with his full complement of goods, then intensified these features into the idea of god, their supreme fulfilment. And again, having formed an impression of a long-lived man, the men of old increased the time-span to infinity by combining the past and future with the present; and then having thus arrived at the conception of the everlasting, they say that god was everlasting too.[12]

We can start with the empiricist interpretation, according to which this whole passage acts as a close parallel to Lucretius, V 1169–82. When Sextus talks of the process starting out from anthropomorphic images received in dreams, these images should be taken as images of anthropomorphic gods. Sextus then asks why this need have given rise to the concept of gods rather than that of super-humans. To fill this lacuna in the argument some, he says, append to the first stage a second. As this is the point where blessedness and immortality are apprehended we seem to have a stage corresponding to Lucretius V, 1172–82. Sextus, however, describes this process somewhat differently from Lucretius. The mind arrives at these attributes by a process of 'transition from men'.[13] Just as we form our notion of a giant by enlarging our concept of a human being, we apprehend the attributes of the gods by intensifying the idea of a happy and long-lived human. Now there are some grounds for doubting that this is the inference process described by Lucretius. Sextus does not provide us with a list of conclusions and their premises, but seems instead to be referring to a non-inferential process of concept formation. We merely intensify the concept of a happy and long-lived human into that of a god. This, it might seem, no more involves an inference process than does forming the notion of a Cyclops from an ordinary human being.[14]

It would be wrong, however, to say that Sextus cannot be talking about a process of inference. A way of bringing his account into line with Lucretius' would be to say that in both texts we start out from dream-images of anthropomorphic gods, without 'seeing' their

---

[12] Trans. Long and Sedley (1987) I 143, modified.
[13] 45: κατὰ τὴν ἀπὸ τῶν ἀνθρώπων μετάβασιν.
[14] See Long and Sedley (1987) II 149 who insist that 'transition' (μετάβασις) in this context is a process of concept formation as opposed to one of inference.

blessedness or immortality directly. In both texts we infer these attributes from the nature of the images and from our experience of human beings. This process, however, involves intensifying our notion of a human being. Just as if we saw enormous human-shaped foot-prints in the ground we might infer that a giant had been walking around; but in reaching this conclusion we would have to intensify a notion we already have. The inferences recorded in Lucretius and the 'transition' process mentioned in Sextus can be seen as compatible and complementary aspects of the same process.

Sextus' account is, like Lucretius', empiricist. Crucially, we first form our notion of god from images of actually existent gods. But here again we come into conflict with Long and Sedley. According to them, when Sextus talks of men receiving anthropomorphic images at the beginning of the process, he is referring not to images of anthropomorphic gods, but of human beings. We then follow our innate disposition to intensify this notion into that of the gods by the process of transition. Now it is true that on its its own, the phrase 'anthropomorphic images'[15] mentioned at the beginning need not be taken as referring to images of anthropomorphic gods but merely to those of human beings. Nevertheless, the way Sextus goes on to describe the process of concept formation conflicts with Long and Sedley's interpretation. In their view, all that we are given empirically are images of men; the process of intensification then takes over to form the concept of the gods. But this is not what happens in Sextus' account. When reporting the Epicurean view, he makes it quite clear that the concept of god is formed from dream images *before* the process of transition has even begun: 'the idea of god's existence originated from appearances in dreams'. Only after this point do the Epicureans invoke the process of transition, and this is to explain something beyond the existence of the gods, namely, the attributes of being imperishable and perfect in happiness. In other words, for Sextus, as for Lucretius, the perception of dream images is alone sufficient to instil the Epicurean concept of the existence of god. It is empirically given, not developed by an innate predisposition of the kind Long and Sedley propose.

However, even if we reject their interpretation, there is another

---

[15] ἀνθρωπομόρφων εἰδώλων.

way in which innatism might play a role in Epicurus' account of concept formation. Throughout the Lucretius and Sextus passages the mode of perception that is at work is of a very special kind: not by means of any of the five senses, but by the mind on its own. One important feature of this kind of perception is that when the mind perceives directly in this way, it plays a more active role than the ordinary senses do when they perceive. As we learn from Lucretius, IV 802–4 it has to make a deliberate act of attention to see the images clearly:

And because they [the dream images] are delicate the mind can only see sharply those of them which it strains to see. Hence the remainder all perish, beyond those for which the mind has prepared itself.[16]

If this is the process by which we conceive of the existence of the gods we need to explain why the mind should focus its attention upon the images of gods and why it does not instead just let them pass by unnoticed. One explanation would be that we have an innate predisposition to select these images for closer viewing. Such a position differs from the empiricist interpretation because it uses an innate disposition to explain why we focus upon the images of the gods out of all the myriad images available to us. It also differs from Long and Sedley's interpretation because it admits that there are biologically existent gods emitting images.

But if this is the correct interpretation, it is extremely mysterious that Lucretius should make no mention of an innate predisposition to focus upon images of gods in this passage. There is anyway a much simpler explanation available. Throughout V 1169–82, Lucretius stresses again and again the extraordinary nature of these images. The figures of gods are 'of marvellous appearance and prodigious size' (1170–1); their voices have 'a dignity to match their splendid appearance and great strength' (1173–4); they are also seen to 'perform many marvellous acts with no trouble to themselves' (1181–2). The mind is confronted with myriad images, a small number of which are so extraordinary that it stops to focus intently upon them. The explanation for why we focus on the gods lies in the images themselves, not in any innate predispositions that we are supposed to have.

But if we have found no hint of any innatism in the accounts of

Lucretius or Sextus, we still have to contend with Cicero, *N.D.* I
44 whose claim that the prolepsis of the gods is *innata* might seem
to overturn the empiricist interpretation we have just defended.
However, we should not be so quick to assume that *innata* corresponds exactly to our word 'innate'. Instead we should take it
as meaning 'natural' as opposed to 'conventional'. That Cicero is
using the word in this way is suggested by the context of *N.D.* I 44
where *innata* is specifically opposed to the formation of a concept
by convention or law. The contrast is not one between external and
internal, but between nature and convention. Now the empirical
process described above can be understood as occurring without
instruction (*sine doctrina*) in this sense (as long as the inferences
involved in it are easy enough to make).[17]

Nevertheless, we may be tempted by etymology to insist that
*innatus* means 'innate'. The word is formed from the Latin word
for 'to be born' (*nasci*) and so, one might argue, any concept that
is called *innatus* must be 'born into' us (*in-nascor*). But there are two
reasons for resisting this. First, *innatus* may well be a translation
of the Greek word *emphutos*, which need not mean 'innate' in our
sense, but was sometimes merely opposed to 'taught' (*didaktos*).[18]
Second, the *De Natura Deorum* itself shows Cicero using the word
*innatus* in the weaker sense that I have proposed. In his account of
Stoic theology in *N.D.* II, the Stoic spokesman Balbus says of the
Stoic concept of god almost exactly the same as Velleius said of the
Epicurean: 'for all have it naturally and virtually engraved in their
minds that there are gods' ('omnibus enim innatum est et in animo
quasi insculptum esse deos'12). Now we have yet to see whether
the Stoics believed in innate moral concepts, but their empiricism
about the concept of god does not appear to be in much doubt. Just
before the sentence quoted Balbus has been showing how the existence of the gods is inferred empirically from the possibility of divination. In the immediately following passage he goes on to list various ways in which Cleanthes thought that the idea is formed in
people's minds. All of them are empirical.[19] When the Stoic Balbus

---

[17] For this interpretation of *innata* see Brunschwig (1964) 353.

[18] Dio Chrysostomus, admittedly writing after Cicero but clearly under Hellenistic
influence, talks of the idea of god as being *emphutos* (XII 27 and 39) but goes on
to say that it is formed empirically rather than by teaching or convention (XII 39).

[19] This in fact tallies with our only other direct evidence on this issue. In *SVF* II
1009–10 roughly the same empirical sources are cited as being responsible for our
notion of the gods.

calls the belief in God *innata* he means that it arises by nature as opposed to convention, and there is nothing to stop us saying the same for Velleius' account in the previous book.

Incidentally, although Balbus calls the belief in the existence of the gods 'natural' he is very clear that it is formed by a process of inference. Right at the beginning of his account (II 4) he says that the belief in the existence of the gods needs no words of his:

For when we gaze upward to the sky and contemplate the heavenly bodies, what can be so obvious and manifest as that there must exist some power possessing transcendent intelligence by whom these things are ruled?[20]

This is obviously a reference to the way the existence of the gods is inferred from the regularity of celestial phenomena. A few lines later, in II 5, he contrasts such (inferred) beliefs with mere superstitions calling the former 'judgements of nature' (*naturae iudicia*). The point is that such beliefs, although inferred, are almost *inevitably* inferred; in a couple of later passages he says that no one, or at least no sane person, could fail to draw the inference.[21]

Perhaps, then, when the Epicurean Velleius calls his notion *innata* in *N.D.* I 44 he has a similar point in mind. This would be a way of tying his account in more neatly with Lucretius' and Sextus'. Here, although inferences are involved, they are so obvious and easy to make, that the whole process is automatic and natural in the sense of being unlike education or convention. In other words, given our experience of humans and of gods, it would be inconceivable for us not to make these inferences.

We have found no good reason in any of these texts for attributing innatism to Epicurus.[22] The process by which the prolepsis of the gods is formed is an empirical one and begins from 'what has

---

[20] Trans. Rackham (1933).

[21] See II 15: 'when a man goes into a house ... and observes in all that goes on arrangement, regularity and system, *he cannot possibly suppose* that these things come about without a cause ...' and 19, 'Again, consider the sympathetic agreement, interconnexion and affinity of things: *whom will this not compel* to approve the truth of what I say?'

[22] Another passage from Velleius' account which is relevant to our interests is *N.D.* I 49:

'... the force and nature of the gods is of such a kind that it is, primarily, viewed not by sensation but by the mind, possessing neither the kind of solidity nor the

repeatedly appeared from outside' though, unlike the formation of many other prolepses, the case of the gods involves some inferential process and intensification of other prolepses. This process is, however, automatic and, given our previous experience, inevitable and so appropriately named 'natural'.

The prolepsis of the gods is the only instance where there was a *prima facie* case for attributing innatism to Epicurus. Before concluding, however, we should take note of a passage in Cicero where later Epicureans are said to have differed from Epicurus by making a different concept innate. According to Cicero's Epicurean spokesman Torquatus, Epicurus had said that there is no need to show why pleasure is desirable and pain undesirable; this is apprehended by perception 'just like the heat of fire, the whiteness of snow and the sweetness of honey' (*Ends* I 30). Then he adds:

Some of our school, however, want to transmit these doctrines in a subtler way; they deny the sufficiency of judging what is good or bad by sensation, saying that the intrinsic desirability of pleasure and the intrinsic undesirability of pain can be understood by the mind too and by reason. So they say that our sense that the one is desirable and the other undesirable is virtually a natural and innate prolepsis in our minds . . .[23]

The word that Long and Sedley translate as 'innate' here is not *innatus* but *insitus*, which means literally 'sown in'. But I agree with them that in this passage, the word must mean 'innate'. Epicurus had already held that the desirability of pleasure is something naturally apprehended. Because these later thinkers

numerical distinctness of those things which because of their concreteness he calls *steremnia*; but that we apprehend images by their similarity and succession [transition], since an endless series of extremely similar images arises from the countless atoms and flows to us, and that our mind, by focusing intently on those images with the greatest feelings of pleasure, gains an understanding of what a blessed and everlasting nature is.' (Trans. Long and Sedley (1987) I 142–3 modified).

I take it that Velleius is talking about the way in which the mind perceives dream images by focusing upon them. Some scholars think that the words 'similarity' and 'transition' refer to the method of transition (ἡ καθ' ὁμοιότητα μετάβασις) which they assimilate to the process of concept formation in Sextus, *M.* IX 45: see Philippson (1916) esp. 602–3 and Kleve (1963) 80–96, esp. 91ff. But if Velleius were referring to such a process he would be talking about how the *prolepsis* or *concept* was formed. Yet, as Brunschwig (1964) 356 has pointed out, he is explicitly talking about how the images (*imagines*, i.e. εἴδωλα) are apprehended. In my view, Velleius is merely referring to the continuous succession of similar images.

[23] Cicero, *Ends* I 31. Trans. Long and Sedley (1987) I 112, modified.

are said to have gone beyond this, they must mean that we have
an innate concept. But, as the context makes amply clear, this is
not a position that Epicurus himself had espoused.

## [3] THE STOICS

The debate about whether or not the Stoics were innatists is
perhaps even longer-lived than its Epicurean counterpart.[24] As
we have seen, there can be no doubt that innatism about moral
prolepses is to be found by the second century AD in Epictetus.
The question, though, is whether it can be dated back to the early
Stoa. The text that suggests that it cannot comes from Aëtius
(*SVF* II 83) where the Stoics compare the mind at birth to a blank
piece of paper and seem to have notions inscribed upon it in true
empiricist fashion. It is not surprising therefore that those who
have proposed the innatist interpretation of the Stoa have been
accused of ignoring the evidence of this fragment.

On the other hand, there are two important pieces of evidence
that suggest that the earlier Stoics did propose some limited form
of innatism for moral notions. I referred to one of these passages,
Plutarch, *Common Conceptions* 1070c–d, in the introduction to this
section (p. 163 n. 11). Here it is again, this time a little more
in context. Plutarch is lambasting the Stoics for making wildly
counter-intuitive claims about the nature of the good:

Has there ever been another argument that does greater outrage to
common experience ... and this too in matters concerning good things
and evil and objects of choice and avoidance and things congenial and
repugnant, the clarity of which ought to be more manifest than that
of things hot and cold and white and black, since the mental images of
these are incidental to the senses, entering from without, whereas the
former are generated connaturally from principles within us?[25]

---

[24] Among those who advocate an innatist interpretation are Bonhöffer (1890) 199–207
and Grumach (1966) 72–6. Bonhöffer argued that Stoic prolepses were seminal moral
concepts whose origin owed nothing to sensation; he was then taken to task by
Sandbach (1971) 27–30. Rist (1969) 134 and Todd (1973) 51 have sided with Sandbach;
see also Gould (1970) 64 with n. 2. Pohlenz (1970) I 56–9 and II 33–5 has advocated
a middle path, though still rejecting any theory of innate *a priori* knowledge; a similar
position is taken by Luschnat (1958) 191–2. Other scholars who are more sympathetic
to the innatist cause, or who at least feel uneasy with Sandbach's position are Watson
(1972) 268 and Irwin (1986) 208–9 with n. 5.

[25] Trans. Cherniss (1976) modified: γέγονε δὲ ἕτερος λόγος ὑφ' οὗ μᾶλλον ἡ συνήθεια
παρανενόμηται ... καὶ ταῦτ' ἐν τοῖς περὶ ἀγαθῶν καὶ κακῶν αἱρετῶν τε καὶ φευκτῶν

Here we find a distinction between between the origin of our ideas
of sensible things, such as hot and cold or black and white, and
our moral notions. Those in the former category are called 'incidental', while those in the latter owe their origin to a 'connatural'
(*sumphutos*) source. This contrast is one between something that
is internal and natural to a person or thing, and something
adventitious.[26] Thus concepts of black and white are not part of our
nature, and their formation is contingent upon external factors;
moral concepts, on the other hand, derive from features inherent
in human nature and will be formed whatever our experience.

Now one might attempt to dismiss this passage on the grounds
that the word *sumphutos*, 'connatural', can have the weaker sense of
'untaught'. But whereas such a strategy worked well with the word
*innatus* when we discussed Cicero, *N.D.* I 44 on pp. 198–9 above, in
the present context, it will not do. The concepts of hot, cold, white
and black are also untaught and formed naturally, and yet here,
because they are being contrasted with moral concepts, cannot be
connatural, *sumphutoi*. Thus 'connatural' in this context must mean
more than just 'untaught'. This puts beyond doubt that some kind
of innateness is being talked about in this passage.

However, this passage is still not sufficient to show that the
Stoics were innatists, because Plutarch could be importing an
assumption of his own to attack them, rather than borrowing a
Stoic assumption as part of an argument *ad hominem*. But there is
another passage that suggests that this was a Stoic assumption:
D. L., VII 53. This passage reports the Stoic account of how various
different kinds of concepts are formed:

οἰκείων τε καὶ ἀλλοτρίων, ἃ μᾶλλον ἔδει θερμῶν τε καὶ ψυχρῶν λευκῶν τε καὶ μελάνων
σαφεστέραν ἔχειν τὴν ἐνάργειαν. ἐκείνων μὲν γὰρ ἔξωθέν εἰσιν αἱ φαντασίαι ταῖς αἰσθήσεσιν
ἐπεισόδιοι, ταῦτα δ' ἐκ τῶν ἀρχῶν τῶν ἐν ἡμῖν σύμφυτον ἔχει τὴν γένεσιν;

   I take 'the former' (ταῦτα) to refer not to the good and bad things themselves, but
to the notions of them. This makes a better parallel with the previous clause ('since
. . . without') and means that we do not have to attribute to the Stoa the view that
both good and evil proceed from within the soul; this would contradict the point of
Galen, *The Doctrines of Hippocrates and Plato* V 5.14 and D. L., VII 89 (among others),
which I discuss below on pp. 204–5.

   Also, I am accepting ἀρχῶν as an emendation of ἀγαθῶν, which makes very little
sense in the context. This emendation has been proposed by Kronenberg (1924)
105–6. As an alternative emendation of ἀγαθῶν, Pohlenz (1959) II 34 has suggested
ἀφορμῶν, which, in the light of what I shall argue on pp. 205–7 below, is almost too
good to be true.

[26] This opposition is reinforced by the words 'from without' (ἔξωθεν) and 'within
us' (ἐν ἡμῖν).

It is by confrontation that we come to think of sense-objects. By similarity, things based on thoughts of something related, like Socrates on the basis of a picture. By analogy, sometimes by magnification, as in the case of Tityos and the Cyclopes, sometimes by diminution, as in the case of the Pigmy; also the idea of the centre of the earth arose by analogy on the basis of smaller spheres. By transposition, things like eyes on the chest. By combination, Hippocentaur. By opposition, death. Some things are conceived by transition, such as sayables and place. *The idea of something just and good is acquired naturally (phusikōs).* That of being without hands, for instance, by privation.[27]

The claim could be made that the adverb 'naturally' (*phusikos*), which applies to the formation of certain moral concepts, indicates innateness. Now, at first sight, it is difficult to see why one should read so much into this one word. After all, in the Aëtius passage the same word merely means that some notions come without any instruction or intellectual effort; so why should we not adopt this simpler reading in this passage as well?

The reason why we cannot do this stems from the fact that this is a list of *different* types of concept formation. Thus the first category, confrontation, by which concepts of sensible things are conceived, is distinct from the category of 'naturally' formed moral concepts. One implication of this is that concepts formed by confrontation do not arise 'naturally'. So in this context, 'naturally' cannot merely mean 'untaught', because sensible concepts are untaught. This leaves us with the question of what it is about the formation of moral concepts that merits their being put in a class on their own, and the most plausible answer is that they arise innately. We reach a similar conclusion if we look at the passage the other way round. If the terms 'naturally' and 'by confrontation' denote separate categories of concept formation, moral concepts cannot be formed by confrontation. This supports an innatist interpretation, because, unlike sensible ideas, moral notions do not depend for their formation on whether we happen to confront

---

[27] Trans. Long and Sedley (1987) I 238. The sentence, 'the idea of something just and good is acquired naturally' (φυσικῶς δὲ νοεῖται δίκαιόν τι καὶ ἀγαθόν), could be interpreted in two ways. It could mean that a particular thing is thought to be good; or it could be referring to the formation of a hazy general notion. Though these may seem very different interpretations, I do not think that it matters too much which one we take, because involved in the formation of a notion of a good thing will be some sort of general notion of goodness, which is not very developed. For a discussion of this see Bonhöffer (1890) 200 and Sandbach (1971) 33–4.

specific objects in our environment. We form them independently
of the particular experiences we happen to have. Just as someone
with an innate disposition for a certain disease does not have to
encounter any specific stimulus to catch that disease, but will do so
in the normal course of events, similarly we do not have to rely on
specific occasions to form moral notions, but we are already 'wired
up' to do so.

This passage suggests that for the earlier Stoics there was a
basic division between two kinds of notion: those that come purely
as a result of perception or 'confrontation', whose formation is
determined by what we happen to experience, and those that
proceed from our intrinsic nature. These notions we shall form
whatever our experience.[28] But how can this position be reconciled
with the apparently empiricist account reported by Aëtius? In the
rest of this chapter I shall attempt to show that the Stoics held a
theory of dispositional innatism, and that this theory is compatible
with Aëtius' evidence. I shall bring out the innatism of the earlier
Stoa in two phases, first showing that they thought we have innate
predispositions to virtuous behaviour, second that we have innate
predispositions to form moral notions.

In chapter 3 we saw how for Aristotle humans are not, by and
large, born with any natural predisposition to moral virtue, even
though he did, in passing, allow for innate character traits.[29] The
Stoics, on the other hand, did think that we are naturally inclined
to virtue. Chrysippus, for instance, thought that we are born
with a natural kinship for moral excellence.[30] When challenged
to account for the fact that children do not automatically do what
is morally right, let alone spontaneously develop into fully virtuous

---

[28] Another passage to which innatist interpreters have appealed is Plutarch, *Stoic
Self-contradictions* 1042a, where Chrysippus has been translated as saying that moral
prolepses are innate or inborn. The word used in this passage, however, is *emphutos*;
and although this can mean 'innate', it can also have the weaker sense of 'natural' or
'untaught' (cf. n. 18 above). The context of this passage gives us nothing to determine
either way.

[29] See pp. 103–5 above.

[30] Galen, *The Doctrines of Hippocrates and Plato* V 5.1–8. The word Galen uses throughout
this passage for natural kinship is *oikeiōsis* and, at first sight, it is tempting to connect
this text to the Stoic doctrine of *oikeiōsis*, or 'appropriateness'. But this would be a
mistake. Galen also uses the word to apply to Plato and Epicurus, so it is thoroughly
unlikely that he is referring to an exclusively Stoic doctrine. In this context, his use
of the word *oikeiōsis* implies no more than that one has a natural leaning towards
something. For an interpretation that attributes a limited form of innatism to the
Stoa by appealing to the doctrine of *oikeiōsis* see Pohlenz (1970) 58. In my view, there
are too many problems involved in doing this. See Scott (1988) 141–2.

adults, he claimed that although we do have a natural kinship with virtue, we can be led astray either by the influence of our associates or seduced by the attractiveness of things around us.³¹

In proposing this theory of inborn dispositions to virtue, the Stoics used a special term. Nature, they said, gives us unperverted 'starting-points' or 'resources' (*aphormai*).³² In other contexts, this word can be translated as '[banker's] capital', and implies something which gets a process going or enables one to launch some operation, military or commercial, for instance.³³ If we have starting-points towards virtue given by nature, then, so long as there is no interference from our particular environment or associates, we shall behave in accordance with virtue. The course of our behaviour is innately disposed towards virtue, though, if things go wrong, the other alternative could still happen. Notice how the image of an innate disease would be quite at home in all this. In the natural course of events, that towards which we have a disposition will manifest itself. The essential point is that, behaviourally, we are disposed towards one thing rather than another, so that the idea of innate selection is well to the fore.³⁴

To say that we have natural predispositions to virtue is, of course, somewhat vague, but the Stoics articulated the idea in more detail.³⁵ For them, virtue could be subdivided into four parts, wisdom, temperance, courage and justice. Each of these

³¹ Galen, *The Doctrines of Hippocrates and Plato* V 5.9–15. See above pp. 201–2 n. 25.
³² D. L., VII 89. *Aphormē* can also mean 'repulsion', (the opposite of *hormē*) but this was a sense coined by the Stoics. 'Starting-point' is the more usual meaning and is obviously the sense of the word that is at work in D. L., VII 89.
³³ See Liddell, Scott and Jones (1968) *s.v.* esp. 3 and 4.
³⁴ For another text ascribing the theory of natural predispositions to virtue to the Stoa see Stobaeus, II 65.7 (= *SVF* I 566): according to Cleanthes, human beings have starting-points towards virtue given by nature; a person is bad if these natural resources are left unfulfilled, good if they are perfected. (πάντας γὰρ ἀνθρώπους ἀφορμὰς ἔχειν ἐκ φύσεως πρὸς ἀρετήν, καὶ οἱονεὶ τὸν τῶν ἡμιαμβείων λόγον ἔχειν, κατὰ Κλεάνθην. I am assuming that both halves of the sentence (πάντας γὰρ ... πρὸς ἀρετήν and οἱονεὶ τὸν ... ἔχειν) are to be attributed to Cleanthes. Without the first half, the second would be Delphic in the extreme.)
³⁵ Stobaeus, II 60.9 (*SVF* III 264 p. 65 lines 1–3): ἔχειν γὰρ ἀφορμὰς παρὰ τῆς φύσεως καὶ πρὸς τὴν τοῦ καθήκοντος εὕρεσιν καὶ πρὸς τὴν τῶν ὁρμῶν εὐστάθειαν καὶ πρὸς τὰς ὑπομονὰς καὶ πρὸς τὰς ἀπονεμήσεις. One scholar, Grilli (1953) 116–17, note 1, has attempted to argue that neither from this evidence, nor from Stobaeus, II 65.7, nor from D. L., VII 89 can we claim that the early Stoa used the word ἀφορμή to mean 'starting-point' or 'inclination'; this use only seeped into the Stoa with Panaetius who advocated a life lived 'in accordance with the ἀφορμαί given to us by nature', van Straaten (1962) fr. 96. In the case of the Cleanthes citation, Grilli adopts a punctuation that attributes only the words οἱονεὶ τὸν τῶν ἡμιαμβείων λόγον ἔχειν to Cleanthes; as

virtues is concerned with its own particular province, wisdom with what is one's duty, temperance with one's impulses, courage with endurance, and justice with distribution. Corresponding to this division, humans beings have natural inclinations to the discovery of their duty, to the steadying of their impulses, to endurance and to distribution. This shows how the rather general claim about natural dispositions to virtue will work out once we have a more detailed account of what the different virtues are.

So far, we have shown that the Stoics believed that we have inborn predispositions towards virtue, i.e. that from our own resources we are naturally disposed to favour certain patterns of behaviour. We now need to ask whether this would commit the Stoics to the further step of having such dispositions towards the formation of moral *concepts*. We still have a gap between behavioural and cognitive innatism.

One way of bridging this gap would be for the Stoics to hold a theory of behaviour according to which action presupposes beliefs and notions, so that if we are innately disposed to act in certain ways then we must be innately disposed to form the beliefs and notions necessary for that action. As it happens, the Stoics did embrace just such a theory of behaviour. According to them, if I follow a particular course of action, I assent to the proposition that it is good to do that action. So innate starting-points or resources towards certain patterns of behaviour automatically lead to and imply the formation of beliefs corresponding to this behaviour. If we have innate dispositions to do something, then we have innate dispositions to believe that it is right to do it.[36]

Furthermore, with or without this theory of behaviour, there is still another way in which the innate starting-points or resources to virtue will imply innate dispositions to form ideas. One thing we have an innate disposition towards is the discovery of our duty.

---

I have argued in the previous note, this is implausible. As for D. L., VII 89, Grilli accepts that the thought expressed is Chrysippus' (because of Galen's testimony in *The Doctrines of Hippocrates and Plato* V 5) but he still denies that the term ἀφορμή can be attributed to anyone earlier than Panaetius. His argument is that as both Stobaeus and Diogenes are influenced by Panaetius (*via* Hecato) their use of the word ἀφορμή could easily be a product of this influence. But this is made implausible by the fact that, as he himself admits, 'starting-point' was the normal meaning of ἀφορμή, and was no less available to Zeno, Cleanthes, or Chrysippus, than it was to Panaetius.

[36] See Plutarch, *Stoic Self-contradictions* 1057a.

So take an example of a Stoic duty – honouring your parents.[37] According to the Stoics we are innately disposed or inclined to form the belief that it is right to honour one's parents, and so on for a whole list of duties. If we are innately disposed to form these judgements, presumably we are innately disposed to form the notions necessary for making those judgements. So both the beliefs and the notions will be innate in the Cartesian sense illustrated by the analogy of a congenital disease.

What I am claiming for the Stoics is that, as a result of the starting-points or resources (*aphormai*) given to us by nature, we are disposed both to certain patterns of behaviour, and to the formation of certain ethical ideas and beliefs. So, in the terms of the dispositional innatism that we discussed at the beginning of this chapter, these notions and beliefs are innate.

This theory of innate dispositions to form moral notions fits extremely well with the text that provided the best *prima facie* evidence for the innatist case: D. L., VII 53. If we form moral notions as a result of starting points given by nature, it is very appropriate for these moral notions to be described as arising naturally, in a way that notions of such things as hot or cold are not. Plutarch, *Common Conceptions* 1070 c–d is also well illuminated by the theory of natural starting-points or *aphormai*. Since the Stoics drew a clear distinction between our internal propensity towards virtue and the influence of external factors which can pervert them, it is hardly surprising that our moral sense is said to have its origin from within us.

But what of Aëtius? Surely we can only get away with all this on pain of disregarding him completely. Not at all. What he says is entirely consistent with what many innatists would say. As long as he is talking of the items in our mind of which we are aware, then his account is an entirely reasonable – and uncontroversial – history of what follows what in the stocking of our minds: perception, memory, concept. It does not, in fact, tell us very much. Are we more likely to inscribe this rather than that on the piece of paper? The most interesting thing about it is the active power it gives to the mind. It is this that does the writing: no mere passivity here. We should note that many innatists like More, Cudworth and Leibniz stressed the active power or sagacity of the

---

[37] The example is taken from D. L., VII 108.

mind. So, the notion that the mind in its writing is influenced by aspects of its own nature to form some concepts rather than others is not ruled out.

To clarify the Stoic position, we can compare it with Lockean empiricism. Locke would have protested vigorously at the Stoic claim that, for instance, we are naturally inclined to believe that it is right to honour our parents, and he would have cited instances of parricides to make his case. There is no belief which we are innately disposed to form. This seems to me to distinguish the Stoics from a Lockean empiricism and to commit them to the dispositional innatism prevalent from Descartes onwards. However, this is not to deny the presence of empiricism in other aspects of their thought. Colour concepts, for instance, owe their origin to direct contact with our environment; and even though moral concepts have an intrinsic source, sense experience will play a crucial role in developing them.[38]

Our task, however, is not yet finished, because, in addition to distinguishing dispositionalism from other forms of innateness at the beginning of this chapter, I referred to a more basic distinction between the uses to which these different types of innateness could be put: the psychological and epistemological versions of innatism (pp. 188–90). As yet, I have only brought out the psychological aspect of Stoic innatism which consists in the claim that we are naturally disposed to form certain beliefs regardless of the particular experience we have. What we now need to show is that, just as claims about our environment can be justified by sense observations, the Stoics expected moral beliefs to be trustworthy because they derive from innate dispositions.

It is not in fact difficult to see that the Stoics went beyond psychological innatism and claimed that the moral precepts that arise naturally are the ones we should follow. When Diogenes refers to the starting-points given by nature in VII 89, he stresses that they not perverted. If one asks why the Stoics should think this, the answer lies, of course, in their view that nature is providential. Our inclinations, like our senses, must be trustworthy because

---

[38] This is made clear in Seneca, *Letter* 120.4ff., where he discusses how we attain knowledge of the good. In what we can now take as a reference to innate dispositions to form moral notions, he starts by saying that Nature has given us 'the seeds of knowledge'. But the rest of the learning process involves making analogies based upon repeated observations.

they are given to us by nature, and nature, after all, is nothing if not good.[39]

This line of argument is very similar to the theological support that some of Locke's opponents claimed for their arguments. A benign God would hardly give us perverted ideas or inclinations to form ideas. This similarity becomes even clearer when we remember that for the Stoics nature and God are equivalent,[40] and when we come to Epictetus we frequently see him talking of the natural resources (i.e. perception and prolepses) that God has given us.[41]

There is, however, another way of showing why the Stoics' innate dispositions could not have been perverse. In Galen as well as in a crop of other texts,[42] the Stoics emphasise that evil cannot be natural to us; perversity must result from things extrinsic to us. The reason they insisted on this must have a great deal to do with the fact that they thought that all men are parts of universal nature, or fragments of it.[43] They also thought that virtue consisted in living in accordance with universal nature.[44] If they thought that these off-shoots are endowed with innate tendencies at all, it is far more plausible that these off-shoots are disposed towards rather than against the whole, that is disposed to virtue rather than vice. Thus for the Stoics, the claim that a disposition to form an idea is natural to man does automatically guarantee justification. For other innatists this guarantee may only have been inspired by a pious and rather feeble hope; for the Stoics it is the natural implication of their physical views.

Perhaps we can take this appeal to Stoic physics further and argue that it does not so much show that, *if* they were innatists, they were of the epistemological variety, but *that* they were innatists. For if we are off-shoots of universal nature, it is more likely that we are inclined towards fitting in with it than that we are moral *tabulae*

---

[39] Nature's providence in endowing us with sense perception is implied by Sextus, *M.* VII 259–60 and Cicero, *Academica* I 42.

[40] Cicero, *N.D.* I 39.

[41] Epictetus talks of God-given prolepses in *Discourses* III 5.8. In the same passage he talks of these prolepses as *aphormai*. But for Epictetus, the word *aphormē*, when used in these contexts, has a rather general meaning. It applies not only to prolepses but also to perception (cf. III 6.8 and IV 10.14–15).

[42] *SVF* III 229–36.

[43] D. L., VII 87 and 143.

[44] Stobaeus, II 75.11 – 76.8; D. L., VII 87–9.

*rasae*, that is, utterly indifferent as to whether we are at one with the whole or alienated from it.

We started this section by recalling the distinction between Platonic recollection and a doctrine that was to be prevalent in the seventeenth century, the theory of innate ideas. Unlike Plato's theory, this is one that uses innateness to explain the formation of concepts and beliefs that are operative in everyone's thinking. It also shows strong optimistic tendencies in its view that so many of our ordinary beliefs and concepts are the result of the work of God or Nature. Our task has been to discover who first developed this theory. That it was around in ancient times was clear from Cicero and, later, Epictetus, but there were indications that the theory might have been the work of Epicurus or the Stoics themselves. If we now piece together our conclusions about the Stoics – their qualified optimism about common consent and their dispositional innatism – we can see that the theory was theirs. That the Stoics, rather than Plato, were responsible for such an influential piece of philosophy has for too long gone unnoticed. The point of the last two chapters has been to set the record straight.

*Interim Conclusions*

One of the results of the preceding chapters has been the distinction between two theories of innateness in antiquity, Platonic recollection and Stoic dispositionalism. Some of the differences between these two theories are obvious: for instance, Plato has the soul endowed with memories, the Stoics with dispositions. But a further difference is that, unlike Plato, the Stoics used innateness to account for the formation of common ethical conceptions. In doing so they also gave those notions an enhanced status that they never enjoyed in Plato's theory. It is this difference that will give us the momentum for the next two chapters, where we shall find the Stoic theory to have been the true ancestor of the seventeenth-century theory of innate ideas. However, the distinction between these two theories is not the only conclusion that we have reached so far; and before going on, we need to draw together some of the other strands of the argument as well. This will also be an opportunity to look across the different theories we have discussed and make some comparisons that have so far been left implicit.

## [1] INNATISM AND EMPIRICISM

In the general introduction, I set out three issues around which the study would be structured, the first of them being the distinction between innatism and empiricism (pp. 4–5). At the beginning of section I, I argued that the theory of recollection should be seen as a variety of innatism. When it came to locating the positions of the other philosophers on this issue I had to prepare the ground more carefully. In the first part of chapter 3, I distinguished different types of innatism, singling out the dispositional variety for special attention. I also argued that we need a more subtle account of

the distinction between between innatism and empiricism than is
often given. An empiricist need not say that we have no innate
dispositions at all, as the analogy of the blank slate might suggest,
but that any innate dispositions which we may have play only a
minor role in the development of understanding.

Aristotle is an empiricist of this more cautious variety. He does
make reference to innate dispositions, especially innate character
traits, and talks about an innate *desire* to know, but his accounts
of learning give the emphasis to perception and experience. In
Epicurus' theory, the only place where a *prima facie* case could
be made for innatism arose in connection with the prolepsis of
the gods. But here we have found that there is no evidence of
innate dispositions at work. The Stoics, on the other hand, give
a significant role for such dispositions to play in the formation
of moral concepts, and, if we are in a mood to make diachronic
comparisons, then, we might present Plato and the Stoics as alike
in belonging to the innatist camp. But where Plato thought that
knowledge is already in us, presupposing a prior state of awareness,
the Stoics were content merely to ascribe innate cognitive predispositions to the mind. This comparison makes the Stoic theory
appear as the more economical and, once again, Gregory Vlastos'
phrase, 'Plato's wildest metaphysical flight', comes to mind as the
appropriate epithet for recollection.[1]

On pp. 16–17, when I argued that recollection should be seen as
a variety of innatism, I raised the question of why Plato should
have chosen this variety rather than any other. The more aware
we become of other, more economical theories of innateness, the
greater the urgency of this question. In particular, does Plato
attempt to provide an *argument* for the pre-existence of our innate
knowledge, or does he, once committed to the general thesis of
innatism, simply prefer the theory of recollection because he
already happens to accept the pre-existence of the soul?

Plato does indeed opt for proof rather than assertion, and he
does so in the *Phaedo*. It is, after all, part of his purpose in this
dialogue to argue not merely that we have innate knowledge,
but that this knowledge pre-exists our present life. The crux
of the argument – the point where Plato tries to show that
we must have had the knowledge before we were even born –

[1] See above p. 100

comes at 74e9–75c5. We analysed the argument on pp. 62–3 and need not rehearse it here, but we should remember that it is problematic for a number of reasons. Apart from the fact that the crucial stage of the argument, 74e9–75c5, is extremely condensed, the argument as a whole rests on distinctively Platonic premises about the relationship between particulars and forms and the comparison 'we' make between them. In addition, it depends on two further and very questionable premises: firstly, that our innate knowledge of the forms can only be awakened by the stimulus of sense perception; secondly, that if we are reminded of one thing by something else that resembles it, we must consider how close that resemblance is (74a5–7). For all these problems, however, we should not lose sight of the fact that Plato was aware of the need to provide a proof for the claim that our innate knowledge pre-exists our birth.

But Plato had already proposed the theory of recollection in the *Meno*, where he was not yet committed to the theory of forms or the other assumptions that support the argument in the *Phaedo*. Here the theory is at a tentative stage, as Socrates makes clear at 86b, and it would be a mistake to look for a determinate argument to show why recollection, as opposed to other varieties of innateness, is preferred in this dialogue. But if we cannot find such an argument, we can at least come to understand the considerations that led Plato in the direction that he took.

When we examined the problem that prompted Plato to put forward recollection in the *Meno*, we found him committed to the principle that in an inquiry we should only proceed in terms of what we already know (75d). This 'fore-knowledge' principle re-appears at the beginning of Aristotle's *Posterior Analytics* as the claim that all learning and discovery must derive from pre-existent knowledge, a claim that looks very much like an epistemological version of the Eleatic ban on something coming to be out of nothing. Unable to find the pre-existent knowledge in an earlier point in our present lives, and unwilling to enlist the aid of experience or any other external source, Plato looks further back into the history of the soul itself. In the end, his solution looks as Eleatic as the problem with which he started. There is no point at which knowledge begins.

To the dispositionalist, of course, this will all seem extremely strange. Surely, they will protest, the pre-existent state does not have to be a prior state of knowledge before birth. We are born with dispositions to form beliefs and these can then act as the seeds of future discovery. When asked to explain how these beliefs can have the reliability to play such a role, the dispositionalist may invoke God or Nature to act as their guarantor.[2] Thus, in effect, the theory satisfies the fore-knowledge principle by supplying another being, God, as the pre-existent knower. For Plato, however, it is as if the pre-existent knower cannot be anyone else but the learner himself.[3] There can be no knowledge by proxy; not even God can do our knowing for us.[4]

## [2] LEVELS OF LEARNING

The second concern of this study has been the question of the level of learning that the ancient philosophers were attempting to explain. The argument of section I showed that although Plato does have an account of how ordinary thought is developed, an empiricist one, he spends very little time on it, concentrating instead upon the movement from the ordinary human perspective to the philosophical. Aristotle, following Plato's lead, has equally little to say about ordinary learning and almost all the passages we considered were concerned to tackle scientific or ethical discovery. But one thing that should have become very clear from section III is the strength of the interest that the Hellenistic philosophers showed in the development of mundane concepts. Lucretius, V 1169ff., for instance, is all about the formation of quite primitive notions of the gods; the same goes for Sextus' report in *M.* IX. Similarly, one of the most important pieces of evidence for the Stoic theory of learning, Aëtius (*SVF* II 83), concentrates on the earliest stages of concept formation. This means that it was

---

[2] I said above that dispositionalist theories appear more economical than Platonic recollection. But as they start to invoke divine providence to warrant our innate dispositions, this boast becomes more difficult to make.

[3] Brown (1991) 617–19 has claimed that in the *Meno* Plato does not actually ascribe a previous state of awareness to the soul. But if so, why does Plato refer so frequently to *recollection*? One might answer that such talk is to some extent metaphorical. But this is undermined by 85d6–7 where Plato states explicitly that he understands recollection to be the recovery of the knowledge already in the slave boy (τὸ δὲ ἀναλαμβάνειν αὐτὸν ἐν αὑτῷ ἐπιστήμην οὐκ ἀναμιμνῄσκεσθαί ἐστιν;). The sense of 'recovery' (ἀναλαμβάνειν) here is that of getting *back* (ἀνα-) something that had been there previously. Since what the slave boy will be recovering is a state of awareness there must have been a previous state of awareness to be recovered.

[4] In the myth of the *Phaedrus* human souls do not have their vision of the forms *from* the gods but in company with them.

Epicurus who introduced early learning so conspicuously onto the agenda, and the time has come to find out why.

Epicurus, like the Hellenistic philosophers in general, had a primarily practical aim in philosophy, the attainment of happiness *via* tranquillity, *ataraxia*. The attainment of *ataraxia* is no ordinary achievement, but requires one to travel far beyond the point that most people normally reach. In part, this journey is an epistemological one, because achieving happiness of this kind involves a process of discovery, ridding oneself of false beliefs and understanding, among other things, the true causes of natural phenomena. This in turn involves reaching far beyond the cognitive state of ordinary people. Thus, when Epicurus came to epistemology and to questions about the growth of knowledge, his ultimate aim was, like Plato before him, the explanation of philosophical discovery. His interest in ordinary learning, however marked, was subordinate to his attempt to explain higher learning.[5]

Why should his interest in explaining philosophical discovery have led to an interest in the earliest phases of learning? The answer lies in the theory of prolepsis. Prolepses are criteria of truth and hence the bases of higher discovery. They are formed early on in our lives, naturally and without instruction or any cultural intervention, and it is precisely from this natural origin that they derive their reliability. Now, if they are to play so crucial a role in higher learning we must be given some reason to place confidence in them. We can be, but only so long as we are convinced of the naturalness of their formation. This made it essential to have an account of their formation and, as this takes place early in our lives, that means an account of early learning.

But this still leaves the question of why neither Plato nor Aristotle had much to say about earlier learning. In Plato's case the answer is clear. Like the Hellenistics, his interest in epistemology was motivated, at least originally, by the need to explain a kind of moral development that goes far beyond what most ordinary people achieve in their lives. So questions about learning were primarily about higher learning, and if he were to be interested in early learning it would be because of this prior interest. But why should he? Why go to any trouble to explain the development of mundane concepts if we are not going to use them in the

[5] If, in the Hellenistic period, interest had tranferred wholly to earlier learning, it would be strange to call the Hellenistic theories rivals to recollection, as I have done.

development of philosophical understanding? If the results of ordinary learning are so unreliable, there is little to be gained by giving an account of it.

With Aristotle, however, the question is more pressing. First of all, his range of interests was exceptionally broad; as one who wrote about memory, dream images, divination in sleep, to name but a few of his prodigiously wide-ranging interests, he might be expected to show an interest in early learning, whether or not it helped answer questions about higher learning. Furthermore, one would also expect an account of early learning as part of his interest in explaining higher learning. Since he finds a continuity between later learning and the concepts of ordinary thinking, it is puzzling and somewhat disappointing that we find so little in his works about how ordinary concepts are formed.

It may be that we have simply lost those works in which he did tackle the question. Nevertheless, this problem can be eased by the following consideration. What made it necessary for Epicurus to give an account of early learning was the opposition that he saw between nature and culture. It is the naturalness of our concepts that gives them their reliability and so it becomes crucial to distinguish the role of nature from the accretions of culture in the formation of those concepts. As we have just seen, this process occurs early in our lives, which explains why Epicurus needs to give an account of early learning. For Aristotle, however, the opposition between nature and culture is not nearly as strong; political, cultural and intellectual developments are all facets of *natural* development. Witness the way, for instance, he sees the development of the *polis* as a process of nature;[6] similarly the growth of arts and sciences is a cumulative natural process. As a result, he would not find so strong a conflict between nature and culture in the formation of ordinary concepts, and so would have had less of a need to give an account of our early cognitive development.

### [3] OPTIMISM AND PESSIMISM

The other issue that we raised in the general introduction concerned the relation or distance between two cognitive levels,

---

[6] See *Politics* I 2 where he talks of the genesis of the city state out of families and then villages as something that happens by nature.

the more familiar to us and the more familiar in nature (pp. 6–7). When we first set this distinction out, we saw how there were two extremes with the possibility of different positions lying in between. Plato took a position very close to the pessimistic extreme. That he does so in the cave allegory in the *Republic* should be uncontroversial. What I have argued is that he had already done the same in proposing the theory of recollection, especially in the *Phaedo*. The senses are explicitly said to deceive us, and so the Platonic equivalent of the more familiar to us is something on which philosophy turns its back, wax to be scraped away. In contrast, Aristotle attempted to reinstate a cautious optimism about the reliability of the perspective given in perception and common intuition. This is not to put him at the opposite extreme entirely, or to say that he preserves the appearances just as they stand; he does, however, allow them in a modified form to play an important role in determining the course of the inquiry. In his ethical work, there are certainly moments when this method is stretched to its limit but, overall, he had a good record of putting it into practice. From what we can gather, the Stoics professed to have had essentially the same approach to the appearances as Aristotle. They expected an inquiry to be guided by them without slavishly following them in all details. It does look, however, as if they were less committed than Aristotle to following through these promises in practice. This contrast is epitomised in their different reactions to the case of the virtuous person who is tortured on the rack. Notoriously, the Stoics argued that, even in these conditions, such a person would not lose their happiness. Aristotle, on the other hand, is brusquely dismissive. Just after appealing to the generally held view that a happy life is pleasant – that pleasure and happiness are 'woven together' – he adds, 'those who say that the victim on the rack or the man who falls into great misfortunes is happy if he is good, are, whether they mean it or not, talking nonsense'.[7]

Epicurus' theory of learning has turned out to have a more revisionary aspect than either Aristotle or the Stoics. Admittedly, he did think that each of us has proleptic knowledge that plays a role in our ordinary thinking, and in allowing the foundational

---

[7] See *N.E.* VII 13, 1153b19–21 with p. 143, n. 19 above. For the Stoic view see Cicero, *Tusculan Disputations* V 73–83 and *Ends* III 42. The latter passage directly contrasts Peripatetic and Stoic views.

knowledge to play an active role in this way, he shows more optimism than Plato. But this does not preclude a strong dose of pessimism and ultimately a counter-intuitive philosophy. Despite the presence of the criterion before people's minds they are too apt to superimpose false beliefs and to confuse them with their prolepses.

This brings out certain Platonic tendencies in Epicurus. Both philosophers thought in their different ways that even at the beginning of an inquiry we are in possession of certain items of foundational knowledge. But in the case of the prolepsis of the gods Epicurus moves another step closer to Plato: everyone does indeed have the knowledge already, but it has become overlaid by excrescences which they must remove. This, of course, recalls the analogy of Demaratus' tablet.[8] Both Plato and Epicurus think that the task of philosophy is to strip away a layer of surface accretions and to point to the presence of knowledge that we already possess. For Plato and Epicurus, unlike Aristotle and the Stoics, common sense is normally an obstacle to philosophical progress. As we turn to the question of ancient influences at work in the seventeenth century, it is specifically this difference between Plato and the Stoics, and the way it distinguishes their approaches to innateness, that comes to the fore.

---

[8] Plato's theory differs from Epicurus' in that the layer of accretions completely obscures the message underneath. This difference can be illustrated by using a slightly different analogy for recollection. Imagine a detective cross-examining a group of witnesses. In Plato's case, the detective's task is to catch out the lying witnesses, to reject their story and unearth the truth that is being concealed. The Epicurean task is subtly different. The detective has to take some witnesses who claim to have seen something, and to distinguish what they think they saw from what they actually saw.

# *Innatism in the Seventeenth Century*

# Introduction

The seventeenth century has often been seen as the hey-day of innatism, and not without reason. We have already introduced some of the *dramatis personae* in chapters 3 and 8 – Descartes and Cambridge Platonists among the proponents of innatism, and, as its most famous critic, Locke, whose polemic in the first book of his *Essay concerning Human Understanding* prompted Leibniz to mount an elaborate defence in his *New Essays on Human Understanding*. But the theory was not confined to the philosophically illustrious, but was extremely popular with other thinkers as well, many of whom commanded influence both in universities and in the church. Seeing the foundations of morality and Christianity under threat, these thinkers were especially concerned with moral and religious principles and attempted to reverse the damage by appealing to principles allegedly stamped on our minds by the hand of Nature.

All those who contributed to this debate would have realised that it was one with an ancient pedigree. Leibniz admits as much in the preface of his *New Essays on Human Understanding*:

There is the question whether the soul in itself is blank like a writing tablet on which nothing has as yet been written – a *tabula rasa* – as Aristotle and [Locke] maintain, and whether everything which is inscribed there comes solely from the senses and experience; or whether the soul inherently contains the sources of various notions and doctrines which external objects merely rouse up on suitable occasions, as I believe and as do Plato and even the Schoolmen, and those who understand in this sense the passage in Saint Paul where he says that God's law is written in our hearts (*Rom.* 2: 15). The Stoics call these sources *Prolepses*, that is fundamental assumptions or things taken for granted in advance. (Remnant and Bennett (1982) 48–9)

A casual reader of these lines might be tempted to form an over-simplified picture of the history of the innateness debate: right at the beginning, Plato and Aristotle marked out two clearly opposed positions and thereafter philosophers simply rallied to one cause or the other. But the idea of Plato allowing innatists all and sundry to his ranks should strike us as dubious given the conclusions of the previous chapters. We have seen how innatism in the ancient world had its own distinction between the Platonic and Hellenistic theories, so that Plato would have been ambivalent, to say the least, about welcoming the Stoics into his camp. Furthermore, I have asserted in previous chapters that he would have been equally wary about the seventeenth-century theory of innate ideas. Chapter 9 will substantiate this in more detail. Starting with those philosophers who advocated the innateness of metaphysical ideas and principles, I shall show that questions about the formation of mundane concepts were as much on their agenda as more advanced types of learning. Then I shall turn to the discussion of moral principles and show that it was the Stoic rather than the Platonic form of innateness that held sway.

In chapter 10, I shall turn away from the proponents of innatism to Locke's critique of the theory in the *Essay concerning Human Understanding*. Not surprisingly, his polemic is to some extent a creature of its time and his target is the theory that was then prevalent, the Hellenistic version of innatism. But what is so remarkable is the way in which he attacks this brand of moral innatism. He fastens on to precisely those features of the theory that distinguish it from Platonic recollection – the obviousness of the allegedly innate principles and their widespread acceptance – and uses remarkably Platonic arguments against it. Paradoxical as it may sound, Locke's critique of moral innateness has many features which can only be called Platonist.

CHAPTER 9

# The inner core and mortar of our thoughts

## [1] METAPHYSICAL INNATISM

The best known philosophers to argue for the innateness of metaphysical ideas in the seventeenth century were Descartes, Leibniz and, among the Cambridge Platonists, More and Cudworth. All of them were familiar with Plato's theory of recollection and acknowledge as much explicitly. Sometimes their references are made in a spirit of congratulation, but More, Cudworth and Leibniz are also at pains to register what they see as the essential difference between Plato and themselves, the acceptance or rejection of the literal theory of recollection.[1] What is at issue in this chapter, however, is the further difference about which they are silent, namely that, unlike Plato, they expected a theory of innateness to explain mundane concept formation.

When we discussed Descartes's dispositionalist variety of innatism in chapter 3, we referred to his *Notes directed at a certain Programme*.[2] This was in fact a series of replies to some criticisms of his *Meditations* made by an erstwhile follower, Regius, and it had been in the third *Meditation* that Descartes had espoused the innateness of ideas, thus provoking his opponent's empiricist reply. The *Notes* act as a useful commentary on the third *Meditation*.

Here he is in *Meditation* III announcing a threefold division of our ideas:

[1] For a reference to the *Meno* in Descartes's writings see Adam and Tannery (1897–1913) VIIIb 167. On the rejection of recollection see Cudworth (1678) 693 and More (1651) 88–90. Leibniz voices his criticism of recollection in both the *Discourse on Metaphysics* and the *New Essays*: see Parkinson (1973) 36; Remnant and Bennett (1982) 52, 78–9 and 106. For a discussion of the Cambridge Platonists' objections to recollection see Scott (1990) 85–91 and (1994) 145–7. The story in More's case is complicated by the fact that although he rejects recollection he nevertheless accepts the pre-existence of the soul.
[2] See pp. 92–3.

But among these ideas, some appear to me to be innate, some adventitious, and others to be formed [or invented] by myself; for, as I have the power of understanding what is called a thing, or a truth, or a thought, it appears to me that I hold this power from no other source than my own nature. But if I now hear some sound, if I see the sun, or feel heat, I have hitherto judged that these sensations proceeded from certain things that existed from outside of me; and finally it appears to me that sirens, hippogryphs, and the like are formed out of my own mind. (Haldane and Ross (1911) I 160)

As examples of innate ideas Descartes gives 'thing', 'truth' and 'thought'. But the third *Meditation* is concerned primarily with the idea of God which, as the end of the work makes clear, is also innate, placed within us 'like the mark of the workman imprinted on his work'.[3]

There can be little doubt that when Descartes talks about the innateness of such ideas as God, thing, truth and thought, he means his theory to cover the formation of ideas operative in everyone's thought. This point is confirmed by his subsequent commentary on this passage in the *Notes*, where at one point he talks of the innate ideas as equivalent to our faculty of thinking. A little later on where he focuses upon the idea of God, he makes it very clear that it is an idea shared by almost everybody. He has argued against Regius that if we had no innate ideas, all we would have to implant an understanding of God in us would be statues, pictures or words. He adds 'but that with regard to God we can comprehend nothing beyond a name or a mere bodily effigy, no one can affirm, save a man who openly professes himself an atheist and moreover destitute of all intellect.' This makes it clear that the 'we' is not some select few.[4]

But the application of innateness to ordinary thought may extend wider even than this. In *Meditation* III Descartes used the term 'innate' to describe ideas that were neither adventitious nor fictitious. But in attempting to clarify his position to Regius he went on to use it in a broader sense making all ideas innate:

in our ideas there is nothing that was not innate in the mind or faculty of thinking, except only these circumstances which point to

---

[3] Haldane and Ross (1911) I 170.

[4] Descartes expected innateness to explain higher learning as well, and thought that although everyone uses their innate resources to some degree, they had a great deal more work to do. Innateness is invoked to explain the knowledge of geometry in Haldane and Ross (1911) II 227–8.

experience – the fact, for instance, that we judge that this or that idea, which we now have present to our thought, is to be referred to a certain extraneous thing, not that these extraneous things transmitted the ideas themselves to our minds through the organs of sense, but because they transmitted something which gave the mind occasion to form these ideas by means of an innate faculty, at this time rather than another. For nothing reaches our mind from external objects through the organs of sense beyond certain corporeal movements ... but even these movements and the figures which arise from them are not conceived by us in the shape they assume in the organs of sense, as I have explained at great length in my *Dioptrics*. Hence it follows that the ideas of the movements and figures are themselves innate in us.[5]

In Descartes's view of the physical world there is no place for secondary qualities, nor even for primary ones as we perceive them. In perception, the organ is affected by certain movements from outside; these provide the occasion for the mind to form its own ideas even of the primary qualities, such as shape and movement, and still more of the secondary qualities, like colour and sound. Elsewhere, he compares a perceiver to a blind man with a stick who translates the signals from the stick into representations of his own. Now this aspect of Descartes's theory seems to create problems. We were told in the third *Meditation* that there was a distinction between innate ideas and adventitious ideas. Now, it seems, 'adventitious' ideas are innate as well. I shall not attempt to solve this problem here, because from the point of view of this study we have more than we need. Descartes's innatism, unlike Plato's, extends to many, if not all, of the concepts involved in ordinary thinking.

A similar lack of Platonism on this issue can be found in some of the Cambridge Platonists, particularly More and Cudworth who wrote most extensively about metaphysical innatism. More's most detailed discussion of innate ideas comes at the first book of his *Antidote against Atheism*. As part of his proof of the existence of God he wants to establish the claim that the idea of one omnipotent, omniscient, provident God is natural to man, and this leads him into a discussion of other ideas and beliefs that are natural or innate to human beings.[6] His first examples are from geometry.

---

[5] Haldane and Ross (1911) 442–3. For a discussion of the apparent discrepancy in Descartes's use of the term 'innate' see Adams (1975) 77–8.

[6] More (1662) 17–19 = Patrides (1969) 222–5. His purpose is to show that the idea of God as necessarily existent is just as natural and inevitable as our ideas of mathematical

We have never seen perfect circles or triangles, yet from our own faculties can derive all sorts of demonstrations of necessary truths. Here More seems to be talking about higher learning, but then he goes on to tackle the problem of how certain elements in ordinary human understanding could possibly have arisen if all we had for their explanation was sense experience. Here he is arguing against the claim that relative ideas, such as those of similarity and dissimilarity, are produced by sense experience:

they [*sc.* relative ideas ] may be produced when there has been no *Physicall Motion* nor alteration in the Subject to which they belong, nay indeed when there hath been nothing at all done to the Subject to which they doe accrue. As for example, suppose one side of a room whitened the other not touch'd or medled with, this other has thus become unlike, and hath the notion of *Dissimile* necessarily belonging to it, although there has nothing at all been done thereunto.[7]

If there is no physical impression from without, the ideas must proceed from within the mind. It is clear from the example that he is discussing ideas used in mundane judgements, exactly as defenders of the 'Kantian' interpretation thought Plato was doing in the *Phaedo*.

A similar set of interests can be attributed to Cudworth. In his *Treatise on Eternal and Immutable Morality*, he attempts to establish that moral concepts are unchanging, and hence not dependent on matter or anything else that is itself subject to change. In the course of this he investigates the nature of the human mind where these concepts are lodged and finds it to be, not a blank tablet, but a source of innate truth. Like More, he insists that relational ideas are innate but also includes what he calls 'cognitive' ideas, such as wisdom or folly.[8] He then goes further than More had done in the *Antidote* by arguing that even in the formation of sensible ideas there has to be a contribution from the mind.[9]

But to see the contrast between Plato's and Cudworth's interests at its clearest, look at the following passage where Cudworth is arguing that our universal notions or 'intelligible ideas' must be innate:

and logical notions. Therefore, we should accord our idea of God as much respect as we accord our idea of the perfect circle.

[7] More (1662) 16 = Patrides (1969) 224–5.
[8] Cudworth (1731) 148–9.
[9] Cudworth (1731) 214–9. There are clear parallels here with Descartes's position in Haldane and Ross (1911) I 442–3.

It is an error that they suppose the intelligible ideas to be made out of these sensible ideas and phantasms thus impressed from without in corporeal manner likewise by abstraction or separation of the individuating circumstances, as it were by the hewing off certain chips from them, or by hammering beating or anvelling of them into thin intelligible ideas: as if solid and massy gold should be beaten out into thin leaf gold.

To which purpose they have ingeniously set up and contrived an active understanding, like a smith or carpenter, with his shop or forge in the brain, furnished with all necessary tools and instruments for such a work. Where I only would demand of such philosophers, whether their so expert smith or architect, the active understanding, when he goes about his work, doth know what he is to do with these phantasms beforehand, what he is to make of them, and unto what shape to bring them? If he do not, he must needs be a bungling workman; but if he do, he is prevented in his design and understanding, his work being done already to his hand: for he must needs have the intelligible idea of what he knows or understands already within himself; and therefore now to what purpose should he use his tools, and go about to hew and hammer and anvil these phantasms into thin and subtle intelligible ideas, meerly to make out what he hath already, and which was native and domestick to him?[10]

Here Cudworth is arguing that universal notions must be innate, and he does so by deploying a relative of Meno's paradox. But notice how different Cudworth's problem is from Plato's. When discussing the *Meno* I argued that there were no anxieties about ordinary concept formation; rather, the priority of definition gave rise to a problem about how we could ever transcend our opinions and convert them into knowledge (pp. 27–9). Cudworth on the other hand is doing exactly what the 'Kantian' interpretation would have expected Plato to do; he attempts to explain how human beings ever get from their first sense impressions towards the formation of mundane concepts.[11] That Cudworth should be approaching the topic with these interests does in fact have a

---

[10] Cudworth (1731) 220–1. Compare, more recently, the challenge to the empirical abstractionist view of concept formation which holds that the similarity of things emerges by abstraction from the things themselves. Such abstraction however presupposes a concept according to which abstraction will take place. See Geach (1957) chs. 6–11 and Sugarman (1974) 5.

[11] Cudworth does go on to invoke innateness to explain higher learning in Cudworth (1731) 226–7 where he turns to consider the acquisition of 'universal axiomatic truth'.

Another passage that brings out Cudworth's interest in the formation of ordinary concepts comes in Cudworth (1678) 693 where he attempts to demolish the claim that the notion of God was originally invented by astute politicians as a means of subduing their subjects. He objects first that this theory cannot explain why the concept of God is so similar in all places, and then asks how these politicians could impose the idea

Platonic explanation, but not one connected with the *Meno* or the *Phaedo*. A very interesting fact about the *Treatise* is that it strongly influenced by the *Theaetetus*, whose argument it follows with remarkable closeness; and in the course of arguing for innate ideas Cudworth praises *Theaetetus* 184b–6e as an accurate assessment of the limitations of sense perception. As we saw on pp. 83–4, this was a passage in which Plato himself was moving towards the kind of considerations that the 'Kantian' interpretation was reading back into the theory of recollection.

All these philosophers include ordinary ideas and beliefs among the innate resources of the mind. The same can be said for Leibniz. This could actually have been predicted from the context of his principal work on the subject, *New Essays on Human Understanding*, which is a point-by-point reply to Locke's *Essay concerning Human Understanding*. There is no doubt that Locke had targeted easily understood propositions, because much of his polemic is aimed at those who claim innateness for propositions that command universal assent or receive assent upon first hearing. So in his reply, Leibniz includes among innate principles those involved in ordinary thought. At one point he talks of the mind relying on certain principles constantly, these serving as 'the inner core and mortar of our thoughts'; such innate principles are the necessary conditions of thought, and in using them we know them 'fundamentally'.[12]

His fullest statement as to where he stands on this issue, however, comes a little earlier in I i:[13]

Some innate principles are common property, and come easily to everyone. Some theorems are also discovered straight away; these constitute natural sciences which are more extensive in some people than in others. Finally . . . any truths which are derivable from primary innate knowledge may also be called innate, because the mind can draw them from its own depths, though often only with difficulty.

This passage demonstrates as clearly as we could wish that Leibniz, like the other philosophers we have mentioned, expected innatism

of God on subjects who did not already have it. It is impossible, he insists, for ideas simply to be poured into people as if they are mere vessels. It is evident both from the nature of the claim he is attacking and from the arguments he uses to do so that it is the common conception of God that is at issue.

[12] Remnant and Bennett (1982) 84. See also 51 where he talks of the ideas of being, unity, substance, duration, change and action as innate to us.

[13] Remnant and Bennett (1982) 78.

to explain human learning at all its levels, whether it be our awareness of the obvious or the discovery of the abstruse.

## [2] MORAL INNATISM

So far I have been showing that the formation of ordinary concepts was very relevant to the interests of those who defended metaphysical innatism in the seventeenth and early eighteenth century. One might go further and say that, because of this, the theory showed some strong Stoic affinities. This would be misleading, however, because the texts we have been looking at were concerned with metaphysical ideas and propositions, whereas the Stoics confined their innatism to moral prolepses.[14] But now I wish to turn to the moral innatism of this period, and bring out the Stoic affinities as much as the Platonic differences. In turning to moral innatism I shall be dealing with a slightly different crop of thinkers, notably those clerics who advocated the theory in England prior to Locke's *Essay*. Descartes now bows out of the story because his innatism is almost always focused on metaphysical notions. To a lesser extent the same is true of More, who tends to air his innatist views when discussing the existence of God and other metaphysical topics. This is not to deny that these thinkers would have abandoned their innatism when they came to moral philosophy; just that morality does not enter so much into their explicit discussions of the topic.

It would anyway be a distortion to confine ourselves to better known philosophers as there is a whole crop of lesser known figures

[14] There was, however, an awareness of Stoic theory among those who advocated the innateness of metaphysical ideas. Descartes had strong Stoic leanings in ethics and makes allusions to Seneca in his writings. If Descartes was a reader of Seneca he would doubtless have come across the passage dealing with innate ideas, *Letter* 120.4, which refers to the seeds of knowledge (*semina scientiae*: cf. p. 208 n. 38 above) and he does indeed talk of there being seeds of knowledge (*semina scientiae*) in us 'just as there are seeds of fire in a flint; philosophers extract them by reasoning, poets take possession of them by the imagination': Adam and Tannery (1897–1913) X 217. In *Rules* IV he talks of 'primary germs of truth implanted by nature in human minds' – 'veritatum semina humanis ingeniis a natura insita': Haldane and Ross (1911) I 12. See also Haldane and Ross (1911) I 121.

As he indicates in the preface to the *New Essays*, Leibniz also sees innatism as a Stoic doctrine: see Remnant and Bennett (1982) 49. Interesting too is the way Cudworth (1678) 691, talks of the idea of God as a prolepsis; in Cudworth (1731) 218 he talks of the soul having innate ideas 'proleptically'. I discuss the seventeenth-century use of Hellenistic terminology on pp. 238–9 below.

to be taken into account. In an important work, *John Locke and the Way of Ideas*, J. W. Yolton has sought to explain why Locke should have spent so much time attacking innatism in the first book of the *Essay*. Yolton brought to light a large number of thinkers, most of them eminent churchmen, who espoused the innateness of moral principles.[15] What I wish to show is that, if we look at the views of the thinkers in Yolton's study, as well as one or two others, we shall find some remarkable affinities with the Stoic variety of innatism.

The theory that was popular among such thinkers was a fabric of many different strands. One of the most important was the concept of natural law, a notion often thought to have its origins in the Stoics and Cicero and which subsequently influenced Scholasticism. On one interpretation of this theory, there is a moral law that applies to all rational creatures, all human beings as such, and is therefore binding and obligatory on all peoples of all times and places. Furthermore, this law is distinct from the revealed law of the Old and New Testaments. Truths about religion and morality are disseminated by God prior to and independently of revelation, and are known through the light of reason implanted in us at the moment of our creation. This can be expressed in a naïve form by saying that God has implanted in us at birth a knowledge of the dictates of natural law or, in the more subtle dispositionalist form, by saying that He has implanted dispositions in us to acknowledge the requisite notions. Such truths shone in their full brightness to Adam before the Fall, and although they may have become darkened thereafter, they were not wholly obliterated. Being natural to human reason in itself, they are common to all mankind, unlike revelation, and immediately assented to upon first hearing. In this way they were seen as being just like the speculative maxims of non-contradiction and identity.

Those who advocated this theory appealed, for their authority, to what was for many a *locus classicus* in the Christian natural law tradition, Romans 2:14–15. In the course of talking about a law which applies to all people alike (i.e., on this interpretation, a natural law) Paul mentions 'the work of the law written in our hearts':

When Gentiles who have not the law do by nature what the law requires, they are a law to themselves, even though they do not have the law. They

---

[15] See Yolton (1956) ch. 2.

show that what the law requires is written on their hearts, while their conscience also bears witness and their conflicting thoughts accuse or perhaps excuse them on that day when, according to my gospel, God judges the secrets of men by Christ Jesus.

This brand of innatism was thus a particular epistemological application of natural law theory. It was also connected to the notion of conscience because the laws of nature, inscribed as innate principles by the hand of God, were assimilated to the dictates of conscience.

Such a theory emerges clearly from the sermons of the father of the Cambridge Platonist movement, Benjamin Whichcote.[16] Religious truth comes to man from two sources.[17] God teaches man first by instilling principles into his very nature and then by biblical revelation. This second source is necessary because man, after his fall, needs to be recalled to the natural principles from which he has apostatised. The light of nature which gives rise to our innate ideas, or our predispositions to form them

is connatural to Man, it is the light of God's creation, and it flows from the principles of which Man doth consist, in his very first Make: this is the soul's complexion.[18]

As examples of the principles involved he cites 'good Affection and submission towards God, the instances of justice and righteousness towards men, and temperance to himself'.[19] This doctrine of innate ideas is also associated with the idea of man being made in the image of God. The concreated principles flow from man's essentially deiform nature. Whichcote stressed that man was made in God's image and saw his reason as a 'deiform seed'. Just as Caesar's coin bore Caesar's image on it our souls bear God's impression, and this impression is made at the moment of our creation.[20]

Whichcote makes the connection with natural law, claiming that the principles of first creation are common to and binding upon all

[16] Whichcote's innatism is a subtle version of the dispositionalist variety. For a fuller discussion of this see Scott (1990) 78–83.
[17] See *Aphorism* 109 in Patrides (1969) 327.
[18] (1751) III 20.
[19] (1751) III 28.
[20] (1751) III 190 and IV 74.
[21] (1751) III 183; he cites Romans 2:15 on 344–7.
[22] (1751) III 22, 29–30.

men.[21] He sees these principles as obvious, easily discovered[22] and self-evident.[23] He also makes much of universal consent, and even argues from the alleged fact of such consent to the truth of the principles.[24] Those who attempt to dissent from the principles in question are treated dismissively:

if any rise up against them then they have been incompetent; and so of no moral consideration.[25]

Another writer who synthesises these elements is Robert Sanderson, a scholastic thinker who lectured at Oxford on natural law (among other things) and was later bishop of Lincoln. In his influential work, *Lectures on Conscience and Human Law* (1660),[26] he tackles the question of how we know about the law of nature (or how we discover the 'immediate rule of conscience') and answers that it is by the light of the mind. This he divides into three: an innate light, an imparted one (i.e. revelation) and an acquired one (i.e. authority and tradition). Of the innate light Sanderson says:

[it] proceeds from the law of Nature; for upon the first creation of things, God endued the brute and inanimate creatures with a natural *instinct*, which should incline them to support and preserve their being, to be as a law to them ... So a sort of natural law is imposed upon man, and proportioned to the nature of a rational creature, which is more noble and sublime, and (if I may so speak) more Divine than what was laid upon the other creatures of this lower world; and this Law incites him ... to live according to reason. Now this law is a natural impression, and as it were a copy of that original law in the Mind of God and a part of that *Divine Image*, in which man at first was created by God.[27]

He goes on to say that although this innate light was much obscured by the Fall of Adam,

[23] (1751) III 29.

[24] Whichcote appeals to universal consent both to confirm belief in the existence of God and justify practical principles. In (1751) IV 352–3 he argues for the former quoting from Seneca, *Letter* 117.6 (cf. p. 179 above).

[25] (1751) III 31. He never claims that there are principles with which literally every individual agrees; rather, 'the universal acknowledgment of a thing for truth' lies in 'the due and even proportion that it bears to the universal reason of mankind': (1751) III 32. In other words, he selects only opinions that 'any sober man in the due use of reason hath entertained', as he says a few lines later. On the dangers of this approach see p. 264 below.

[26] References are to Wordsworth (1877).

[27] Wordsworth (1877) 107–8.

it escaped with less hurt than many of the other faculties; for it has pleased God that certain propositions and practical principles, which the philosophers call *common notions*, and *natural maxims*, and *St Basil* excellently calls a *spark of the divine image concealed within us*, preserved, as it were, in the ashes of the general conflagration, should still remain in our breasts, as witnesses of His Will to us. These *common* notions are that Law of God which the Apostle says is *written in the hearts of men* . . .[28]

Sanderson then argues that although there are many practical principles, they reduce to one, namely that Good is to be done and Evil to be avoided. From this a number of very general principles can be deduced, for instance, 'God is to be worshipped' and 'no man is to be injured'. Such principles command assent as soon as proposed and

because of their undeniable evidence, oblige our assent. No one can reasonably dispute their certainty; nor is it possible, if we understand the sense of the words, to mistake about them.[29]

In this work, therefore, we can see how religious and moral innate principles were embedded in a whole network of other ideas: the distinction between revelation and the light of nature implanted at Creation, together with the notions of conscience and natural law, all supported by a reference to Romans 2:15.

Whichcote and Sanderson were only two out of a large number of thinkers who espoused this combination of doctrines. Another is Robert South. Preaching in 1662 he held that the truths of first inscription were prior to revelation and shone in their full brightness for Adam who 'had these notions firm and untainted, had his own law in his heart and to have such a conscience as might be its own casuist'. He also appeals to Romans 2:15 and affirms that the God-given principles are universally acknowledged and, as the 'foundations of all religion' and 'grounds of all vertue', self-evident.[30] Several of these themes can be found in the Cambridge

---

[28] Wordsworth (1877) 108. In using the phrases, 'common notions' and 'natural maxims', Wordsworth is translating the Greek expressions, *koinai ennoiai* and *prolepses phusikai*, which Sanderson used in the original edition. On the use of Hellenistic terminology in this period see pp. 238–9 below.

[29] Wordsworth (1877) 109. See also 17 where Sanderson likens practical principles to the speculative maxims (e.g. 'the whole is greater than the part') whose truth 'occurs immediately to the mind . . . without the least assistance of thought or instruction'.

[30] South (1692) I 66–7.

Platonist John Smith[31] and in most of the figures whom Yolton identified as the leading proponents of innatism at that time, including Ferguson, Hale and Wilkins.[32]

In establishing what type of innatist theory was at issue at the time we need not confine ourselves to defenders of innatism but can also see what sort of innatism opponents of the theory thought they were attacking. One critic, for instance, Burthogge, portrays his opponents as believing in innate principles that are indubitably true and the foundation of all other moral truths.[33] He himself agrees that certain moral principles command universal assent, but traces this not to innateness but a common tradition stemming from Adam.[34] Again, Samuel Parker, in *A Demonstration of the Divine Authority of the Law of Nature*, takes it for granted that innate principles would be invoked to explain our knowledge of natural law and that Romans 2:15 would be invoked by innatists in support of their claims.[35]

The most famous attack on innatism in this century was, of course, made by Locke in his *Essay concerning Human Understanding*. We shall be discussing this in more detail in the next chapter, but for the moment we should note that more evidence of the type of theory current at the time emerges from the way in which the theory continued to be held after the publication of the *Essay*. In his *Treatise of Moral and Intellectual Virtues*, a work that makes no reference at all to Locke's *Essay*, John Hartcliffe cheerfully affirms the existence of a natural and instinctive knowledge of the rules of virtue. Like an animal's drive to self-preservation these notions have no need of reason, and so are self-evident; they are easy to understand and command universal assent. Arguing that all men would be bound by these rules with or without revelation, he appeals to Romans 2:15 and also connects the whole theory to conscience.[36]

[31] See Patrides (1969) 149: truths of natural inscription are connected with natural law and hence with Romans 2:15 as well as with Cicero. He also says of the common notions of God and virtue that 'they are more clear and perspicuous than any else; and if they have not more *certainty* they have more *evidence*, and display themselves with less difficulty to our *Reflexive* faculty than any Geometrical Demonstrations . . .', Patrides (1969) 138.

[32] Ferguson (1675) 23 and 42, Hale (1677) 61–4, Wilkins (1675) 57.

[33] Burthogge (1678) 55, where he also connects innatism with the doctrine of conscience.

[34] Burthogge (1675) 339–41.

[35] Parker (1681) 5–7.

[36] Hartcliffe (1691) 352–5. The same connection between innate principles, natural law, conscience and Romans 2:15 can be found in John Burnet's remarks on Locke. See Watson (1989) 58.

Of course, most supporters of the theory writing after 1689 were responding to Locke. Henry Lee in *Antiscepticism* (1702), a work notable for its subtle defence of dispositional innateness, reaffirms the innateness of a law of nature which is implanted in us prior to revelation.[37] Commanding universal assent, practical principles emerge as easily and naturally as the speculative maxims; Lee reaffirms the self-evidence of innate principles, saying that though they may require verbal explication, no proof is required once the words are understood.[38] Likewise, James Lowde, who is responding to Parker as well as Locke, expects innate practical principles to be God-given, obvious and self-evident.[39] John Milner claims the same attributes for innate principles,[40] as well as making the connection to natural law and to Rom. 2:15.[41] Finally, William Sherlock's *Discourse concerning the Happiness of Good Men* defends the theory and makes a reference to the pre-revelation state in which Adam's innate ideas were 'sparkling and bright'.[42]

What should now be clear is the similarity between the Stoic brand of innatism and the views being expressed by these writers. Of course, there is a peculiarly Christian aspect to the innatism of the seventeenth century in that the theory of natural law is combined with the doctrine of revelation; also, the notion of conscience is considerably more recent. Nevertheless, the crucial features of seventeenth-century innate practical principles – universality, obviousness and self-evidence – have clear analogues in Stoic theory.[43] The obviousness of these notions recalls the ease with which Stoic prolepses emerge as implied by Aëtius[44] when he says that prolepses come naturally and without instruction before the age of reason, and contrasts them with notions that come by teaching and diligence; the universality of innate principles reminds us of the way in which Stoic prolepses, the common notions, were widely shared; their self-evidence picks up the foundational role

---

[37] Lee (1702) 11 and 20.

[38] Lee (1702) 16–17.

[39] Lowde (1694) 56–7.

[40] Milner (1700) 177.

[41] Milner (1700) 60 and 159.

[42] Sherlock (1704) 128.

[43] Another Stoic theme worth mentioning is that of seeds (cf. Seneca, *Letter* 120.4), which crops up in some of this literature. Whichcote, for instance, sees reason as a seed sown by God and as a 'seminal principle' (III 211). Cf. also Sanderson in Wordsworth (1877) 18 and Sherlock (1704) 131, 161.

[44] IV 11 = *SVF* II 83; Long and Sedley (1987) I 238.

of the original Stoic prolepses; and the Stoics, like the innatists of the seventeenth century, thought that the notions derived directly from Nature, i.e. God.[45]

The Stoicism of these writers is also shown by their use of Hellenistic terminology and, in some cases, sources. Many of them used the expression 'common notions' (often in the original Greek, *koinai ennoiai*), as well as the words 'prolepsis', 'proleptic notion', 'anticipation' and 'prenotion'. A prime example is Sanderson who, as we have seen, not only uses the Greek terms *koinai ennoiai* and *phusikai* ('natural') *prolepseis* but also refers to Cicero's phrase 'rudimentary beginnings of intelligence' (*inchoatae intellegentiae*) from *Laws* I 30.[46] But almost all the other innatists mentioned use, either in Greek, English or both, variants on the central terms 'common notions' and 'prolepses'.[47] The same goes for the critics of innatism, Burthogge and Parker.[48] And though our topic is now specifically concerned with moral or practical principles, we should note how Hellenistic themes and terminology pervade seventeenth-century discussions of the idea of God and speculative maxims. The use of arguments from universal consent for the existence of God in Cicero's *N.D.* I 44, together with its apparent attribution of innateness to Hellenistic prolepsis, proved to be a favourite quarry for seventeenth-century theists, perhaps most notably Edward Stillingfleet;[49] and the use of the terms 'common notion' and 'prolepsis' is as widespread as in the case of practical principles.[50] Finally, we should note that the assumption that innatism meant Stoic innatism also led to some misinterpretation

---

[45] Throughout this section, I have concentrated on the convergence between Stoic and seventeenth-century innatism. What I have not done is to go into the ways and means by which Locke's contemporaries may have been influenced by Stoicism. This is a treacherous area. Claims about influence are easy to support when an author quotes a Hellenistic source directly, but less so when this is not the case. Stoicism could have crept in at many stages in the history of philosophy and theology, from the birth of Christian thought to the Stoic renaissance of the late sixteenth century.

[46] Wordsworth (1877) 108. See also *Laws* I 27, cited on p. 161 above in n. 4. Sanderson also makes use of the Stoic distinction between an appropriate action (καθῆκον) and a right one (κατόρθωμα) as reported by Cicero, *Ends* III 20–5: Wordsworth (1877) 110.

[47] For the use of such terms see Ferguson (1675) 26, Hale (1677) 60 and 61, Lee (1702) 28, Milner (1700) 177, Sclater (1611) 236, Smith in Patrides (1969) 128, 132 and 138 and Wilkins (1675) 55.

[48] Burthogge (1678) 55–8; Parker (1681) 7.

[49] Stillingfleet (1710) II 243. See also Bates (1722) 15–16.

[50] Cudworth (1678) 691, and Charleton (1652) 102. For a reference to Sextus' report in *M.* I 57 that having a prolepsis is a necessary condition for even asking a question, see Charleton (1652) 105–6.

of Plato. In his *Free and Impartial Censure of Platonick Philosophy* Samuel Parker interprets the theory of recollection in terms of 'proleptic notions' and 'congenite anticipations' and assumes that Plato is talking about obvious and self-evident speculative maxims.[51]

Both in substance and terminology, then, the innatists of this century show their true lineage to be more Hellenistic than Platonic. What we shall now go on to discover is that although Platonism was receiving little help from those usually supposed to be its friends, it did find an unwitting ally in a most unlikely philosopher, John Locke.

[51] Parker (1666) 57–60.

# CHAPTER 10

# *Locke and the posture of blind credulity*

Locke, no friend of innate principles, would normally be considered, *a fortiori*, no friend of Plato. But while there are undeniable and obvious differences between the two philosophers, this chapter is intended to bring out some remarkable affinities between them. To do this we shall be focusing on Locke's attack on moral innatism in the first book of the *Essay concerning Human Understanding*. After first sketching out the background to this attack, I wish to show that, as we might by now be expecting, when Locke comes to attack moral innatism, he selects something far more like the Stoic theory than the Platonic as his target. Admittedly, he does not simply do this because that was the theory that happened to be around at the time; he himself believes that if there were to be an innatist theory, that would be the most plausible; and he actually supplies arguments of his own to show this. But despite this limited concession to those who espoused the Stoic form of innateness, he then turns against it using arguments that sound strangely Platonic.

## [I] BACKGROUND TO ESSAY I iii

Locke starts his attack on innatism in the second chapter of book I and his overall strategy remains clear and systematic throughout: the second chapter deals with speculative maxims, the third with practical (i.e. moral) principles and the fourth with ideas such as those of God and substance. Another way of seeing the division of labour is that the second and third chapters deal with principles or propositions alleged to be innate, whereas the fourth concentrates mostly on ideas. Locke seems mainly concerned with the innateness of propositions, and his reason for dealing with ideas in the fourth chapter is that the denial of innate ideas will furnish another argument against the innateness of propositions: if no ideas are innate then nothing constituted out of them – i.e. propositions – can be innate either.

As our subject is moral epistemology the interest will be focused on the arguments of the third chapter, a chapter that has been rather neglected in discussions of Locke's polemic against innatism. This is unfortunate, because moral epistemology was a topic of immense importance for him. Initially things may look different. A common view of the *Essay* sets it in the context not of moral knowledge but of scientific knowledge, i.e. the new science, whose success was epitomised by Boyle and Newton and fostered by the newly formed Royal Society. Here was a new movement in search of a new epistemology; Locke conveniently supplies it with the *Essay*. While this is far from being false it is not the whole story. Locke was prompted to write the *Essay* by a discussion among a small number of friends, as he tells us in the 'Epistle to the reader' (p. 7). When this discussion reached an impasse Locke realised that an inquiry into the nature and extent of the understanding was called for. What he does not say in the *Essay*, but what was later claimed by one of those present is that the discussions were 'about the Principles of morality and reveal'd Religion'.[1] The epistemological problems involved seemed therefore to have been originally moral and religious in nature.[2]

Another indication of the importance of moral epistemology to the *Essay* is Locke's intention to add on a fifth part concerned with the importance of the understanding in human conduct. Although this intention was never realised the material was published posthumously and separately as *Of the Conduct of the Understanding*. But it is enough for the present point simply that Locke should have thought of concluding the whole work with so practical and prescriptive an ending.

In addition to Locke's intentions subsequent to *Essay* I–IV there is evidence from previous writings, among them the earlier draft of the *Essay*, draft B, as it is known, probably written in 1671.[3] In

---

[1] The person in question was James Tyrrell, one of the circle of friends meeting at Exeter House in London, who wrote the comment in a marginal note to his copy of the *Essay*. See Tully (1988) 17 with note 12.

[2] One writer who has done much to highlight the ethical aspect of Locke's philosophy is Colman (1983). See especially the Introduction and ch. 3.

[3] The most recent edition of draft B is Nidditch and Rogers (1990).

the attack on innate principles found in this draft, much of the material of *Essay* I is already there, but there is an almost exclusive emphasis given to moral principles with practically no discussion of speculative maxims at all.[4] Admittedly, the first thing Locke does is to attack the claim that the idea of God is innate, which in the *Essay* is left until the fourth chapter,[5] but from the way he presents his argument in draft B it is quite clear that his purpose in denying the innateness of the idea of God is to deny that there are any innate practical principles:

If then (as it seems probable to me) there be noe innate notion of a god in the mindes of men I cannot see how there can be any innate principles of morality or sense of obligation to any duty borne with us. For without a law-maker there can be noe sense of a law, or obligation to obedience . . .[6]

Locke then goes on to attack innate principles directly, setting out the gist of what is to appear in *Essay* I iii.

In fact, Locke's interest in moral epistemology goes back further even than early drafts of the *Essay*. In about 1664 Locke wrote but never published a set of essays on the law of nature, a topic that many people, as we saw in the previous chapter, connected to the theory of innate ideas.[7] In it he argues that the law is capable of being known and then considers a number of hypotheses about how it is discovered – that it is known innately, by sense perception or by universal consent. Locke accepts the second alternative, rejecting both the first and the third. The attack in the third of the *Essays* on innate knowledge is clearly a first run of the arguments that are finally to appear in the *Essay* and most of the points he makes in the earlier work are to reappear. Among them is the claim that the principles alleged to be innate command neither

---

[4] For example, whereas I ii 6–23 of the *Essay* itself discuss the use of reason and immediate assent with reference to speculative maxims, the equivalent passage in B is with reference only to practical maxims.

[5] I iv 8–16.

[6] Nidditch and Rogers (1990) 109.

[7] They were probably given as lectures when he was the senior censor at Christ Church, Oxford, but were only published in 1954 in W. von Leyden's edition.

Interestingly enough, the *Essays on the Law of Nature* were clearly written under the influence of Robert Sanderson. On this see von Leyden (1954) 30–4 who points to the unmistakable influences of Sanderson on the *Essays*. On the issue of innateness, of course they disagreed, so that Sanderson is a most likely target in these essays. If so, he would remain a target in *Essay* I. (That Locke is still thinking of natural law in the course of his polemic against innatism in *Essay* I is clear from I iii 13).

universal obedience nor consent (iii 136–9).

None of this is to deny that for Locke an epistemology of the new science was of great importance, but it is to emphasise that moral epistemology had a special urgency. Anyway, if his main interest was the empirical science of the new movement the conclusions he reaches in the *Essay* would be far from a celebration of its achievements, actual or potential. By the fourth book he makes it clear that in empirical matters certain knowledge is unattainable; only probability is available (IV xii 10). Rather Platonically, he holds that true knowledge can only be found in mathematics and morals (IV xii 8). He also adds, without intending to downgrade experimental science, that morality is the proper business of mankind (IV xii 11–12).

### [2] OUTLINE OF THE ARGUMENT OF I iii

At the very beginning of his polemic against innatism, Locke attributes to his opponents the belief that there are 'certain *innate Principles*; some primary Notions, Κοιναὶ ἔννοιαι [common notions], Characters, as it were, stamped on the Mind of Man' (I ii 1). As his use of terminology might lead us to predict, when he comes to attack moral innatism in *Essay* I iii, his target has abundantly clear similarities to the Hellenistic version of innateness and could scarcely be further away from Platonic recollection.

Locke's strategy in this chapter is one of extended *modus tollens*. He argues that if a moral principle were to be innate it would have to have certain characteristics; moral principles lack such features, and so cannot be innate. The features in question turn out to include being God-given, obvious, universally accepted and self-evident.

That an innate principle would have to have been implanted in us by God is clear from iii 6 where he complains about the variety of different (and conflicting) practical principles and asks how could this be 'if practical principles were innate and imprinted on our minds immediately by the hand of God'. In iii 19, pointing out that any innate principle containing the idea of virtue would be too vague, he adds: 'it will scarce seem possible, that God should engrave principles in men's minds, in words of uncertain signification . . .' That Locke should make this assumption is easily explained by reference to his own moral theory; moral principles are laws given to us by God. Were there no law-maker there would be no obligation to follow the laws.[8]

The obviousness of innate principles is spelt out very early in chapter iii when he uses the difficulty which people find in seeing the allegedly innate principles as an argument against their innateness:

> But the Ignorance wherein many Men are of them, and the slowness of assent, wherewith others receive them, are manifest Proofs, that they are not innate, and as such offer themselves to their view without searching. (I iii 1)

The reason that the principles would have to be obvious is that, if they were innate, they would have to have been instilled in us by God for the purpose of making us behave morally; from this he infers that they ought on the whole to be effective and useful in running our lives.[9] It then follows that if practical principles are to be effective they ought to be obvious to us.

The principles will have the further characteristic of commanding universal assent. God implants the principles in all his creatures; they are obvious to all; so they must be acknowledged everywhere. That innate principles should command universal consent is in fact stated as an introductory remark to the whole polemic as applying both to speculative and practical principles:

> There is nothing more commonly taken for granted, than that there are certain Principles both *Speculative* and *Practical* (for they speak of both) universally agreed upon by all Mankind: which therefore they argue must needs be the constant Impressions, which the souls of Men receive in their first Beings, and which they bring into the World with them, as necessarily and really as they do any of their inherent Faculties. (I ii 2)

Locke himself vigorously denies that because a principle is universally acknowledged it is innate. Such universality arises from

---

[8] See e.g. I iv 8: when introducing the discussion of the idea of God he says: 'If any *Idea* can be imagined *innate*, the *Idea of God* may of all others, for many Reasons, be thought so; since it is hard to conceive, how there should be innate Moral Principles without an innate *Idea* of a *Deity*: without a notion of a Law-maker it is impossible to have a Notion of a Law, and an Obligation to observe it.' Locke's theological and legalistic ethics can also be found in the *Essays on the Law of Nature*: see von Leyden (1954) 110–11, 172–3.

[9] See I iii 17: 'this [*sc.* the principle "virtue joined with piety is the best worship of God"] can be but a very uncertain rule of human practice and serve but very little to the conduct of our lives, and is therefore very unfit to be assigned as an innate practical principle'. See also iii 20.

the nature of things themselves. What he does agree with is the reverse implication: 'If they [*sc.* principles] are innate they must needs have universal assent' (I ii 24). This point remains well to the fore in chapter iii. In the very first paragraph he promises to show that there is no moral rule that commands universal assent 'whereby it is evident that they are farther removed from a title to be innate'.

The last criterion of innateness on our list is that an innate principle would have to be self-evident and 'not need any proof to ascertain its truth, nor want any reason to gain it approbation' (I iii 4). Locke holds up the principle of non-contradiction as the paradigm of self-evidence (though not, of course, innateness) to which every innate principle would have to aspire and then objects that, as moral principles are not self-evident, they cannot be innate.[10] One reason why he expects innate principles to be self-evident stems from the assumption that they would have been given to us by God; for, if God were to give us any principles as our birth-right, he would presumably select the most important, namely, those that act as the foundation of all other knowledge (I ii 21 and 25).

## [3] THE EDUCATIONAL CRITIQUE

Locke's use of the Greek term *koinai ennoiai* (common notions) in the introduction to his argument was a good foretaste of what was to come. The theory that he attacks in I iii is representative of his time and redolent of the Stoic version of innateness. We have also seen that Locke does not target this theory merely because that was what happened to be believed at the time but he himself thinks that if there were to be an innatist theory, it would have to be very similar to the one espoused by the Stoics and later by his contemporaries. This shows that, in a conditional sense, there is a certain amount of common ground between Locke and his innatist opponents. Nevertheless, as he goes on to attack the Stoic theory, certain strongly Platonic themes begin to emerge in his arguments.

---

[10] The requirement that innate principle be self-evident is in addition to and distinct from the claim that they would have to be obvious. A self-evident principle is an axiom, something for which no evidence can possibly be given; that is not to say that it is obvious and easily understood by anyone.

His argument partly consists in showing that none of the features that would have to belong to innate beliefs do in fact belong to moral beliefs. Hence moral innatism is false. Universal consent is one of his favourite targets (I iii 2, 9–10) and obviousness is denied in I iii 12 (if there are these obvious truths, why is there such widespread disagreement?). The alleged self-evidence of moral principles is attacked in I iii 4:

Another Reason that makes me doubt of any innate practical Principles, is, That I think, *there cannot any one moral rule be propos'd whereof a man may not justly demand a reason*: which would be perfectly ridiculous and absurd if they were innate, or so much as self-evident; which every innate Principle must needs be, and not need any Proof to ascertain its Truth nor want any Reason to gain it Approbation.

Moral principles cannot be self-evident because any moral claim can and should be supported by grounds or argument. This claim should be connected with Locke's expectation that morality could be just as much a demonstrable science as mathematics or geometry. This, as we have seen, is stated in IV xii. At one point, for instance, he says:

and I doubt not, but if a right method were taken, a great part of Morality might be made out with that clearness, that could leave, to a considering Man, no more reason to doubt, than he could have to doubt of the Truth of Propositions in Mathematicks, which have been demonstrated to him. (IV xii 8)

Nevertheless, important though these arguments are to chapter iii as a whole, I shall be concentrating on another line of attack in which he claims that ethical innatism is not merely false, but dangerously false. This line of argument is no less important to him than, say, the argument against universal assent; if anything it is the argument about which he is most passionate. It is also crucial for the sake of our ancient parallels.

The passage in question, I iii 22–7, comes as the conclusion of the discussion of moral principles. In the course of attempting to explode the myth of universal assent in the earlier part of the chapter, Locke has exploited not just the diversity of moral principles but also the absurdity of many of them. So he is naturally led to ask how people came to hold such diverse and often ridiculous notions in such awe as natural and written by the hand of God or as he puts it, how it may really come to pass, that Doctrines that have been derived from no better original, than the Superstition of a Nurse, or the authority of an old Woman, may by length of time and consent of neighbours *grow up to the dignity of Principles* in religion or morality. (I iii 22)

Accounting for this phenomenon is the business of the final section of I iii (22–7). He starts by claiming that such principles are inculcated as soon as children can understand anything and are confirmed in all subsequent education, especially by their contact with those they respect; and these people will not allow such principles ever to be questioned, but only to be seen as the basis and foundation for everything else. By this process of social conditioning, notions can attain the status of 'unquestionable, self-evident and innate truths'.

In 23 Locke gives a further explanation of how these principles come to be considered innate. As the children described in the previous paragraph grow up, they seek to find the origin of these principles, but can find nothing in their memory that antedates them; whence they conclude

that those propositions of whose knowledge they can find in themselves no original were certainly the impress of God and Nature on their minds . . .

That is, innate. And so they come to venerate these principles as if they were their parents. The preceding paragraph explained how the principles came to seem unquestionable; 23 explains how they come to be held in such awe, and it is their alleged innateness that is held responsible.

But how is it that so few people sit down and examine their principles? Locke thinks that everyone needs some principles as the basis of their reasoning; and there is nothing wrong with that. The problem is that people for the most part borrow their principles and take them on trust, and this for a number of reasons: lack of skill, time, inclination, or because they have been taught not to question principles (24).

The next paragraph, 25, develops this point and brings out most clearly how the doctrine of innate ideas is a major culprit in this process. It is a fact of life that most people have not the time or patience to question principles – especially when one principle is that principles ought not to be questioned. But even if someone had the will or the time, would he really be prepared to renounce so many of his former beliefs and to risk the ridicule, or worse, of his fellows? Moreover,

he will be much more *afraid to question those principles*, when he shall think them, as most men do, the standards set up by God in his mind, to be the rule and Touchstone of all other opinions. And what can hinder him from thinking them sacred, when he finds them the earliest of all his own thoughts, and the most reverenced by others?

Give someone all the sabbatical that they could wish, and yet there is still something to stop them questioning principles: a belief that they are innate, hence the fit objects not of examination, but of reverence. The myth of innate principles is thus the enemy of honest and open inquiry. Of course, Locke need not deny the truth of these principles, and in I iv 15 freely admits that as far as principles about God are concerned, many of these are excellent in themselves. But they were originally thought out by a few wise people; subsequently they were taken up by the lazy mass of mankind and enshrined as innate, with the result that no one would have to do what others had once done, i.e. think for themselves.

This line of thinking begins to show why Locke attacks the doctrine of innate ideas with such indignation and at such length. But further explanation of his strategy can be found. I iii 22–7 has brought out the dangers of innatism by showing how the doctrine prevents an individual from questioning his own principles. In I iv 24, however, Locke turns the knife in the wound by claiming that innatism is used by some as a means of indoctrinating others. Once again he claims that labelling something innate is used to relieve the lazy from the pain of search. But then he adds:

it was of no small advantage to those who affected to be Masters and Teachers to make this the Principle of *Principles*, That Principles must not be questioned; For having once established this Tenet, that there are innate Principles, it put their Followers upon a necessity of receiving some Doctrines as such; which was to take them off from the use of their own Reason and Judgement, and put them upon believing and taking them on trust, without farther examination; In which Posture of blind Credulity, they might be more easily governed by, and made more useful to some sort of Men, who had the skill and office to principle and guide them. Nor is it a small power it gives one Man over another to have the Authority to be the Dictator of Principles, and Teacher of unquestionable Truths; and to make a Man swallow that for an innate Principle, which may serve to his purpose, who teacheth them.

That this argument comes at the culmination of the entire polemic shows that book I is not merely to be seen as an essay in epistemology or psychology. It is a tirade against the educational evils of innatism.

Unlike the first two parts of *Essay* I iii, Locke's educational critique is not a direct refutation of moral innatism. It does not follow the pattern of claiming that an innate principle would have to have a particular feature, moral principles do not, therefore they are not innate. But it has an analogous structure. It assumes that innate principles would have to have certain features; it then argues that if such attributes are foisted upon moral propositions, the consequences will be educationally pernicious. The principal features in question are universal consent, self-evidence, and divine origination, each playing a crucial role in the educational critique. The act of labelling a principle innate is an attempt to render it immune from examination (or at least it has that effect). Because innate principles command universal assent anyone who considers questioning one will be accused of being whimsical; its self-evidence means that such a person is simply attempting the impossible, and, of course, its divine origination renders that person atheistical and wicked.[11]

Furthermore, the claim that innatism is morally pernicious is not just a conclusion hammered home at end of chapters iii and iv but is integral both to book I and to the *Essay* as a whole. Locke's condemnation of those who accept principles on trust is one of his more deeply-rooted and pervasive philosophical convictions. It stems from his belief that the acid test of whether we have knowledge or merely true opinion is whether we have examined things for ourselves:

The floating of other Men's Opinions in our brains makes us not one jot the more knowing, though they happen to be true. What in them was Science is in us but Opiniatrety, whilst we give up our Assent only to reverend Names and do not as they did employ our own Reason to *understand* those *Truths* which gave them reputation. (I iv 23)

If we are to make any headway in the enlargement of our knowledge, thinking for ourselves is of paramount importance. That this is a crucial theme for the entire *Essay* hardly needs pointing out.

The main purpose of the book is to set out the nature of human understanding and so aid the process of enlarging our knowledge. Anything that gets in the way of that will be a prime target for attack. No surprise, then, to find Locke advocating the principle of thinking for yourself right at the beginning of the work – even as early a place as the *Epistle to the Reader*: in the second paragraph, Locke commends anyone

> who has raised himself above the Alms-Basket, and not content to live lazily on the scraps of begg'd Opinions, sets his own Thoughts on work, to find and follow the Truth, . . .

Encouraging people in the course of reading the *Essay* to think for themselves he adds

> 'Tis to them [*sc.* thine own thoughts] . . . that I referr myself: But if they are taken upon Trust from others, 'tis no great Matter what they are, they not following Truth, but some meaner Consideration . . .

The improvement of the understanding depends crucially on think-ing for yourself and the doctrine of innate ideas stands in the way of this. The content of book I is linked to the essential strain of the entire work. And just as that theme appears on the very first page, it recurs at the end – in book IV. Appropriately enough, Locke returns to his condemnation of borrowed principles in the chapter on 'The Improvement of our Knowledge' (IV xii) and again in the chapter on 'Wrong Assent, or Errour' (IV xx). In IV xii 4, for instance, he remarks

> *Nothing* can be *so dangerous* as *principles* thus *taken up without questioning or examination*; especially if they be such as concern Morality, which influence Men's lives and give a biass to all their Actions.

This brings out with all clarity not only why Locke was so concerned about innatism, but why his most pungent remarks came whilst he was discussing practical principles (i.e. in 22–7 of I iii). The doctrine was not just bad epistemology but also morally harmful.

But not only is the polemic of book I linked to more general preoccupations of the *Essay* as a whole, but these preoccupations

---

[11] The educational emphasis of Locke's polemic has not received the attention it deserves. But there are exceptions, notably Greenlee (1972) and Tully (1988) esp. 20–4.

in turn recur in places other than the *Essay*, notably in Locke's posthumous work *Of the Conduct of the Understanding*. Its theme is the importance of the understanding in human conduct, and the book has a more practical and prescriptive slant to it than the *Essay*, although it remains philosophically close to it. In §3 of the *Conduct*, Locke spells out some familiar points about how and why the reasoning faculty can go wrong. The first of them is that there are some people who seldom reason at all but

do and think according to the Example of others, whether Parents, Neighbours, Ministers, or who else they are pleas'd to make choice of to have an implicit Faith in, for the saving of themselves the pains and trouble of thinking and examining for themselves.[12]

Locke will return to his attack on borrowed thoughts later on in the *Conduct*, but not before he has had something to say about the acceptance of questionable principles as unquestionable. This he attacks at length and with unflagging vigour in §6, on 'Principles'. He once again abhors the way we uncritically accept as foundations such thoughts as 'it hath long been received in the World, therefore it is true'.[13] He acknowledges, in tones very reminiscent of *Essay* I iii 24, that we all need principles, but stresses that we must examine them for ourselves.

In the *Conduct* Locke offers some practical advice about the use of habit and exercise for breaking our reliance on such dubious principles. Similar remarks can be found in §10 on 'Prejudice' as well as in the two succeeding chapters 'Indifferency' and 'Examine':

We take our Principles at haphazard upon trust, and without ever having examined them, and then believe a whole System, upon a Presumption that they are true and solid; and what is all this but childish, senseless, shameful Credulity?[14]

Locke's condemnation of such credulity also finds its way into his more specific proposals for education. In the *Conduct* itself he has a section on the value of reading (§19) and, not surprisingly, inveighs against the practice of cramming 'ourselves with a great load of Collections'. 'We are of the ruminating kind' and need to meditate on what we read for ourselves. By reading without such

---

[12] Yolton (1993) 7.   [13] Yolton (1993) 21.   [14] Yolton (1993) 44.

thinking we merely accumulate 'so much loose matter floating in our brain'.[15]

Such a Knowledge as this is but Knowledge by hearsay, and the ostentation of it is at best talking by roat, and very often upon weak and wrong Principles.

In the end, then, *Essay* I iii does more than merely argue for the falsity of ethical innatism. In pointing out the dangers of the theory it reveals in its closing sections an intensity and energy that is motivated by Locke's fiercely-held views on education, and in particular moral education.[16]

## [4] LOCKE'S PLATONISM

The Platonic resonances in Locke's argument should now be so clear that, paradoxical as it may once have seemed, it becomes appropriate to talk about Locke's Platonism. Of course, these are two philosophers between whom there are many areas of disagreement, one of them being the way in which Locke conditionally endorsed the Stoic version of innatism: 'if you had to be innatist' he seems to say, 'you would have to adopt this version'. Plato, on the other hand, would vigorously attack the claim that if a proposition is innate it need have all the features attributed to it by Locke and his innatist contemporaries. But once Locke starts to attack the theory in the way we have just outlined we begin to see some striking affinities between the two.

First of all, there is a similarity in the way both see moral reasoning. We saw how Locke is very much a theorist in ethics, claiming that morality could be as demonstrable as mathematics. If we wanted to find a parallel for this we would not have to look very hard before the Plato's name came to mind. In *Republic* VI–VII he sketches the nature of a science whose first principle is that

---

[15] Yolton (1993) 60–1. Cf. *Essay* I iv 23: 'the Floating of other Men's Opinions in our Brains'.

[16] Locke was by no means alone in encouraging people to think for themselves more. Ironically, it was something of a rallying cry for the Cambridge Platonists as well, who were constantly exhorting people to the use of reason in religion. Their belief was that rather than accepting religious dogma on hearsay we should always consult our reasoning faculty, which is conveniently stocked with innate truths. But Locke is in effect attempting to turn the tables on them by showing how an apparently innocent appeal to reason is really an appeal to a group of entrenched opinions. See Cudworth (1731) 137 and, for other references, Scott (1990) 91–4 and (1994) 147–50.

of the form of the good, and which surpasses even mathematics in the clarity and rigour of its construction. But the *Republic* is anticipated in this to some extent by the *Meno* which also expects moral knowledge to turn out to be substantially similar to mathematics or geometry. When explaining how to give a definition in ethics, Socrates has no hesitation in drawing examples from geometry (73e3–76a7); the theory of recollection is introduced in order to show that moral knowledge is attainable, but the example used in the slave-boy demonstration comes again from geometry; finally, the method of hypothesis which is used to help make discoveries about virtue derives originally from the geometers.[17]

A second affinity, linked to the first, is that both philosophers expect moral claims to be subject to scrutiny and supported by reasons. Locke, as we have just seen, was adamant on this point, but Plato also insisted that beliefs about morality, even if they happen to be true, are not enough; explanatory reasoning must be called in. This is the point of the distinction between knowledge and true belief made at the end of the *Meno*.[18] This distinction can be seen as a development of Socrates' insistent use of the *elenchus* in the first part of the dialogue. What drives Meno to want to give up the inquiry into virtue is precisely Socrates' refusal to let any statement of mere opinion stand unexamined.

The third and, for us, most salient affinity now falls into place. Both Plato and Locke are deeply concerned to fight off laziness, in particular that of borrowing one's principles from others. Laziness, or the failure to think for oneself, features prominently in the *Meno*. It is associated with the dialogue's two epistemological innovations, the theory of recollection and the distinction between knowledge and true belief. In the first case, we saw how, in addition to using the theory to solve the paradox, Socrates also uses it as a way of preventing Meno from

[17] 86d3–87c3. Of course, we should not overdo the similarities between Plato and Locke here. Locke claims in iii 4 'there cannot any one moral rule be propos'd whereof a man may not justly demand a reason', that is, for every moral rule there is some further demonstration; it follows from this that no moral proposition could be self-evident. The first principles of ethics are therefore not themselves ethical. In the *Republic*, at least, Plato would have disputed this, even though he would have agreed that the vast majority of moral propositions require demonstration.

[18] The similarity between Plato and Locke on this issue has been noticed by Burnyeat (1987) 20, note 26.

succumbing to intellectual laziness (p. 32). Meno's paradox would 'make us lazy and is music to the ears of weaklings. The other doctrine [i.e. recollection] produces energetic seekers after after knowledge' (81d6–e1). As well as this comment we saw how Socrates ended the whole episode with another passionate attack on laziness: if we believe that we have a duty to inquire after what we do not know, we shall become better, braver and less lazy than if we decide to give up the inquiry (86b7–c2). The slave-boy demonstration provided a reinforcement of this point. From the beginning of the examination Socrates insists that he is not instilling the opinions into the slave boy, and at the end claims that to complete the recollection process the boy needs not just to draw the opinions from himself but also *for* himself (85d4). Laziness in the form of borrowed principles then re-occurs at the end of the dialogue with the analogy of the road to Larissa. The salient distinction between knowledge and true belief is between someone who has heard from others and someone who has worked things out for themselves.

These passages will all be familiar from chapter 1, but since intellectual laziness has now turned out to be such an important issue it is worth showing that it pervades the *Meno* even more extensively than even these passages suggest. The rejection of hearsay has in fact been a preoccupation of the first ten pages of the dialogue where Socrates shows a strong concern about Meno's laziness, precisely the kind of laziness that relies on hearsay. When Socrates first asks Meno what virtue is, both see the task as a matter of remembering what his mentor Gorgias said on the subject. What happens up to the point where Meno wants to give up is that he finds he can no longer rely on ready-made answers, because he is unable to defend them for himself. Let me show how this happens in more detail.

When Socrates admits his ignorance about virtue Meno is surprised, and still more so when Socrates claims that he has never met anyone who does know what it is (71b5–d2):

MENO: What, didn't you meet Gorgias when he was here?
SOCRATES: Yes.
MENO: And you still didn't think he knew?
SOCRATES: I'm a forgetful sort of person, and I can't say just now what
    I thought at the time. Probably he did know, and I expect you know

what he used to say about it. So remind me what it was, or tell me
yourself if you will. No doubt you agree with him.

The examination is apparently going to be a matter of Meno
recalling what Gorgias has said.

In fact Meno makes three attempts to define virtue, all of
which seem to be derived from someone else – in the first two
cases from Gorgias.[19] The third definition, 'virtue is the desire
for and ability to obtain noble things',[20] may not be Gorgias',
but it is nevertheless borrowed from an unnamed poet. As with
the previous two attempts, Meno fails to defend his answer. The
original authors might have been able to do better, but that is not
what Socrates is seeking. Meno must be able to think for himself,
and this he manifestly fails to do.[21]

We are told at 96d6 that Meno was taught by the sophist Gorgias
and the evidence that we have about the historical Gorgias'
teaching methods fits well with Plato's tacit criticism of Meno's
education. According to Aristotle, Gorgias was keen on giving his
pupils set speeches on favourite topics to learn by heart (*Sophistical
Refutations* 183b36–184a8):

For the training given by the paid professors of contentious argument
was like the practice of Gorgias. For he used to hand out rhetorical
speeches to be learned by heart, and they handed out speeches in the
form of question and answer which each supposed would cover most of
the arguments on either side. And therefore the teaching they gave to
their pupils was rapid but unsystematic. For they used to suppose that
they trained people by imparting to them not the art but its products,
as though anyone professing that he would impart a form of knowledge
to obviate any pain in the feet, were then not to teach a man the
art of shoe-making or the sources whence he can acquire anything of
the kind, but were to present him with several kinds of shoes of all
sorts – for he has helped him meet his need, but has not imparted
an art to him.

---

[19] Aristotle attributes the first definition to Gorgias in *Politics* I 13, 1260a25–8; for evidence
that Gorgias held the second definition see *Gorgias* 452d5–8.

[20] 77b2–5.

[21] It is interesting to note the device that Plato uses to emphasise this point. When
Socrates first asks Meno to recall what Gorgias has said, he ironically adds that
Meno will be giving his own opinion as well (71c10–d2). After the downfall of the first
definition, Socrates asks Meno to remember what Gorgias said, but quickly adds 'and
you with him'; now the suggestion that Meno has thought for himself is less marked
than before (73c6–8). When Socrates makes a third allusion to Gorgias at 76b1, the
irony wears even thinner, and he omits any reference to Meno's own views: 'you're
not willing to recollect what Gorgias said'.

Similarly, Meno will simply reproduce a set-speech on the topic of the day without the ability to create the product afresh from his own resources. As a result, memorised speeches, which may have served him well on many other occasions (as he says at 80b2–3), fail him when he encounters an awkward customer in Socrates. Given all this, it should come as no surprise that when Socrates comes to making his distinction between knowledge and true belief later on in the dialogue he places the rejection of hearsay at its very centre.

It should now be clear what Locke's Platonism consists in. Where Plato saw himself engaged in a battle against the acceptance of opinions on hearsay, whether those were the opinions of a sophistic mentor or simply the commonplaces of society,[22] Locke found himself in a very similar battle with the seventeenth-century innatists. But if Locke and Plato are so close, why is one attacking and the other defending theories of innate knowledge? The answer is that they are concerned with very different innatist theories and that, when Locke attacks innatism in the passages discussed, he is fastening onto precisely those features that are lacking in Platonic recollection.

The educational argument of *Essay* I iii would not only leave Plato untouched, he would no doubt have enjoyed using it himself. Like Locke, he would have rounded on any theory that tended to insulate principles from examination by appealing to their apparent self-evidence, ease of discovery or general acceptance. Committed to such a theory we would be highly unlikely to go wherever the argument led; there would in fact be no argument at all. That Plato would have vigorously rejected any innatist theory that glorified common sense in this way was the main thrust of our interpretation of recollection in section I.

In the last two chapters we have used some of the conclusions of sections I–III to revise some views about the relations

---

[22] In the *Meno* the opinions that are being received on hearsay seem to be those not of society in general but of one particular sophist, Gorgias. Does this not mark a considerable difference between Plato and Locke who places so much emphasis on universal consent? However, a closer look at the opinions that Gorgias has been instilling in Meno shows them to be nothing if not conventional. At 71e3–4, for instance, a man's virtue is said to involve 'doing good to his friends and harm to his enemies' – a fifth-century commonplace if ever there was one. On this issue see Canto-Sperber (1991) 223, note 37.

between ancient philosophy and the seventeenth-century debate over innateness. We saw how metaphysical innatism, even though some of its proponents were called Platonists, had some remarkable dissimilarities with Platonic recollection. We then saw how the inspiration behind the moral innatism of the century was again not Platonic but Stoic. This led us to expect that Locke would be attacking a Stoic target, but what was striking was that he should have done so by using considerations that were at the front of Plato's mind when he first proposed his own version of innateness in the *Meno*. In the introduction to this section, I quoted Leibniz's view of where the historical affinities lay in the innateness debate. It should now be clear that the true position is rather more complicated.

# Conclusion

This study has been shaped in part by the contrast between two very different interpretations of Platonic recollection. I have tried to show how opting for one of these interpretations also raises new questions about the course of the learning debate as it ran through Aristotle and the Hellenistic philosophers. We took stock of our conclusions about that debate after section III, and so shall not repeat the task here. In the last section, we showed how some of these conclusions affect the way we view the lineage of the theory of innate ideas in the seventeenth-century. In chapter 9 we traced out the affinity between Stoicism and the seventeenth century theory of innate ideas, and in the following chapter found a remarkable alliance between Plato and Locke. The explanation for this lies partly in the fact that the theory Locke was attacking was very different from recollection. What was also important was that Plato and Locke shared a similar attitude to the status that ethical common notions should have in philosophical inquiry. This last point brings out the way in which the debate about moral learning in the seventeenth century, like its ancient equivalent, was not simply one about the origin of ideas or principles, but also about the status of ethical common sense. In this conclusion, I wish to show how this second issue, that so divided Plato from both Aristotle and the Stoics, has developed more recently.

The debate about the status of common sense and the role it should play in ethical reasoning is now often referred to as the debate about moral intuitionism. An intuitionist in this context is someone who thinks that there are widely-shared beliefs that should have a criterial role to play in ethical reasoning; other moral beliefs must be judged by conformity to them. This means that such prevalent and deeply held views are to act as criteria for any

moral theories that philosophers may from time to time produce.[1]
Now, although I have avoided using the term 'intuitionism' so
far in this study, the style of ethical reasoning to which it refers
should be very familiar. The theory that Locke was attacking was
not just innatist but also, in this sense, 'intuitionist'; similarly,
Stoic innateness differs from Platonic recollection by, among other
things, its commitment to some form of intuitionism. And because
intuitionism is detachable from innateness *per se*, an Aristotelian
could be described as an intuitionist.

The context in which the debate about moral intuitionism has
persisted is the debate over the merits or otherwise of utilitarianism. This may seem like territory very remote from any of the
issues we have been discussing, but a brief look at the attitude of
some of the most famous utilitarians and their critics will show
that the argument that Aristotle had with Plato, and the fight
that Locke had under the guise of attacking moral innatism
has continued, albeit in an adapted form. The anti-intuitionist
utilitarians in question are J. S. Mill and R. M. Hare, who have
both put forward arguments strikingly similar to those of Locke's
educational polemic, but without tackling the innatist issue at all.

Mill's attitude to intuitionism is well known. He sees it as one
of the major contrasts with utilitarianism, a theory in which all
ethical rules can be derived systematically and scientifically from
one principle, the principle of utility. Mill was adamant that there
is only one ultimate principle. As he explains in both *Utilitarianism*
and the *System of Logic*,[2] having more than one principle would
mean that moral conflicts cannot be resolved; ultimately there
would have to be a single criterion to decide the priority between
principles.

But there is also a much more Lockean strain to his discussion
of the use of intuitions in ethics. In general, he sees their use as a
means of entrenching irrationality and prejudice, and of imposing
these in a tyrannical manner on those in one's power.[3] This view of
intuitions as tending towards irrationality and prejudice is one he
shares with Bentham, who also sees an essential contrast between

---

[1] For discussions of intuitionism in this sense see Rawls (1971) 34–40 and Williams
(1985) ch. 6.

[2] *Utilitarianism* ch. I = Ryan (1987) 273–4; *System of Logic* VI xii 7 = Robson (1974) 951.

[3] See *On Liberty* ch. I = Collini (1989) 9 for a particularly eloquent account of how
culturally formed opinions can acquire the status of self-evident and self-justifying
natural principles.

the highly systematic approach of utilitarianism and intuitionism.[4] In fact, in his *Autobiography*, Mill cites anti-intuitionism as the first and most striking thing he found in Bentham:[5]

What thus impressed me was the chapter in which Bentham passed judgment on the common modes of reasons in morals and legislation, deduced from phrases like 'law of nature', 'right reason', 'the moral sense', 'natural rectitude' and the like, and characterised them as dogmatism in disguise imposing its sentiments upon others under the cover of sounding expressions which convey no reason for the sentiment but set up the sentiment as its own reason. It had not struck me that Bentham's principle put an end to all this.

Although Mill's views on intuitionism are scattered throughout his works, they are given a sustained airing in his critique of Whewell, one of the foremost intuitionist philosophers of the day.[6] It is in this work that Mill's Lockean tendencies are strongest. Right from the start, Mill makes it clear that his objection to Whewell's intuitionism is bound up with the nature of Whewell's professional aspirations. The universities of Oxford and Cambridge were run by the clergy, the beliefs that they intended their alumni to hold were therefore prescribed from the start. What mattered was not whether what you believed was true, but whether it was orthodox. A worse starting-point for education could scarcely be imagined. Mill goes on to apply this indictment of the universities to Whewell in particular, accusing him of shaping 'the whole of philosophy . . . into a form adapted to serve as a support and justification to any opinions that happen to be accepted'. His intuitionism consists in ascribing self-evidence 'to all moral propositions familiar to him from his early years'.[7] Compare Locke's remarks in *Essay* I iii 22–3 about the way opinions with which we are brought up from our earliest memories assume, by some sort of illusion, the status of natural truths.

The Lockean theme of thinking for oneself crops up again a few pages later when Mill is defending Bentham's disciples against Whewell's attack. These 'were and are persons in an

---

[4] See *An Introduction to the Principles of Morals and Legislation*, I xiv = Ryan (1987) 68–9.

[5] Ch. III = Robson (1989) 67.

[6] William Whewell, intuitionist, poet, polymath and Master of Trinity College, Cambridge, was also, interestingly enough, the first person to publish an edition of Robert Sanderson's *De Obligatione Conscientiae* for over a hundred years. Mill's *Whewell on Moral Philosophy* is reprinted in Ryan (1987).

[7] Ryan (1987) 230.

unusual degree addicted to thinking and judging for themselves;
persons remarkable for learning willingly from all masters, but
swearing blind fealty to none':[8] shades of Locke's 'posture of
blind credulity'. Another Lockean theme that appears in this
work is that of universal consent. Mill rounds on Whewell's claim
that principles that command universal assent must be right. He
immediately objects that the most appalling superstitions and
practices have received widespread assent. And as for universal assent, there is no such thing: in an apophthegm of which
Locke would have been proud, he concludes 'the universal voice
of mankind, so often appealed to, is universal only in its dis-
cordance'.[9]

But Mill has already mentioned universal assent when com-
plaining of the way that intuitionists think that their opinions
are self-justifying.[10] He acknowledges that some intuitionists, no
doubt embarrassed by the arbitrariness of this, attempt to claim
universal assent for their principles, declaring that they are part
of human nature. But the reality is that when they come to
count the votes they simply ignore or write off any who dissent
on the grounds of perversity or insincerity.[11] Why do they resort
to such tactics?

The explanation of the matter is, the inability of persons in general
to conceive that feelings of right and wrong, which have been deeply
implanted in their minds by the teaching they have from infancy
received from all around them, can sincerely be thought by anyone
else to be mistaken or misplaced. This is the mental infirmity which
Bentham's philosophy tends to correct, and Dr Whewell's to per-
petuate.[12]

Given the degree of cultural conditioning involved in the implant-
ing of moral principles, no one of them can be immune from
examination and criticism of the sort provided by Bentham. In
the conclusion to this section, Mill talks of the contest between
Bentham and Whewell as being one

[8] Ryan (1987) 238.
[9] Ryan (1987) 262.
[10] Ryan (1987) 243–4.
[11] Compare, yet again, Locke *Essay* I iii 20, criticising those who, in their failure to
establish universal consent, claim that the principles in question have become perverted
and darkened by custom. In effect, he says, they are making 'their private Perswasions
... pass for universal Consent', and thereby 'cast by the Votes and Opinions of the rest
of Mankind, as not worthy the reckoning.'
[12] Ryan (1987) 243.

of reason and argument against the deification of mere opinion and habit. The doctrine that the existing order of things is the natural order, and that being natural all innovation on it is criminal, is as vicious in morals, as it is now at last admitted to be in physics, and in society and government.[13]

Like Locke before him, Mill weaves together the themes of self-justification and universal consent; one conspires with the other to establish the alleged naturalness of certain opinions, thus insulating them from all examination. The result is the debilitation of our critical faculties.

The parallels between Locke and Mill show how the seventeenth-century debate over innatism had become intertwined with an issue that was to become central to ethics and, it seems, to remain so; for the anti-intuitional stance of the early utilitarians has been taken up by some of their contemporary successors, most notably by R. M. Hare. In *Moral Thinking* he sets out a distinction between two levels of moral thinking, the critical and the intuitive.[14] The latter refers to what we do in most everyday moral thinking – reacting to situations with deeply ingrained moral convictions for which we may or may not have any rationale. Hare contrasts this with critical thinking which, on his theory, means utilitarian reasoning in accordance with his principle of universalisation. The advantage of critical thinking is that it is able to resolve moral conflicts, whereas intuitive thinking has nothing to contribute beyond presenting a clash of principles. However, it is obvious that we are not able to engage in critical thinking all the time, so instead we may use critical thinking for 'the cool hour of reflection' in which we select what principles we shall appeal to in everyday situations and in which we can reflect on moral conflicts and dilemmas. Thus, in everyday situations we act as if we are intuitionists, but ultimately it is critical thinking that ought to have the last say.

Like Mill before him, Hare has some very rough things to say about those who stop at the intuitive level, as some deontological opponents of utilitarianism do.[15] And like Mill, it is not just their

---

[13] Ryan (1987) 244. On 'deification' of opinion and prejudice see Locke *Essay* I iii 26: someone who raises his own prejudices to the status of natural principles is 'taking Monsters lodged in his own Brain for the Images of the Deity'.

[14] Hare (1981) ch. 2.

[15] See, for example, Hare (1981) 12.

inability to resolve conflicts that he criticises, but the fact that the intuitions on which they rely may be little else than mere prejudice. Intuitions are not self-justifying, but the products of upbringing and past moral decisions. Here is a passage where he dismisses the proposal that we could use intuitive thinking without ever having to appeal to the critical level:

For the selection of prima facie principles, and the resolution of conflicts between them, critical thinking is necessary. If we do not think that men can do it, we shall have to invoke a Butlerian God to do it for us, and reveal the results through our consciences. But how then would we distinguish between the voice of God and the voices of our nursemaids (if we had them)?[16]

Parenthetic concessions to the twentieth century aside, Locke's 'superstition of a nurse or the authority of an old woman' is still here to haunt us.

An important point about both Mill and Hare is that, unlike Locke, they explicitly acknowledge the Platonic ancestry of their anti-intuitionism. Mill had an enormously high opinion of Plato; he called him the 'master-mind of antiquity' and was appalled at the general ignorance of him at the time, not least at the two great seats of learning and hot-beds of intuitionism, Oxford and Cambridge.[17] In addition to publishing annotated abridgements and translations of the *Apology, Protagoras, Gorgias* and *Phaedrus*, he wrote an extended review of Grote's *Plato* in which he set out his own views in some detail. What is so interesting about his perception of Plato is the emphasis he gives to the critical side of Plato's philosophy. In the introduction to the *Protagoras*, for instance, he asserts that it is only when talking about epistemology or philosophical method that Plato shows himself to have definite views. Otherwise he is elusive. In a passage that has remarkable relevance to the *Meno* (86bc and 97dff.) he says:

when the topic under discussion is the proper *mode* of philosophizing – either the moral spirit in which truth should be sought, or the intellectual processes and methods by which it is to be attained; or when the subject matter is not any particular scientific principle, but knowledge in the abstract, the differences between knowledge and ignorance, and between knowledge and mere opinion; *then* the views inculcated are definite and consistent, are always the same,

---

[16] Hare (1981) 45–6.
[17] *Notes on Some of the More Popular Dialogues of Plato* = Robson (1978) 39–40.

and are put forward with the appearance of earnest and matured belief.[18]

These comments are made about Plato's writings in general, but it is interesting to note that when he comes to talk of the purpose of the *Protagoras* in particular, he claims that it is not to ridicule the sophists

but to show that it was possible to go much beyond the point which they had attained in moral and political philosophy; that, on the whole, they left the science of the mind and of virtue in an extremely unsatisfactory state; that they could not stand the test of the rigorous dialectics which Socrates carried into these inquiries; and that the truth could only be ascertained by that more accurate mode of sifting opinions which the dialectic method . . . furnishes but which speech-making, and the mere delivery of doctrines from master to student (the practice of the sophists) absolutely preclude.[19]

In his review of Grote's *Plato* he makes a rather similar point, but now about Plato's philosophy in general:[20]

The enemy against whom Plato really fought, and the warfare against whom was the incessant occupation of the greater part of his life and writings, was not Sophistry either in the ancient or modern sense of the term, but Commonplace. It was the acceptance of traditional opinions and current sentiments as an ultimate fact; and the bandying of the abstract terms which express approbation and disapprobation, desire and aversion, admiration and disgust, as if they had a meaning thoroughly understood and universally assented to.

Mill thus highlights Plato's pessimistic diagnosis of the intellectual achievements of his day, and describes the purpose of Platonic philosophy as being [21]

to make men conscious of their ignorance of the things most needful to be known, fill them with shame and uneasiness at their own state, and rouse a pungent internal stimulus, summoning up all their mental energies to attack these greatest of all problems, and never rest until, as far as possible, the true solutions are found.

He concludes with a stern reminder that Plato's diagnosis is no less applicable to his contemporaries. So, the Plato of J.S. Mill is

---

[18] Robson (1978) 41.
[19] Robson (1978) 44. This recalls our discussion of Plato's attitude to Gorgias on pp. 254–5.
[20] *Grote's Plato* = Robson (1978) 403.
[21] Robson (1978) 404.

very much Plato the anti-intuitionist and, not surprisingly, Mill finds him a strongly sympathetic philosopher. It is also the Plato who proposes recollection in the *Meno* and who develops it in the way I have described in the *Phaedo* and *Phaedrus*. Indeed, when Mill himself mentions the theory, he contrasts it with contemporary intuitionist accounts of knowledge which, he thinks, Plato would have rejected outright: 'he knew too well how slowly, painfully and at last imperfectly, the knowledge is acquired. The whole process of philosophizing was conceived by him as a laborious effort to recall former knowledge back to mind'.[22]

Hare shares with Mill a strong interest in Plato, though it is a rather more critical one. In his writings too, the anti-intuitional aspects of Platonism are pushed well to the fore. *Moral Thinking* is itself prefaced with a quotation from the *Meno*, the passage in which Socrates speaks of his conviction that there is a distinction between knowledge and true belief (98b); Hare sees this distinction as the ancestor of his own between the two levels of thinking. In his own short introduction to Plato, the distinction of the *Meno* figures quite prominently. Plato's point is that although true opinion does allow us to get by, it is not enough – if it were there would be no purpose to philosophy. The problem in ethics is that 'there is no orthodoxy to appeal to, and we have, however much we should like the comforts of moral assurance, to think the thing out for ourselves'.[23] And when it comes at the end of the book to assessing Plato's achievement, this is one of the main themes:

> by recognizing the distinction between knowledge and right opinion, he was led to demand, as a qualification for knowledge, the ability to give and defend a reason or explanation for the thing known. . . . Whenever anybody, whether in science or mathematics or moral philosophy, makes some statement on the basis of mere intuition, hoping that we shall share the intuition and therefore agree with it, he should be disciplined by means of the Socratic–Platonic demand that he 'give an account' of what he has just said. Even now too many philosophical frauds are unwilling to face the auditors in this way.[24]

Needless to say these 'Platonist' philosophers have not had everything their own way. One intuitionist critic has pointed to the

---

[22] Robson (1978) 423. In the same place Mill describes the *Meno* as a 'gem', the *Phaedo* and the *Gorgias* being 'noble statues'.
[23] Hare (1982) 41.
[24] Hare (1982) 72.

serious difficulties they have had in trying to do without moral intuitions altogether; they are attempting to create a moral philosophy out of nothing. What is so interesting from our perspective is the identity of this critic: David Ross, a figure better known for his prodigious contribution to Aristotelian scholarship.[25] But the hand of Aristotle had already been at work decades earlier when, at the end of the nineteenth century, Henry Sidgwick conceded that utilitarianism could not be created out of nothing, and that the whole system had to be based upon at least one intuition, the principle of utility itself. Then he found that his newly acquired sympathy with intuitionism sent him back to Aristotle: 'In this state of mind I had to read Aristotle again; and a light seemed to dawn upon me as to the meaning and drift of his procedure ... What he gave us was the Common Sense Morality of Greece, reduced to consistency by careful comparison: given not as something external to him but as what "we" – he and others – think, ascertained by reflection.'[26]

Sidgwick's references to 'careful comparison' and 'reflection' perhaps refer to what is one of the most impressive achievements in Aristotle's ethics, his ability to balance intuition and argument and to avoid the kind of enslavement to common sense of which Mill accuses his adversaries. Sidgwick's tribute is also testimony to the way in which modern philosophical debate can be enriched by the continued rereading of ancient texts, whether Platonic, Aristotelian or Hellenistic.

[25] See Ross (1930) chs 1 and 2, esp. 39ff.
[26] Sidgwick (1907) xxi, quoted by Barnes (1980) 495.

# Bibliography

Ackrill, J. L. (1973) 'Anamnesis in the *Phaedo*: remarks on 73c–75c', in Lee, E. N., Mourelatos, A. D. P. and Rorty, R. M., eds. (1973) 177–95
  (1980) 'Aristotle on *eudaimonia*', in Rorty, A. O., ed. (1980) 15–33
  (1981) 'Aristotle's theory of definition: some questions on *Posterior Analytics* II 8–10', in Berti, E., ed. (1981) 359–84
  (1987) *A New Aristotle Reader*. Oxford and Princeton
Adam, C. and Tannery, P. (1897–1913) eds. *Oeuvres de Descartes*. 12 vols. Paris
Adam, J. (1963) ed. *The Republic of Plato*. 2 vols. 2nd. edn. Cambridge
Adams, R. M. (1975) 'Where do our ideas come from? – Descartes *vs.* Locke', in Stich, S. P., ed. (1975) 71–87
Anton, J. P. and Kustas, G. L. (1971) eds. *Essays in Ancient Greek Philosophy*. Albany
Archer Hind, R. D. (1894) ed. *The Phaedo of Plato*, 2nd. edn. London
Arnim, H., von (1903–24) ed. *Stoicorum Veterum Fragmenta*. 4 vols. Leipzig
Asmis, E. (1984) *Epicurus' Scientific Method*. Ithaca and London
Bailey, C. (1947) ed. *Titi Lucretii Cari de Rerum Natura Libri Sex*. Oxford
Baldwin, A. and Hutton, S. (1994) ed. *Platonism and the English Imagination*. Cambridge
Barnes, J. (1972) 'Mr Locke's darling notion', *Philosophical Quarterly* 22: 193–214
  (1975) 'Aristotle's theory of demonstration', in Barnes, J., Schofield, M. and Sorabji, R. (1975) eds. 65–87
  (1980) 'Aristotle and the methods of ethics', *Revue internationale de la philosophie* 34: 490–511
  (1981) 'Proof and the syllogism', in Berti, E. (1981) ed. 17–59
  (1984) ed. *The Complete Works of Aristotle* (The Revised Oxford Translation). 2 vols. Princeton
  (1988) 'Epicurean signs', *Oxford Studies in Ancient Philosophy* Suppl. 91–134
  (1993) ed. *Aristotle: Posterior Analytics*, 2nd. edn. Oxford
Barnes, J., Schofield, M. and Sorabji, R. (1975) eds. *Articles on Aristotle I: Science*. London
  (1979) eds. *Articles on Aristotle III: Metaphysics*. London
Bates, W. (1722) *Works*. London

Bedu-Addo, J. T. (1991) 'Sense-experience and the argument for recollection in Plato's *Phaedo*', *Phronesis* 36: 27–60

Benson, H. H. (1990) 'The priority of definition and the Socratic elenchus', *Oxford Studies in Ancient Philosophy* 8: 19–65

Berti, E. (1981) ed. *Aristotle on Science: The Posterior Analytics. Proceedings of the 8th. Symposium Aristotelicum*. Padua

Blond, J. M. le (1970) *Logique et Méthode chez Aristote*. 2nd. edn. Paris
(1979) 'Aristotle on definition', in Barnes, J., Schofield, M. and Sorabji, R. (1979) eds. 63–79

Bluck, R. S. (1961) ed. *Plato's Meno*. Cambridge

Bolton, R. (1976) 'Essentialism and semantic theory in Aristotle: *Posterior Analytics* II 7–10', *Philosophical Review* 85: 514–44
(1987) 'Definition and scientific method in Aristotle's *Posterior Analytics* and *Generation of Animals*', in Gotthelf, A. and Lennox, J. G. (1987) ed. 120–66
(1991) 'Aristotle's method in natural science: *Physics* I', in Judson, L. (1991) ed. 1–30

Bonhöffer, A. (1890) *Epictet und die Stoa*. Stuttgart

Bostock, D. (1986) *Plato's Phaedo*. Oxford
(1988) *Plato's Theaetetus*. Oxford

Bouffartigue, J. and Patillon, M. (1977) eds. *Porphyre: De l'abstinence*. Budé edition. 2 vols. Paris

Broad, C. D. (1975) *Leibniz: an Introduction*. Cambridge

Broadie, S. (1991) *Ethics with Aristotle*. Oxford

Brown, L. (1991) 'Connaissance et réminiscence dans le *Ménon*', *Revue philosophique* 181: 603–619

Brunschwig, J. (1964) review of Kleve, K. (1963) *Revue des études grecques* 77: 352–6
(1978) ed. *Les Stoiciens et Leur Logique*. Paris
(1981) 'L' objet et la structure des *Seconds Analytiques* d'après Aristote', in Berti, E. (1981) ed. 61–96

Burnet, J. (1900) ed. *The Ethics of Aristotle*. London
(1900–7) ed. *Platonis Opera*. 5 vols. Oxford

Burnyeat, M. F. (1976) 'Plato on the grammar of perceiving', *Classical Quarterly* n.s. 26: 29–51
(1977) 'Examples in epistemology: Socrates, Theaetetus and G. E. Moore', *Philosophy* 52: 381–96
(1981) 'Aristotle on understanding knowledge', in Berti, E. (1981) ed. 97–139
(1987) 'Wittgenstein and Augustine *De Magistro*', *Proceedings of the Aristotelian Society* Suppl. 61: 1–24

Burthogge, W. (1675) *Causa Dei or An Apology for God*. London
(1678) *Organum Vetus et Novum*. London

Bury, R. G., trans. (1933–49) *Sextus Empiricus*. Loeb Translation. 4 vols. London and Cambridge, Mass.

Canto-Sperber, M. (1991) ed. *Platon: Ménon.* Paris
Carré, M. H., trans. (1937) *Herbert of Cherbury: De Veritate.* Bristol
Charleton, W. (1652) *The Darkness of Atheism Dispelled by the Light of Nature.* London
Cherniss, H., trans. (1976) *Plutarch's Moralia* xiii, part 2. Loeb Translation. London and Cambridge, Mass.
Chomsky, N. (1966) *Cartesian Linguistics.* New York
  (1969) 'Quine's empirical assumptions', in Davidson, D. and Hintikka, J. (1969) eds. 53–68
Collini, S. (1989) ed. *J.S. Mill: On Liberty and Other Writings.* Cambridge
Colman, J. (1983) *John Locke's Moral Philosophy.* Edinburgh
Cooper, J. M. (1975) *Reason and the Human Good in Aristotle.* Cambridge, Mass.
  (1987) 'Contemplation and happiness: a reconsideration', *Synthese* 72: 187–216
Cornford, F. M. (1935) *Plato's Theory of Knowledge.* London
Cudworth, R. (1678) *The True Intellectual System of the Universe.* London
  (1731) *A Treatise Concerning Eternal and Immutable Morality.* London
Davidson, D. and Hintikka, J. (1969) eds. *Words and Objections: Essays on the Work of W. V. O. Quine.* Dordrecht
Day, J. (1994) ed. *Plato's Meno in Focus.* London
De Lacy, P. (1980–4) ed. *Galen: On the Doctrines of Hippocrates and Plato.* 3 vols. 2nd. edn. Berlin
Diels, H. and Kranz, W. (1985) eds. *Die Fragmente der Vorsokratiker.* 3 vols. 6th. edn. Zurich and Hildesheim
Diels, H. and Schubart, W. (1905) eds. *Anonymer Kommentar zu Platons Theaetet.* Berlin
Dragona-Monachou, M. (1976) *The Stoic Arguments for the Existence and Providence of the Gods.* Athens
Everson, S. (1990) ed. *Epistemology (Companions to Ancient Thought I).* Cambridge
Ferguson, R. (1675) *The Interest of Reason in Religion.* London
Fine, G. (1992) 'Inquiry in the *Meno*', in Kraut, R. (1992) ed. 200–226
  (1993) *On Ideas: Aristotle's Criticism of Plato's Theory of Forms.* Oxford
Fortenbaugh, W. W. (1975) 'Aristotle's analysis of friendship: function and analogy, resemblance, and focal meaning', *Phronesis* 20: 51–62
Fremgen, A. and Fay, D. (1980) 'Overextensions in production and comprehension: a methodological clarification', *Journal of Child Language* 7: 205–11
Gallop, D. (1975) ed. *Plato's Phaedo.* Oxford
Geach, P. (1957) *Mental Acts.* London
Gigante, M. (1983) ΣΥΖΗΤΗΣΙΣ. *Studi sull' epicureismo greco e romano offerti a Marcello Gigante.* 2 vols. Naples
Glidden, D. K. (1983) 'Epicurean semantics', in Gigante, M. (1983) 1 185–226

(1985) 'Epicurean prolepsis', *Oxford Studies in Ancient Philosophy* 3: 175–217

Goldschmidt, V. (1978) 'Remarques sur l'origine épicurienne de la prénotion', in Brunschwig, J. (1978) ed. 155–69

(1979) *Le Système stoïcien et l'idée de temps*. 4th. edn. Paris

Goodman, N. (1980) 'The epistemological argument', in Morrick, H., (1980) ed. 251–56

Gotthelf, A. and Lennox, J. G. (1987) eds. *Philosophical Issues in Aristotle's Biology*. Cambridge

Gould, J. B. (1970) *The Philosophy of Chrysippus*. Leiden

Graeser, A. (1987) ed. *Mathematik und Metaphysik bei Aristoteles: X Symposium Aristotelicum*. Bern

Greenlee, D. (1972) 'Locke and the controversy over innate ideas', *Journal of the History of Ideas* 33: 251–64

Grilli, A. (1953) *Il Problema della Vita Contemplativa nel Mondo Greco-Romano*. Milan

Grube, G. M. A., trans. (1981) *Plato: Republic*. London

Grumach, E. (1966) *Physis und Agathon in der alten Stoa*. 2nd. edn. Berlin, Zurich and Dublin

Gulley, N. (1954) 'Plato's theory of recollection', *Classical Quarterly* N.S. 4: 194–213

(1962) *Plato's Theory of Knowledge*. London

Guthrie, W. K. C., trans. (1956) *Plato: Protagoras and Meno*. London

Hackforth, R. (1952) ed. *Plato's Phaedrus*. Cambridge

(1955) ed. *Plato's Phaedo*. Cambridge

Hacking, I. (1975) *Why Does Language Matter to Philosophy?* Cambridge

Haldane, E. S. and Ross, G. R. T. (1911) eds. *Descartes' Philosophical Works*. 2 vols. Cambridge

Hale, M. (1677) *The Primitive Origination of Mankind*. London

Hamlyn, D. W. (1976) 'Aristotelian *epagoge*', *Phronesis* 21: 167–84

Hare, R. M. (1981) *Moral Thinking*. Oxford

(1982) *Plato*. Oxford

Hartcliffe, J. (1691) *A Treatise of Moral and Intellectual Virtues*. London

Irwin, T. (1977) *Plato's Moral Theory*. Oxford

(1986) 'Aristotelian and Stoic conceptions of happiness', in Schofield, M. and Striker, G. (1986) eds. 205–44

(1988) *Aristotle's First Principles*. Oxford

Jolley, N. (1984) *Leibniz and Locke*. Oxford

(1988) 'Leibniz and Malebranche on innate ideas', *Philosophical Review* 97: 71–91

Judson, L. (1991) ed. *Aristotle's Physics*. Oxford

Kahn, C. H. (1981) 'The role of *nous* in the cognition of first principles in *An. Po.* B 19', Berti, E. (1981) ed. 385–414

Kant, I. (1928) *Reflexionen zur Metaphysik, in gesammelte Schriften* XVIII 5. Berlin and Leipzig

Kemp Smith, N. (1933) ed. *Kant: Critique of Pure Reason*. London

Kleve, K. (1963) *Gnosis theon: die Lehre von der natürlichen Gotteserkenntnis* in *der epikureischen Theologie* in *Symbolae Osloenses* suppl. 19

Kosman, L. A. (1973) 'Explanation and understanding in Aristotle's *Posterior Analytics*', in Lee, E. N., Mourelatos, A. D. P. and Rorty, R. M. (1973) eds. 374–92

Kraut, R. (1989) *Aristotle and the Human Good*. Princeton
(1992) ed. *The Cambridge Companion to Plato*. Cambridge

Kronenberg, A. J. (1924) 'Ad Plutarchis Moralia', *Mnemosune* 52: 61–112

Lear, J. (1987) 'Active episteme', in Graeser, A. (1987) ed. 149–74

Lee, E. N., Mourelatos, A. D. P. and Rorty, R. M. (1973) eds. *Exegesis and Argument. Phronesis* Suppl. I. Assen

Lee, H. (1702) *Antiscepticism*. London

Leites, E. (1988) ed. *Conscience and Casuistry in Early Modern Europe*. Cambridge

Lesher, J. H. (1973) 'The meaning of *nous* in the *Posterior Analytics*', *Phronesis* 18: 44–68

Leyden, W. von (1954) ed. *Locke: Essays on the Law of Nature*. Oxford

Liddell, H. G., Scott, R. and Jones, H. S. (1968) *A Greek–English Lexicon* (with Supplement). Oxford

Long, A. A. (1971a) 'Aisthesis, prolepsis and linguistic theory in Epicurus', *Bulletin of the Institute of Classical Studies* 18: 114–33
(1971b) ed. *Problems in Stoicism*. London

Long, A. A. and Sedley, D. N. (1987) eds. *The Hellenistic Philosophers*. 2 vols. Cambridge

Lowde, J. (1694) *A Discourse concerning the Nature of Man*. London

Luschnat, O. (1958) 'Das Problem der προκοπή in der alten Stoa', *Philologus* 102: 178–214

Mansion, S. (1976) *Le Jugement d' existence chez Aristote*. 2nd. edn. Louvain
(1979) '"Plus connu en soi", "plus connu pour nous". Une distinction epistemologique importante chez Aristote', *Pensamiento* 35: 161–170
(1981) 'La signification de l' universel d' après *An. Post.* I 1', in Berti, E. (1981) ed. 329–42

Manuwald, A. (1972) *Die Prolepsislehre Epikurs*. Bonn

Martin, C. B. and Deutcher, M. (1966) 'Remembering', *Philosophical Review* 75: 161–96

McKirahan, Jr, R. D. (1992) *Principles and Proofs: Aristotle's Theory of Demonstrative Science*. Princeton

Milner, J. (1700) *An Account of Mr Lock's Religion*. London

More, H. (1651) *The Second Lash of Alazomastix*. Cambridge
(1662) *A Collection of Several Philosophical Writings*. 2nd. edn. London

Morrick, H., (1980) ed. *Challenges to Empiricism*. London

Nehamas, A. (1985) 'Meno's paradox and Socrates as a teacher', *Oxford Studies in Ancient Philosophy* 3: 1–30
(1987) 'Socratic intellectualism', *Proceedings of the Boston Area Colloquium in Ancient Philosophy* 2: 274–85

Nidditch, P. H. (1975) ed. *John Locke: An Essay Concerning Human Understanding*. Oxford

Nidditch, P. H. and Rogers, G. A. J. (1990) eds. *John Locke: Drafts for the Essay Concerning Human Understanding, and other Philosophical Writings* I. Oxford

Nussbaum, M. C. (1986) *The Fragility of Goodness*. Cambridge

Obbink, D. (1992) '"What all men believe – must be true": common conceptions and *consensio omnium* in Aristotle and Hellenistic philosophy', *Oxford Studies in Ancient Philosophy* 10: 194–231

Oehler, K. (1969) *Antike Philosophie und byzantinisches Mittelalter*. Munich

Oldfather, W. A., trans. (1925–8) *Epictetus: Discourses*. 2 vols. Loeb Translation. London and Cambridge, Mass.

Owen, G. E. L. (1975) 'Tithenai ta phainomena', in Barnes, J., Schofield, M. and Sorabji, R. (1975) eds. 113–26

Owens, P. J. (1971) 'The universality of the sensible in the Aristotelian noetic', in Anton, J. P. and Kustas, G. L. (1971) eds. 462–77

Parker, S. (1666) *A Free and Impartial Censure of the Platonick Philosophie*. Oxford

(1681) *A Demonstration of the Authority of the Law of Nature and of the Christian Religion*. London

Parkinson, G. H. R. (1973) ed. *Leibniz: Philosophical Writings*. London

Patrides, C. A. (1969) ed. *The Cambridge Platonists*. London

Pembroke, S. G. (1971) 'Oikeiosis', in Long, A. A. (1971b) ed. 114–49

Philippson, R. (1916) 'Zur epikureischen Götterlehre', *Hermes* 51: 568–608

Pohlenz, M. (1970) *Die Stoa*. 2 vols. 4th. edn. Göttingen

Pohlenz, M. and Westman, R. (1959) eds. *Plutarch: Moralia* VI, 2. Leipzig

Price, A. W. (1989) *Love and Friendship in Plato and Aristotle*. Oxford

Putnam, H. (1980) 'The "innateness hypothesis" and explanatory models in linguistics', in Morrick, H. (1980) ed. 240–50

Quine, W. V. O. (1960) *Word and Object*. Cambridge, Mass.

(1969) *Ontological Relativity and Other Essays*. New York

(1980) 'Linguistics and philosophy', in Morrick, H. (1980) ed. 257–9

Rackham, H., trans. (1931) *Cicero: De Finibus Malorum et Bonorum*. Loeb Translation. 2nd. edn. London and Cambridge, Mass.

(1933) trans. *Cicero: De Natura Deorum and Academica*. Loeb Translation. London and Cambridge, Mass.

Rawls, J. (1971) *A Theory of Justice*. Cambridge, Mass.

Remnant, P. and Bennett, J. (1982) eds. *G. W. Leibniz: New Essays on Human Understanding*. Cambridge

Rist, J. (1969) *Stoic Philosophy*. Cambridge

Robson, J. M. (1974) ed. *J. S. Mill: System of Logic* IV–VI (*The Collected Works of John Stuart Mill*. VIII). Toronto

(1978) ed. *J. S. Mill: Essays on Philosophy and the Classics* (*The Collected Works of John Stuart Mill*. XI). Toronto

(1989) ed. *John Stuart Mill: Autobiography*. London

Rorty, A. O. (1980) ed. *Articles on Aristotle's Ethics*. Berkeley

Ross, W. D. (1924) ed. *Aristotle's Metaphysics*. 2 vols. Oxford
  (1930) *The Right and the Good*. Oxford
  (1936) ed. *Aristotle's Physics*. Oxford
  (1949) ed. *Aristotle's Prior and Posterior Analytics*. Oxford
  (1958) ed. *Aristotelis Topica et Sophistici Elenchi*. Oxford

Rowe, C. J. (1993) ed. *Plato: Phaedo*. Cambridge

Ryan, A. (1987) ed. *John Stuart Mill and Jeremy Bentham: Utilitarianism and Other Essays*. London

Saffrey, H. D. and Westerink, L. G. (1968–87) eds. *Proclus: Théologie platonicienne*. 5 vols. Budé edition. Paris

Sandbach, F. H. (1969) trans. *Plutarch's Moralia* XV. Loeb translation. London and Cambridge, Mass.
  (1971) 'Ennoia and prolepsis in the Stoic theory of knowledge', in Long, A. A. (1971b) ed. 22–37

Savile, A. (1972) 'Leibniz's contribution to the theory of innate ideas', *Philosophy* 47: 113–24

Schofield, M. (1980) 'Preconception, argument and God', in Schofield, M., Burnyeat, M. F. and Barnes, J (1980) eds. 283–308

Schofield, M., Burnyeat, M. F. and Barnes, J., (1980) eds. *Doubt and Dogmatism*. Oxford

Schofield, M. and Striker, G. (1986) eds. *The Norms of Nature*. Cambridge and Paris

Sclater, W. (1611) *Key to the Key of Scripture*. London

Scott, D. J. (1987) 'Platonic anamnesis revisited', *Classical Quarterly* n.s. 37: 346–66
  (1988) 'Innatism and the Stoa', *Proceedings of the Cambridge Philological Society* 3rd. Series 33: 123–53
  (1989) 'Epicurean illusions', *Classical Quarterly* n.s. 39: 360–74
  (1990) 'Recollection and Cambridge Platonism', *Hermathena* 149: 73–97
  (1991) 'Socrate prend-il au sérieux le paradoxe de Ménon?', *Revue philosophique* 181: 627–41
  (1994) 'Reason, recollection and the Cambridge Platonists', in Baldwin, A. and Hutton, S. (1994) eds. 139–50

Sherlock, W. (1704) *A Discourse concerning the Happiness of Good Men, and the Punishment of the Wicked, in the Next World*. London

Sidgwick, H. (1907) *The Methods of Ethics*. 7th edn. London

Smith, J. A. (1917) 'General relative clauses in Greek', *Classical Review* 31: 69–71

Sorabji, R. (1980) 'Aristotle on the role of intellect in virtue', in Rorty, A. O. (1980) ed. 201–19

South, R. (1692–4) *Twelve Sermons Preached on Several Occasions*. 2 vols. London

Stewart, J. A. (1892) *Notes on the Nicomachean Ethics of Aristotle*. 2 vols. Oxford

Stich, S. P. (1975) ed. *Innate Ideas*. Berkeley

Stillingfleet, E. (1710) *Works*. 6 vols. London

Straaten, M. van (1962) ed. *Panaetii Rhodii Fragmenta*. 3rd. edn. Leiden

Striker, G. (1990) 'The problem of the criterion', in Everson, S. (1990) ed. 143–60

Sugarman, S. (1983) *Children's Early Thought*. Cambridge

Taylor, A. E. (1960) *Plato: The Man and His Work*. 7th. edn. London

Thompson, W. H. (1868) *Plato: Phaedrus*. London

Todd, R. B. (1973) 'The Stoic common notions', *Symbolae Osloenses* 48: 47–75

Tredennick, H. trans. (1960) *Aristotle: Posterior Analytics*. Loeb Translation. London and Cambridge, Mass.

Tricot, J., (1962) ed. *Aristote: Organon IV (Les Seconds Analytiques)*. 2nd. edn. Paris

Tully, J. (1988) 'Governing conduct', in Leites, E. (1988) ed. 12–71

Usener, H. (1887) ed. *Epicurea*. Leipzig
  (1977) *Glossarium Epicureum*. Rome

Verdenius, W. J. (1955) 'Notes on Plato's *Phaedrus*', *Mnemosune* 4th series 8: 265–89

Vlastos, G. (1983) 'The Socratic elenchus', *Oxford Studies in Ancient Philosophy* 1: 27–58
  (1994) 'Anamnesis in the *Meno*', in Day, J. (1994) ed. 88–111

Vries, G. J. de (1969) ed. *A Commentary on the Phaedrus of Plato*. Amsterdam

Waitz, T. (1844–6) ed. *Aristotelis Organon*. Leipzig

Walker, A. D. M. (1979) 'Aristotle's account of friendship in the *Nicomachean Ethics*', *Phronesis* 24: 180–96

Wardy, R. (1990) *The Chain of Change*. Cambridge

Watson, G. (1972) Review of Gould, J. B. (1970) *Philosophical Quarterly* 22: 268–9

Watson, G. G. (1989) ed. *Thomas Burnet: Remarks on John Locke*. Doncaster

Westerink, L. G. (1976–7) ed. *The Greek Commentators on Plato's Phaedo*. 2 vols. Amsterdam

Whichcote, B. (1751) *Works*. Aberdeen

Wieland, W. (1970) *Die aristotelische Physik*. 2nd. edn. Göttingen
  (1975) 'Aristotle's *Physics* and the problem of inquiry into first principles', in Barnes, J., Schofield, M. and Sorabji, R. (1975) eds. 127–40

Wilkins, J. (1675) *Principles and Duties of Natural Religion*. London

Williams, B. (1985) *Ethics and the Limits of Philosophy*. London

Witt, N. W. de (1954) *Epicurus and his Philosophy*. Minneapolis

Wordsworth, C., trans. (1877) *Sanderson: Lectures on Conscience and Human Law*. Lincoln

Yolton, J. W. (1956) *John Locke and the Way of Ideas*. Oxford
  (1993) ed. *John Locke: Of the Conduct of the Understanding*. Bristol

# Index of ancient passages

# General index